166

MAKING HISTORY

MAKING HISTORY

The Remarkable Story Behind *Canada: A People's History*

Mark Starowicz

National Library of Canada Cataloguing in Publication

Starowicz, Mark
    Making History : the remarkable story behind Canada, a people's history / Mark Starowicz.

ISBN 0-7710-8257-6

1. Canada, a people's history (Television program)   I. Title.

PN1992.3.C3S73 2003   791.45'72   C2002-904626-2

We acknowledge the financial support of the Government of Canada through the Book Publishing Industry Development Program for our publishing activities. We further acknowledge the support of the Canada Council for the Arts and the Ontario Arts Council for our publishing program.

Typeset in Minion by M&S, Toronto
Printed and bound in Canada

McClelland & Stewart Ltd.
The Canadian Publishers
481 University Avenue
Toronto, Ontario
M5G 2E9
www.mcclelland.com

1 2 3 4 5   07 06 05 04 03

To my daughters,
Caitlin and Madeleine.
To the children of Serge Turbide,
Camille and Reynaud,
and to the children of Gail Boyd,
Daniel and Catherine.
Now, you figure it out.

Contents

Introduction

What you are about to read is one person's record of an extraordinary expedition, one that lasted longer than the First World War, transported more than 150 people into uncharted regions of the thousand-channel universe, and explored the very nature of Canada. It is a story that takes readers from the frozen Arctic to Bay Street boardrooms and into the governor general's official residence, sometimes passing through the bleak landscape of a devastated institution – and a divided country. It was the largest photographic journey across Canada undertaken in a generation and the largest documentary project in Canadian television history. It's a tale full of great battles – some staged, some painfully real – and is often humorous, occasionally ridiculous, sometimes poignant, and at times maddening. It's an account of the remarkable adventures of the English-French team that made the first television history of Canada. Paving the Darien Gap would have been an easier task.

I headed this improbable expedition, called the Canadian History Project, and the result was the television series *Canada: A People's History*; I have written this account principally as a tribute to the remarkable people with whom I shared the journey. I learned from working on the series that nothing survives in history unless someone kept a journal, wrote letters, or left an account in some other form. For many of us, these were the most extraordinary years of our professional lives, and I could not abide the thought that what we achieved and endured would fade away, unrecorded. So I embarked, after the series had aired, on writing one more narrative episode: a people's history, as it were, of *Canada: A People's History*. I asked the seventeen episode teams for their recollections and road stories, combined them with my own tale, and set it in the context of some of the most turbulent years in the CBC's history.

I had a model for this. The best book I have ever read about television is *Television: The Business Behind the Box* by Les Brown, the former *New York Times* television reporter and pre-eminent historian of the medium. His book follows the vagaries, vanities, and turbulence of one television season in New York, as seen through the eyes of network program directors competing against one another. It set the standard for all reportage on the medium. His account is punctuated with observations that are now taught in every media studies course, truisms such as: "Television news is scheduled on the peripheries of the prime-time schedule, where it will do the least possible damage to commercial revenue."

I had the pleasure of meeting and becoming good friends with Les Brown and his wife, Jean. During many dinners in New York and long hikes in Banff National Park during the annual television festival, he taught me the history of the medium. He also gave me the moral framework for tackling the conundrum of whether television is a medium for entertainment or for enlightenment. He gave me the greatest television post-graduate course any person could have. For almost twenty years, Les Brown was my mentor – so, ironically, it was an American who taught me to appreciate Canadian television.

I've tried to write an accessible book, one that demystifies the process of broadcasting, and to write an honest account of a scared person trying to navigate the currents and reefs of network television. This is a powerful medium. It needs description.

I've tried to paint a detailed picture of one television production for the viewer, and also for students of journalism and management as well as those working in cultural policy. I hope the result is interesting to all, and useful to government policy makers, CBC Head Office, and the corporation's board of directors. What I am saying is, This is how television is made, and these are the consequences (good and bad) of your decisions. Some of what you'll read here about cultural policy is heroic, much of it is cause for despair. Many good people at the CBC whom you'll meet in these pages end up discarded in the end.

The CBC allowed me to write this book and gave me access to all the files I needed. I had complete liberty to delve into whatever I needed – indeed, I encountered only generous co-operation. There are few corporations in the country that would give an employee this latitude, and it reflects the CBC's view of itself as a public corporation owned by the Canadian people. No one in management read the manuscript before publication; this is solely my version of events, my views on what happened. I love the CBC, the institution that has nurtured, challenged, and protected me for thirty-two years, although what I have to say about it may – in some pages here – seem more like an account of court politics in Tudor England.

A word about that: The CBC, as I see it, was an occupied institution between 1990 and 2000, injured by ruthless cuts, the target of frequent government and regulatory hostility, often cowed by consultants and managers who had little understanding of or affection for its founding principles. Much of this is skilfully documented in Knowlton Nash's *Microphone Wars*. It was the time of the Great Error, when the marketplace ruled all and public broadcasting was seen as passé. We lost a generation of talent. The story told in this book takes place in that period and recounts how good people sacrificed their careers in order to maintain the dream of public broadcasting.

I'm grateful to my colleagues for sharing their accounts and recollections, particularly to Hubert Gendron. The friendship, energy, and skill of my assistant, Nathalie Bibeau, were indispensable while I was writing, and her stories of the French community in Welland,

Ontario – which portray it as something between Stendhal and the Sopranos – were an inspiration.

Avie Bennett, Doug Gibson, and Dinah Forbes at McClelland & Stewart were believers in the Canadian History Project before anyone else outside the CBC. Dinah shaped this book and gave me the good counsel and generous encouragement anyone writing a first book needs. We at the Canadian History Project were grateful to her for her encouragement and sheer endurance in producing the two illustrated companion books to the series, but assumed she had had her fill of the lot of us. To my amazement, and gratification, she had some patience left over for me.

Sinking Ships

On its very first shoot, the Canadian History Project comprised five drenched people on the deck of a twelve-metre boat that was sinking slowly in the middle of the ocean. It was the dead of night and we were miles from land. "Whatever you do," Keith Bonnell shouted, "do not jump in the water! You'll die of hypothermia in ten minutes." The wheelhouse was billowing smoke, and the boat had sunk so low that sea water was lapping at our shoes whenever we moved. I had been in danger before – once I was even caught in an ambush in Cambodia. But this dark, silent moment in the Strait of Belle Isle off the coast of Newfoundland was the closest I have come to dying.

What made this different from my previous brushes with fate was the slowness. There was none of the sudden confusion of an ambush or the terror of an exploding mortar shell; this wasn't a bewildering surprise. It was more like waiting in line, wondering how soon the boat would slip below the waves and contemplating how death would be. But there is a greater horror than drowning alone. Beside me on the deck was my thirteen-year-old daughter, Caitlin, whom I had brought on the expedition.

When I realized that we were sinking, I panicked for a moment, thinking that I had doomed my own daughter. Then I remembered the tiny rubber dinghy that was tied half-swamped to the starboard side. Caitlin and Louis Martin from Radio-Canada could both fit in it. Surely everyone would agree to save the oldest and the youngest. The dinghy wouldn't hold anyone else. Not the boat's three crew members. Not Gene Allen, the journalist and historian, who was the brains of the project. Not Michael Sweeney, the cameraman who had been to every war zone in the past twenty-five years. Caitlin and Louis would watch us drown.

It was July 28, 1997, and it had taken us two and a half years to get to this dark moment: years filled with corporate intrigue inside a devastated and divided CBC and with dramatic negotiations that took us into the boardrooms of Canadian industrial giants and into the governor general's residence at Rideau Hall. Months of frantic meetings with the head of the National Film Board and late-night discussions with some of the leading names in Quebec journalism and the most respected historians in the country. All this for a project that many warned us would never see air. From our sinking boat, it looked like they were right.

The journey to this night began in 1995, a year when Canada looked like it might come asunder, the CBC was definitely falling apart, and I wasn't feeling so good myself.

This was the year I turned forty-nine, and the prospect bothered me. "I'd rather be fifty," I told my friends. Television commercials were full of fifty-year-olds eating margarine on mountain summits. "You can be a young fifty," I argued, "but you can't be a young forty-nine. That's just a decrepit forty-year-old." The thought of being forty-nine was bad enough, but the anniversary that really made me edgy was coming up in March of that year: I would be inducted into the twenty-five-year club at the CBC. That meant I had spent more of my life in the CBC than out of it, since I had joined when I was twenty-four. And that winter of 1995, the investment of half your life at the CBC was worth as much as a handful of Yugoslavian war bonds – or, for that matter, the Liberal Party's Red Book of promises from the recent election. Because two days before my anniversary, even the president of the CBC bailed out of the ship I had sailed for a quarter-century.

> February 28, 1995
> *For Immediate Release:*
> OTTAWA – Citing purely personal reasons, Anthony S. Manera, CBC's President and Chief Executive Officer, resigned at 9:00 a.m., effective March 31, 1995.
> Editors should expect no further comment from Mr. Manera at this time.
> Robert Pattillo,
> Vice-President, Communications and Public Affairs

The "purely personal reasons" were that the minister of communications who had promised there would be no cuts to the CBC had broken his word. In this, the hapless minister, who has since been discarded by history as so much political Kleenex, could be forgiven since he had been reading out of his own party's election platform of just eighteen months earlier, which promised to reverse the draconian cuts the Tories had imposed. A mere one year and twenty-six days after his appointment as president, Anthony Manera was gone, a victim of believing what our politicians say. In his letter of resignation to the prime minister, he referred to none of this and ended by saying, "I know the CBC is in good hands. There is a strong Board of Directors and equally strong management team."

Well, not quite. Soon after Manera resigned, the "strong" board of directors, many appointed by the long-gone Mulroney government, split into at least two warring factions, each of which conspired with the Prime Minister's Office over the leadership of the CBC. Meanwhile, members of the "strong management team" were assiduously courting both factions and pointing the finger at one another. The French Television heads blamed the English Television heads for everything, and vice-versa, and both Radio heads blamed Television. On top of this, all these heads of the four "media lines," as we know them in the CBC, were held in total suspicion by the heads of finance and human resources at Head Office in Ottawa, who thought of them more as shoplifters than as network heads. The Bosnian cabinet was a more secure administrative apparatus than the CBC.

The air had been poisoned in the CBC ever since the Conservative government imposed a four-year plan of painful cuts in 1992. At the time the Liberals were indignant about the cuts and promised to save the CBC if they were returned to power, but when they won the election in 1993, they stunned the arts community by confirming the Conservative cuts. The vast CBC system was torn apart by fear and recrimination, as regional stations faced elimination and entire network departments disappeared. The process of hacking away at the corporation had started in 1992, under the calamitous regime of the previous president, Gérard Veilleux, and had driven more good people out of the CBC than I could count, among them Trina McQueen, who was head of news and current affairs. I held one man significantly – not largely, but significantly – responsible for this: Robert Pattillo, the vice-president of communications who had signed the announcement of Manera's hurried exit. Pattillo, who once worked for Pierre Trudeau's government, is thin, dark-haired, and impeccably dressed in silk suits "so fashionable," Trina would say, "that you thought the silkworms were still chomping on them." Pattillo, who was devoted to his two pet Dobermans, had been Gérard Veilleux's "special adviser" and one of the masterminds behind the 1992 combining of *The National* and *The Journal* into one lumbering package called *Prime Time News* – thereby killing the two most respected brand names in Canadian television and executing its leading current affairs program – and marching the news hour boldly to 9:00 P.M. It was one of the biggest disasters in CBC Television history. By the winter of 1995, the news ratings were in the toilet, the regions were living in terror of being eliminated, the current affairs department was totally demoralized. For months, television columnists had feasted like sharks on daily rumours from *Prime Time News* that the hosts, Peter Mansbridge and Pamela Wallin, loathed each other.

The political climate at the CBC wasn't only toxic, it was also absurd. Veilleux had gone to a senior post at Power Corporation in Montreal, and Pattillo moved to Toronto, provoking a minor but memorable crisis. He was now vice-president of communications, and CBC protocol says that vice-presidents get toilets in their offices. But his new office in Toronto did not have one, so considerable replumbing was undertaken by the building services department to honour his status. This was awkward in a period of the impending layoff of hundreds of people, so it became legend around the building.

I had the opposite problem. After I became head of the documentary unit, I was moved to an office that had a toilet. Since I was not a vice-president, work crews appeared, the toilet bowl was removed, the drainpipe sealed off, and the room it was in was briskly sealed off behind a wall of plasterboard. The small documentary unit staff made a miniature bathroom out of dollhouse furniture and presented it to me as a memento of that terrific winter of 1995. At the time I could not imagine ever being grateful to Robert Pattillo for anything but a ringside seat to his political demise. But, as it turned out, by the time the events recounted in this book were coming to an end, I was praising him – and sincerely so – across the country.

The CBC was rudderless and seemed to be drifting toward the scrapyard. Outside the world of the CBC, there was little cause for cheer either. The whole country seemed to be adrift too, headed not to the scrapyard but into a political hurricane. There was a testy, unsettled feeling in Canadian political life. Everyone expected this year would bring the second Quebec referendum, and the rhetoric was becoming more toxic as each month went by. The Reform Party was gathering strength in the west, and the country was more politically balkanized than it had been since the Great Depression six decades earlier. It seemed absurd to many for the government to be slashing the biggest national cultural institution, the CBC, just as the cracks in the Canadian federation were widening, but the Liberals were determined to bring the deficit into line. As the CBC-TV budget shrank, we became more and more dependent upon finding foreign co-producers to fund series, dramas, and documentaries, which meant watering down the national content. So it was particularly ironic when, on May 10, 1995, it was a sovereignist Bloc Québécois MP who rose in the House of Commons to puzzle aloud about this contradiction.

> *Mr. Bernard Deshaies (Abitibi, BQ):* Mr. Speaker, this morning's Toronto Star announced that the CBC's English network is forced to co-produce television shows with foreign companies, especially from the United States. Therefore, we will slowly but surely watch the Americanization of the CBC. This is neither a coincidence nor a deliberate change in the CBC's programming.
>
> Could it be that the budget cuts affecting the English and French networks of the CBC are dramatically reducing the production of Canadian television shows? It is very likely that this is the case. The English network no longer has the means to produce its own shows. The Liberal government is therefore presiding over the systematic dismemberment of what has long been cherished as a pillar of Canadian culture. The English Canadian culture, with the unwilling help of the CBC, is on its way to becoming a carbon copy of the North American culture.

He was right. Within the cash-poor CBC, the mantras were "co-production" and "partnering," and anyone who could persuade a foreign broadcaster to come in on a production was held up as an example of entrepreneurship. As head of the documentary unit, it was my job to go around the United States and Europe with a briefcase full of documentary proposals and persuade foreign networks to put money into them. After a while, this exercised a significant gravitational pull on the kind of programs the CBC made. We could attract interest in projects like the hunt for Czar Nicholas's bones, the Ebola outbreak, pornography on the Internet – but it was impossible to sell a story set in Sudbury or a chronicle of the death of Newfoundland's fishing communities. Canadian stories were, in the jargon of the trade, "not financeable." The stories that were "financeable" were nature films, or portraits of pedophiles or serial killers. I

told a broadcasting conference that year, "All we are doing is export-
ing our polar bears, our rapists, and our psychopaths."

It was depressing to walk around the tenth-floor studios in the
new Broadcast Centre in Toronto. Here were beautiful, state-of-the-
art studios the size of half a football field each, with soaring ceilings
and banks of lights, testament to a vision – reasonable just ten years
earlier – of Canada as a major player on the world television stage.
Now these studios were either empty or rented out to American
movie companies. Some critics pointed to these studios as a monu-
ment to a bygone age, the folly of a corporation that failed to understand that the industry was transforming. But they were wrong. The
CBC building, the most modern digital production plant in the
country, was state-of-the-art for the entire industry, which was why
the Americans were using it. What it wasn't was state-of-the-politics.
Ottawa, not technology, had decided to make the CBC building
redundant. The dark truth that few could bring themselves to believe
was that the federal government had given up on national broadcasting. "You don't get it," I kept arguing with colleagues. "You think this
is just an aberration, something that you could correct if only you
could get the ear of the minister for thirty minutes, and she would see
the unintended consequences of her policies. This is not an aberration, this is not an accident. This is the national cultural policy."

It was also depressing to take foreign network visitors through
our documentary unit. Sure, on the wall in our lobby there were portraits of the documentary genius Donald Brittain, of the CBC
founders Graham Spry and Alan Plaunt, and of the real inventor of
radio, Reginald Fessenden, as well as posters advertising great documentaries of long ago and plaques recalling former glories. But there
was little else to show them. "You have to understand," I would tell
the Australian or German or British visitor, "we don't actually make
documentaries here. We commission them from private production
companies. We have no cameramen, no directors, no journalists of
our own."

The helplessness of working within this arcane documentary
funding system was maddening. If a million people were being

slaughtered in Rwanda, as they had been the previous year, you couldn't pick up the phone and assign the best director and camera-men you know, as we could have done a decade ago. You would have to invite an independent to write a proposal, strike a budget, and submit the idea to Telefilm, the government funding agency, which only pronounces on the thousands of proposals it receives twice a year. You have to show how it will make a profit; you have to go through a development stage and produce a full production report. With luck, you'll have an answer in six months. By then, Rwanda is a graveyard.

My colleagues Marie Natanson and Hilary Armstrong of *Witness* would stare at the corkboard covered with index cards of scheduled documentaries and air dates, and despair as project after project melted before our eyes. Everything depended on whether it would pass Telefilm, or some provincial fund, or some program meeting at the A&E network in New York. We could no longer deliver a rational schedule, a rational balance of topics, a rational balance between Canadian and international stories. The independents, whose advo-cates we were and whose personal lives we shared, were just as help-less, just as anguished. Their lives, their mortgages, their creative passions were hostage to a system that resembled a lottery more than a national cultural policy. It made no sense, given the new commu-nications universe that was emerging.

This was not the era in which to fragment our industry. Time Inc., the second-largest communications conglomerate on the planet, felt that it was too small to compete in the global information war and amalgamated with Warner Communications, the third-largest global power in information and dramatic content. The merger was an attempt to compete with Bertelsmann of Europe, the conglomerate of six hundred companies in all aspects of publishing, music, news, and television production. In a world where Time and Warner considered themselves too small to compete, what were we doing in Canada, dismembering the CBC, the only world-class broadcaster we owned?

It was also obvious that, in this new information order, owner-ship of content was everything. Bricks and mortar didn't matter.

Who owned the rights to *Casablanca*? Who owned the production apparatus and the talent that could produce drama and documentary? Wealth, in this new communications world, was measured in the capacity to produce and own content – in other words, *software*, not hardware. This was a global competition in software assets, where Ted Turner bought MGM just to own the movie vaults to feed his superchannel. But Canadian policy assured that the CBC owned virtually nothing. Because of Telefilm and other funding systems, we didn't even own the documentaries or dramas we put money into; the independent producer did. CBC doesn't own *Anne of Green Gables* or *Da Vinci's Inquest* or most of the documentaries on *Witness* and *Life & Times*. Ownership has been dispersed among dozens of production companies, some big, some small. If there was a formula by which Canada was certain to lose the global competition, we had found it.

The mid-1990s, when we have some historical perspective on them, will be seen as the time of the Great Fever. The idea that the market rules all had seized the nation, and anyone urging caution couldn't be heard over the noise of the parade. Defending public institutions was seen as organized panhandling. The dot-com bubble was starting to inflate, and several friends of mine were day trading on the Internet and scheming to get rich by creating new specialty channels for the thousand-channel digital universe that lay ahead. In the meantime, wave after wave of consultants washed through the CBC, and after each one, more departments and more veteran producers and journalists disappeared.

One day in that sad year of 1995 showed just how little loyalty had come to mean in the new order. It was Tuesday, June 27, 1995, and in a large windowless boardroom in the Broadcast Centre, those facing layoffs were being paraded through. The way layoffs work in the CBC, as in most unionized institutions, is this: Specific functions and positions, even entire departments, are declared redundant and are eliminated. But the people holding those positions are not necessarily the ones to lose their jobs. If they have some seniority, they have the right to bump someone else who has lower seniority. The result is a cascade of dislocation – a pinball effect – in which one person displaces another, who displaces another, until the institution is filled with chaos and paranoia that doesn't settle for months. Lives are put on hold, mortgages imperilled, families stressed to the limit. In our own household, my wife, Anne Wright-Howard, was facing layoff when *Undercurrents* went through one of its recurring cancellations. When the bumping finished ricocheting through the system, we ended up with the real victims' list. Executive producers and department heads were then given a sad list of those facing layoff and asked if they had any vacant positions which they were prepared to give to anyone on the list. But, by the very definition of layoffs and budget cutbacks, almost no department head or executive producer had any vacant positions. It was Catch-22.

Michael Harris, an executive in the English network management, was given the thankless task of organizing a last-chance auction of the doomed. Some twenty-five or thirty executive producers and unit heads were instructed to go to the boardroom, where the tables had been organized into a very large, hollow rectangle. The doomed were paraded, one by one, thirty minutes apart, in front of this council. Their resumés were distributed, then they were led into the room and asked to sit down alone at the far end of the rectangle, to answer any questions and to make their pitch for redemption.

One by one, they came in: producers and reporters who had been caught out by secondments, disability leaves, or maternity leaves, or because they simply weren't wanted for one reason or another, legitimate or not. When each one left, there was a debate. If the person who had just appeared had higher seniority in his or her field than a member of your department's staff, you had to demonstrate that, despite his or her credentials, there was an overriding reason why you were not prepared to allow this person to bump someone in your unit. So the double cruelty was that not only was the person made to plead their case in front of thirty potential customers who might save them from termination, but the unit head may have to argue, after the person has left, why the supplicant was really not as good as the person on your staff with less seniority.

I was sitting next to David Studer, executive producer of *the fifth estate*, who had been senior producer at *The Journal* during the 1991 Gulf War. We had called each other about one person on the list, Eric Rankin, a reporter who had worked at *The Journal* and played a pivotal role in our coverage of the war. We had no idea how he had got on the list of the doomed, except that he had displeased the management of the news department. Neither Studer nor I had any reporter vacancies, but we were determined that the committee was going to hear just whom the CBC was planning to jettison.

Rankin is a thin, handsome man with close-cropped blond hair, and he walked into the room like all the others, momentarily taken aback by the number of people. "This is definitely the mother of all boards," he said. "It will make any future job interviews remarkably easy." I don't think he saw Studer or me sitting about twelve metres away. David began.

"Mr. Rankin, four years ago, on Tuesday, January 16, 1991, you were the reporter with a *Journal* documentary unit that had been sent to Baghdad, Iraq, when your editors received word that an air strike was imminent on Baghdad, is that correct?"

"Yes," he said hesitantly, obviously perplexed about where this was going, and trying to make out who was asking the question.

"You received a call from Toronto, from myself and from your executive producer, Mark Starowicz, is that correct?

"Yes."

"You were advised that we had received information that the bombing of Baghdad was imminent, and furthermore, that some international news crews were fleeing the city. In fact, the entire CBC News crew in Baghdad fled, abandoning its camera equipment at the airport in the confusion, is that correct?"

"Yes."

I took the next part: "You were advised that the rest of the CBC had left, and that you and your *Journal* unit were the only remaining CBC presence. You were told you had complete permission to leave."

"That's correct."

"You were told you had the right to leave, without any reservation, but that if it was possible, *The Journal* requested that you stay.

You were the only Canadian television crew left in Baghdad. What did you decide?"

"We decided to stay."

"Let's review that," I said. "The CBC News team, like dozens of other news organizations, had fled for their safety. Your hotel was adjacent to the defence ministry, which was a priority target, and the peril to your life was real. However, you, your producer, your cameraman, and your soundman took a vote and informed *The Journal* that you would stay and cover the story."

"Yes."

"How long did it take for you and your unit to make that decision?" I asked. Then I continued, "Let me answer that for you, because it was me on the other end of the line in Toronto asking you to stay. It took you thirty seconds."

Studer asked Rankin to describe what happened next, and Rankin spoke of the sky exploding, the desperate attempt to file his report, then the descent to the bunkers below the hotel, the masses of people huddling, begging time on the BBC satellite phone to get a report through to the CBC. Then how the crew managed to hire a van, and then drive through the desert with some Palestinian refugees who were trying to escape, toward the Jordanian border, passing mobile Scud missile launchers, more checkpoints, being arrested by the Iraqis at the Jordanian border, and finally being saved by the Palestinians they had travelled with.

"There was an international alert because you had disappeared for three days, feared dead," Studer interjected. "You were then interviewed live on *Nightline* recounting your remarkable journey, is that right?"

Rankin nodded.

"Did you ever receive a bonus or any recognition outside your program unit for what you did?"

Rankin didn't say anything.

"And what are you looking for here this morning?"

"A job as a reporter, either in Vancouver or Toronto – anything."

Studer closed off: "Thank you, Mr. Rankin, I think that's all."

As far as Studer and I were concerned, if you had the courage and the professionalism to stick to your post when the rest of your organization had fled and if you risked your life for your corporation, then the corporation should take care of you, not just because you did an exemplary job but because it was a message to the rest of the people in the system: if you risk your life for us, we will take care of you. Rankin was a good, dependable reporter who, when called upon to do the extraordinary, did it quietly, competently, and professionally. When we send the message that we will not be loyal to you after such an act, then we have destroyed the fundamental construct that allows extraordinary acts. (In 1991, we had put Eric's name forward for the President's Award that year. We never even heard back from Head Office.)

Also at the table was Sig Gerber, producer of *Marketplace* and the most senior executive producer in the current affairs department, with three decades in the CBC. He would be made head of the department soon. "It was the most degrading experience I ever had," he said later. "Here were individuals who were productive people one day, reduced to panhandlers the next. We all felt degraded. Dirty."

Eric Rankin got a job with Newsworld in Vancouver. He vividly remembers that day in 1995: "You just knew the bean-counters were now in charge. Everything I respected was being killed off. The place was shutting down, there was no place to go. A few years before, if you worked really hard, you could thrive in the CBC and work with terrific people. Now everything creative came to a halt. Paranoia was everywhere. Everybody was watching their backs, wondering who's next. If anyone, absolutely anyone had called me that day in 1995, offering me a job outside the CBC, I would have taken it."

Many of us went on the road that year, speaking to schools and conferences in defence of public broadcasting. The hardest thing to explain was that a radio or television network was not like a department store; it's more like a theatrical company, or a symphony orchestra, which has to recruit and nurture its own talent. I finally started to make analogies to sports, which worked better than comparisons to orchestras and theatres. "If you are the Blue Jays organization," I said, "and you have to play New York next Thursday, you don't get on the phone to the labour market and see if such-and-such a closing pitcher is free that Thursday. And you don't work your way through your Rolodex to see who's the least bad designated hitter available to play in Toronto that day. You build, carefully, a complex team which assures that you have these talents available to you. You also have an intricate system of scouts, farm teams, training seasons, and special-ist coaches – not to mention the front office, the medical staff, the community development staff.

"Yet the model everyone is toasting for national television is that you should have only a front office, and the minimum overhead, and pick up a writer, a cameraman, an editor, a graphic artist, and a com-poser out of your Rolodex – interchangeable labour units. This model is not the way to produce a great documentary or drama, no more than it is a model for beating the New York Yankees."

In Stratford, I told the story of John Hirsch, when he was artistic director of the Stratford Festival. After a performance, he held a question-and-answer session with the audience, and one woman objected to Stratford receiving government support, arguing that "the theatre should operate to make a profit, like every other busi-ness." Hirsch exploded into the most concise – if blasphemous – defence of the arts I ever heard.

"Christ, lady!" he erupted, arms flailing. "Do the bloody schools make a profit? Do the highways make a profit? Do the goddamn *sewers* make profit? Why the hell should the *theatre* have to make a profit? Some things you need just to be a *civilization!*"

I also remembered Stratford for the gala press reception which preceded the opening of the new theatre season, where I fell afoul of the local member of Parliament. He was also the minister of defence in the Mulroney government. He berated me in front of a dozen people for a report on *The Journal* that had questioned the need to purchase submarines from the British. I thought he was quite rude to go on a tirade at a reception, making sweeping charges about bias at the CBC in front of everyone. I couldn't get a word in edgewise to defend the report, and finally I just walked away. What a pompous, thin-skinned little martinet, I thought, grateful I would not have to see him again.

In April 1995, I was in London with my colleague Don Richardson for negotiations with the BBC. My boss in Toronto, Bob Culbert, rang me in my hotel room late at night. "Get up," he said. "Perrin Beatty has just been named president of the CBC." I woke up Don Richardson and we went down to the bar, an irritating pseudo-Russian affair, with waiters dressed as Cossacks and seventeen different kinds of flavoured vodka at outrageous prices. We felt justified in sampling most of them. The CBC was now being run by a chair who was the owner of a Quebec pulp mill and a president who was a defeated Tory cabinet minister and whose hero was Margaret Thatcher.

"Well, you were born here, Mark. You have a British passport," Don consoled me. "I'll have to ask for political asylum."

Our mission in London involved the biggest co-production ever undertaken between the CBC, BBC Television, and the History Channel in the United States. It was a six-part documentary epic called *Dawn of the Eye*, on the history of newsreels and television news, from Thomas Edison to O.J. Simpson, to coincide with the centenary of cinema. A hundred years of deceit, distortion, and scandal.

It was good to be away from the CBC for a couple of weeks and to have a project that was immune from the savagery going on in Toronto, because it had foreign co-production money. It was good to be researching, visiting archives, and screening famous footage – in short, being creative again. It was even better to be embarking on a global television stage, where I thought the CBC should be pushing with all its documentary talent. In effect, we would be doing the history of British newsreels and television news, along with our British colleagues. We would be writing the history of American television for American television. That felt good.

The BBC had been beaten and cowed by Margaret Thatcher's government, but even bruised and battered, it was a pretty impressive sight. My hotel room overlooked Broadcasting House, the oval building where Edward R. Murrow stood on the roof and described the Blitz live to America, and which contained the studios where

Winston Churchill delivered his broadcasts. The BBC has so many buildings all over London that you could spend half the day in a cab travelling among them. One building, Kensington House, was devoted entirely to documentary programs and series, outnumbering us about fifty to one in annual documentary production. Every morning, I'd get out of a black London taxi in front of the massive building at White City, which housed the current affairs units, and look at the BBC flag billowing on the flagpole, with the BBC coat of arms and the motto "Nation Shall Speak Unto Nation," and think how Canada was almost 30 million people, and Britain 60 million. It is twice the size of us, but its public broadcasting institution is ten times as large, and its place on the world stage a hundred times bigger. The British had invested wisely in their broadcasting assets. They held the high ground when it came to period dramas, documentaries, history. Why were we ceding all this to the British? We could compete in all these fields, with the advantage of being able to produce in French and English, if Ottawa could only realize that *this* was the new global industry: films, news, nature programming, children's programming, documentaries. This was the new information order.

The team I had assembled for the series were mostly *Journal* veterans, happy to be plucked from the sinking *Prime Time News*. And I was happy to be reunited with colleagues who had covered the death of Communism, survived the deserts of Sudan, and lived the melodrama of the Constitution. They were the elite team: the cameraman was Mike Sweeney, the editor was Murray Green; the producers were Laine Drewery, Alan Mendelsohn, Bill Cobban, and Julia Bennett; visual research was headed by Ron Krant; and the senior producer was Gene Allen, a newcomer who had been foreign editor of the *Globe and Mail*. We dreamed of invading the international documentary industry. Mendelsohn, who looked like Stalin and talked like Jackie Gleason, called *Dawn of the Eye* "our training wheels series," invariably adding, "The next one will be really big, BIG!" Well, $3 million and the BBC made it pretty big already, and we had our hands full. But in the bar of the Langham Hotel opposite Broadcasting House in London we did fantasize about "the really big one," and that was going to be the history of Canada. But not for a long time, obviously, given the climate in Ottawa.

Many of our CBC colleagues thought the documentary unit was simply the surviving remnant of *The Journal*, reliving old glories – which, in truth, we were. *The Journal* "underground" – after all, four hundred people had passed through it in a decade – was a powerful force, with many of its veterans in high places, all linked by the kind of loyalty only intense fraternity under fire can forge. It was the Resistance within the CBC. Graham Spry's and Donald Brittain's portraits were on our walls, and the whole gang of consultants were the interlopers. In the bar of the Langham Hotel and the Acme Bar and Grill in Toronto, we schemed and dreamed. We were going to build a tight, fast, and mobile production machine that could compete with the world and put Canada on the production map again.

That is, if Canada as we knew it was still on any map.

Joe Clark was right when he warned that Canada was sleep-walking into disaster. In September and October of 1995, English Canadians started to wake up and realize that something historic was imminent. Two weeks before the Quebec referendum, there was a palpable disquiet everywhere in Toronto. People in the office were talking about how they had just moved their mutual funds out of Canadian equities; others had converted their savings to American dollars. I didn't have any significant assets to convert, but I did think the interest rate would skyrocket after a Yes victory, so I went to the bank and borrowed $10,000 at 8 per cent, just as a hedge. I could always repay the loan the following week.

I decided that I couldn't just watch the referendum from Toronto. I was raised in Quebec, I spoke French, I had been there the day René Lévesque walked out of the Liberal Party convention and set up the fledgling Mouvement Souveraineté-Association. I called my closest friend, Nick Auf der Maur, to find out where my old Montreal gang would be watching the results. I should have saved myself the effort: "At Winnie's, of course," he said with the contempt of someone who has just been asked where the Pope lives. Winnie's – the Sir Winston Churchill Pub on Crescent Street – was the gathering place for

Montreal's anglophone journalists, writers, sports columnists, one Cuban gunrunner, and several gentlemen who had a lot to do with stolen cargo and who tended to keep to themselves. Mordecai Richler made Winnie's famous in his writings and could usually be found there arguing with Auf der Maur. "Everyone's going to be here," Nick promised, "including live television crews." He made it sound like the Restaurant at the End of the Universe.

I decided I should take Caitlin, my elder daughter, who was twelve and had been in French immersion since Grade 1. I told her, "We may see the birth of a new country begin tomorrow, and though it won't be the happiest day for me, it's your generation that will deal with that future. You might as well get to know your counterparts now, and be able to say that you were there to see the beginning."

In the mid-1960s I worked at the Montreal *Gazette*, first on the police beat, then covering the FLQ bombings, the rise of René Lévesque, and all the turbulence of the Quebec nationalist movement. I was comfortable in a world where you switched from English to French in mid-sentence, and I loved the mongrel English-French-Greek-Italian-Scottish-Jewish city. It worked. You could never have designed it or planned it, but a natural civility and tolerance of diversity was more the rule than the exception. Maybe that's why the gulf separating French and English Canadians bothered me more than most. You wouldn't notice it if you hadn't lived in Montreal. We live in such hermetically sealed solitudes that we don't even know it.

After twenty years working in broadcasting, and from travelling around the country extensively, I began to see the magnitude of radio and television's failure. On the airwaves, French and English simply didn't exist for each other. In the early 1990s, I took my observations on the road, speaking to high schools, Canadian Clubs, and universities. I had it down to a good act. In English Canada, this is how it went.

"Do you realize," I'd tell an assembly, "that the only time you see a French Canadian on English television, he or she is complaining about something? Except for hockey games, and the odd variety special, there are no French Canadians on English-Canadian television, public or private, and certainly none on all the American channels we watch. French Canadians exist only in newscasts and public affairs shows, and hockey games." I'd pull out a stopwatch. "Let's try a quiz. Name me, or describe them if you can't name them, the last French Canadian you saw on English television, public or private, network or local, *outside a hockey game or a news or public affairs show*. It can be a character in a sitcom, or a drama, or a movie of the week, or a cartoon, or a children's show. Anything but a news or public affairs show." Then I'd start my stopwatch. Aching silences would follow in huge auditoriums. One minute would go by. Two. Up to four minutes, before I gave up. The shortest stopwatch session was at Jarvis Collegiate in Toronto, and that was two minutes forty-seven seconds, before someone named a singer on a variety show. Sometimes someone would name Trudeau or Chrétien or Bouchard on an episode of *Air Farce* but would concede that this evaded the point.

In Quebec schools, I did the opposite. Name me an English Canadian you saw outside of a newscast, etc. The sessions were marginally shorter only because someone would call out an English name. Without exception, they were all Americans on American shows, and sometimes the intervener didn't realize it.

Then I'd say: "Is there a country in the world where you could duplicate this result? I've been in South Africa. That's an apartheid state, but there are all sorts of black characters on television, in their soap operas and dramas. We, in Canada, have a more hermetically sealed exclusion of each other's presence than the South Africans. But, because we live inside it, we don't know it. We only see each other in newscasts, when we're complaining, or when there's a snowstorm. You're certainly not going to see Halifax on Radio-Canada unless a snowstorm buries it, and you won't see Chicoutimi on CBC – or the privates – unless a school bus rolls over." I admitted this was an exaggeration, but the point remained: it was striking how no one could name anybody.

"Surely," I argued, "this is corrosive of our national soul, and of our capacity to arrive at political civility. We don't just live in French or English skins. We are also teenagers who resent our overbearing fathers or mothers, or we are construction workers, or poets, or new-comers to our country confronting the same problems of assimilation. Don't you think there is something wrong when a teenager in Saskatoon will never see a teenager in Trois-Rivières, in a drama, dealing with the same issues of family or love or hate or sexuality that the teenager in Saskatoon faces? Don't you think it's corrosive that the only teenager outside of Quebec a fifteen-year-old girl in Trois-Rivières will see lives in Los Angeles? This is called culture. Living and exchanging and mediating our common experiences. That's how we negotiate our space. There are 500,000 blacks in Toronto. Some are descendants of Loyalists, but most are from the Caribbean nations, which have totally different cultures and experiences from inner-city America. Yet the only blacks you'll see on Canadian TV live in Bel Air or are being led away in handcuffs on cop shows. Never mind a Calgary teenager seeing a Trois-Rivières teenager in a movie; she'll never see a teenager in the Maritimes, unless it's a hundred years ago on *Anne of Green Gables*. This is the most cabled and satellite-served country on earth, with more fibre optic miles per person than New York City. But the neural paths of national social and cultural discourse are severed. This is dysfunctional." I finally had to retire the quiz, but not the talk, once Céline Dion became an international star.

The escalator from Central Station leads up to Boulevard René-Lévesque. As we stood waiting for a taxi, I pointed to the street sign and said to Caitlin: "I knew him before he became famous. He was a friend. He started all this." I always feel a mix of emotions standing in that spot, seeing someone I knew in ordinary life, sitting next to him in a bar on a boring Tuesday evening, his name now emblazoned on the street corner opposite the Roman Catholic cathedral. This Monday afternoon, just hours before the referendum that might complete his vision, I felt a little empty, arriving in Montreal like a total stranger to the denouement of a story that had once been so large a part of my life.

It was around five o'clock, and there were some essentials I knew we'd need if the night unfolded the way they used to in my day. We took a cab to Rue Saint-Denis and found a shop with fleur-de-lys flags, which wasn't hard. We bought two small ones and a blue fleur-de-lys balloon. In Montreal at night, a crowd of a thousand celebrants can form rather quickly in the street, and, as I learned many a time in my youth, it's best to blend in. So Caitlin and I made a pretty spectacle stumbling up the stairs of Winnie's with our suitcase, coats, flags, and balloons, to be greeted by Nick, leaning at the bar wearing his trademark fedora.

Nick Auf der Maur had been chief copy clerk at the *Gazette* when I joined as junior copy clerk, and he introduced me to a life I had never even imagined existed. He took me with him to the bohemian underground of east-end Montreal, where he knew every artist and hothead in the city, and thoroughly corrupted the life of a studious immigrant teenager from the west end. He was my oldest friend and my older brother. We covered the rise of nationalism together, interviewed all the leading players, covered all the riots and demonstrations. He had gone on to become a folkloric figure in the city, a television personality, a newspaper columnist, a city councillor, a federal candidate, an author, and a much-sought-after commentator on Quebec affairs. He was tall, good-looking, with a grin like a beaver, and a magnetic appeal for women, which infuriated the rest of his friends, who always went home alone. He preferred to call himself a "boulevardier."

In Winnie's that night, all the old gang was there, but there were also some people I had never seen before. "Meet my friend from Norway!" said Nick, pulling a sheepish-looking man over. "I'm going to be on Norwegian television tonight!" He pointed to a couple of cameras set up on tripods – not just the Norwegians, it seemed, but somebody from the BBC and, I think, Argentina. "Oh God," I said, "not again." Nick knew what I meant and instantly recounted the time he and I had been interviewed by French television during Charles de Gaulle's visit to Quebec in 1967, causing a scandal because we were presented as being representative of English-Canadian opinion.

Caitlin was impressed by none of this, but my eyes fell on my friend Jacob Richler across the room, and I moved around the bar to introduce Caitlin to Jacob Two-Two. Knowing René Lévesque was one thing. But that I knew Jacob Two-Two impressed her for the first time that day – or any day since.

The TV set at the bar was already blaring, and within minutes the electronic map of Quebec was showing a tide of Yes sweeping from east to west with incredible speed. Every region except Hull was voting Yes, and the future of Quebec would all be decided on the densely populated island of Montreal. I couldn't continue watching this at Winnie's. History wasn't going to happen here, it was going to happen a few blocks away at the Palais des Congrès, where the Oui side was massed in its thousands, watching the results on giant screens. Caitlin and I flagged a taxi, and I was afraid everything would be over in the ten minutes it took us to get there.

It was dark and crowded inside the vast space, the far end of the hall dominated by two giant projection screens carrying the TV coverage and two huge numeric screens carrying the total votes and percentages, which changed several times a minute like a stock exchange board. By the time we had worked our way to the front, the excitement had built to such levels that the cheers surged like giant waves on a beach. The vote percentages for the two sides were even, flickering a fraction below or above 50 per cent. Then the Oui began to hover longer and longer at 50, then 50.5, then 51. The roaring became constant. "On veut un pays!" (We want a country.) Whatever happened next would be divisive. A very narrow victory or a very narrow defeat would resolve nothing and held the potential for ugliness.

The chants of "On veut un pays" grew longer and more rhythmic, and I kept snapping pictures. I suddenly felt very strange. I was back in 1965, the chant was the same, the passion was as heartfelt, and I was the only person in the whole room who had aged thirty years. I felt like some ghost looking through plate glass at history unfolding.

Then within two minutes, everything changed. The huge digital counter stopped racing, moving only sluggishly, as if in some tawdry B-grade movie which shows the countdown on a nuclear bomb. Half a percentage point short of a Yes, the count froze. The chanting stopped and people milled around, uncertain. Was it over? Would some ballot box somewhere tip the total past 50? The mood had gone from mounting excitement to unbearable suspense and then, suddenly, numbed nothingness. The counter refused to budge.

While we were in the cab back to Winnie's, Parizeau was making the vulgar concession speech that blamed immigrants and big money. By morning, to Quebec's credit, denunciation of his remarks by commentators was so widespread that a clamour was already building for his resignation. There was no joy at Winnie's. This crowd of Quebec Anglos had been too savvy to share in Ottawa's overconfidence before tonight. But half a percentage point! When you lived on the linguistic fault line of the country every day, you knew this was no victory.

The next morning we boarded the train back to Toronto. On the five-hour trip I wrote the first of many drafts of a memo.

TO: Bob Culbert, Head of News, Current Affairs and Newsworld
     Norm Bolen, Head, Current Affairs
     Vince Carlin, Deputy Head, NCAN
RE: A People's History of Canada
     When I went to Montreal on Referendum day, I took my elder daughter with me, and on the train – with Xeroxes from encyclopaedias – I tried to tell her how we got here: Conquest, American invasion, Upper and Lower Canada, Act of Union. . . . Poor kid.

     And it underscored for me that I can buy her two television histories of the Civil War, or the History of Baseball, or the War of the Roses, five boxed sets on World War Two, two on the Vietnam War, and one on the Civil Rights Movement, three on Sexual Technique, the complete Edward R. Murrow Collection and two sets on Mutual Fund management. But I cannot give my children the History of Canada. It is missing, effectively, from the television archive of our country.

     We have not done, for this generation, the most important story of all. . . . The nation is undergoing not only tremendous crisis, but also fundamental change from Quebec sovereignty to

Free Trade. There is no current material that can show our audience the exciting and dramatic evolution of our country.... This is more than a pity, because of the excitement inherent in the story, this is a social and even political problem. This is a failure of cultural policy, and it's happening on our watch.

The shock of the referendum was not the genesis of the Canadian History Project. I had been actively talking about the idea for years, and in the documentary unit, we hoped it would be the next project for the *Dawn of the Eye* team. But until now, I had zero confidence I could sell it in the acrid climate in the CBC. I began to think that now might be the moment to make the formal move. The shock of the referendum, I was betting, would change the climate in the CBC, because it had given us all a brush with history. Over the next three weeks, I crafted the memo to Bob Culbert, who I knew would support the project. The memo gave Culbert the tactical instrument that would allow him to begin staking out the ground for us and begin to mobilize support. The memo went on to describe the series, showing that we had already developed a pretty clear idea of the approach – but massively underestimated its eventual length, by twelve hours:

> It is, essentially, a twenty-hour special television series on the history of Canada. It would be a kind of series which we hope the best historians and the best directors – inside and out – would be honoured to work on. Its style would be documentary, and change with the period. The twentieth century episodes would be closer to *Tenth Decade* and *The Champions* style; the 19th, being a century of photography, mostly in *Civil War* style; the 18th and 17th would use conservative re-enactments.
>
> It would be *A People's History of Canada*, a narrative history emphasizing the diaries and letters of farmers, explorers, traders and immigrants, rather than a diplomatic history. This is the core approach of Shelby Foote's *A Narrative History of the Civil*

War and Peter Watkins's *Culloden*. It is vibrant, story-driven and exciting. It is also very good historiography.

This series would assemble a committee of historical advisers which would be the best in the country. Within the series, every name, every line from a letter, every scene would be impeccably accurate. It would begin with the history of the aboriginal people, and end with the 1980's. We're certain we can make this a must-see national event. This is not intended to be didactic.

I'm always uncomfortable whenever I am asked when I got the idea for the project. It was hardly an original idea.

When I first met Peter Herrndorf in the mid-1970s, when he was vice-president of English Television, he told me, "There are two great ancestral projects which we have to do someday. The first is a history of Canada. The second is the twenty great classics of Canadian literature." I wasn't even thirty yet, and not even in television. It would take the conjunction of the millennium, the near-collapse of the country on October 30, 1995, and the virtual collapse of the CBC as we knew it before anyone could roll this boulder over the hill. And it took the most improbable team the CBC and Radio-Canada had ever seen to get the boulder there.

2

The Hail Mary Pass

Nineteen ninety-six was a critical year in the evolution of Canadian broadcasting. The regulatory body, the CRTC (Canadian Radio-television and Telecommunications Commission), was poised to give out licences to the last tier of cable specialty channels that spring, in what would be the equivalent of the Kansas land rush. A licence to create a history channel or a women's channel or another entertainment channel would be worth millions of dollars almost the instant it was granted. Snagging licences was critical to networks – CBC, CTV, or Global – as well as to production houses such as Alliance, as it was then known.

But the CBC was paralyzed, not only by the government but also by the thinly disguised hostility of the CRTC to any thought of adding to the CBC's existing channels. The specialty channels brought almost guaranteed income from subscription fees, but this fertile source of funding was being reserved for the private sector. The message from the government and from the CRTC to the CBC was, Stay out. (The only exception would be, possibly, a French equivalent of Newsworld.)

After the referendum, I concentrated again on *Dawn of the Eye*, and I finally got to meet our new president, Perrin Beatty. I had received an e-mail from him saying that he knew I had written a lot on broadcasting and inviting me to send him my ideas, so we could discuss them sometime in the next few weeks. We arranged to meet for lunch in Ottawa.

As it happened, the lunch fell on the day before he would be appearing on closed-circuit television across Canada, to announce to all staff how the board would administer the next instalment of cuts. All the devastation that had already ravaged the place was to meet *previous* cuts. Now the real destruction was to begin. Beatty had arranged for lunch in a modest Italian restaurant, and I was relieved that he didn't seem to remember our encounter in Stratford. He was charming, unpretentious, and as committed to public broadcasting as anyone I had met. But it became clear that his room for manoeuvre was virtually nil. He was genuinely troubled by the scale of the announcements that would come out the next day. At one point he said, "Mark, I wish tomorrow would never come."

We talked instead about the future. Specialty channels were everything right now, I argued. In the so-called thousand-channel universe, CBC had no shelf space – in English, just one channel plus Newsworld. Soon we would be just two out of seventy channels. The basic error the CRTC had made went back fifteen years, as far as I was concerned, when the commission turned down a second channel for the CBC. In Britain, the BBC had two channels, one more populist, one more intellectual. In Italy, RAI had three channels, Germany had several public channels, as did France. "Mark," Beatty said, "even if you're right, there isn't the remotest chance that the CRTC would give us a second channel." What was happening had only partly to do with deficit reduction by the government. Both the government and the CRTC wanted a smaller and weaker CBC at all costs.

"Got any ideas of what you'd like to do after *Dawn of the Eye?*" he asked toward the end of lunch. I hesitated. I knew Jim Byrd, the head of English Television, thought we should have a redeeming idea to give hope in this time of despair, but if I wasn't careful, I might lose what remote hope we had by mentioning it here. I had built up no support within the CBC for it, I hadn't checked with the French, and I hadn't made any external alliances yet. Well, I thought, the reason Gretzky scores the highest is that he takes the highest number of shots on goal, so . . . "I have an impertinent idea, but it would cost a lot of money. Perhaps we could do it as a millennium project. I'd like to do the first history of Canada in the television age, and I'd like to do it in French and in English."

His eyes widened, and he said, "Now you're talking my language!"

At the end of the lunch, as we got in his car, he said, "Maybe something like this, on this scale, can give some hope inside the CBC and send the message that we're not folding our tents."

On my way back to Toronto, I thought maybe, just maybe, the puck had slipped into the net. But I knew it would be a long time before we heard. It would take weeks and weeks of editorial research just to come up with a detailed treatment for the series, and right now we were scrambling to produce three separate versions of *Dawn of the Eye* for three different countries. I reported Beatty's reaction to Jim Byrd and went back to my job.

The announcements of the cuts, while no surprise, ground staff morale into hopelessness. That winter, we worked on *Dawn of the Eye* with designers, photo editors, and sound mixers who all thought this was their last job in the CBC. It was like working in a factory that was fulfilling one last order in the shipping department, while the movers and the liquidators had already moved onto the shop floor. I had been through that with *The Journal* four years earlier and was getting tired of this recurring experience.

March break was coming up. Our family just had to get away from the gloom, if only for a bit. We decided to rent a house on Sanibel Island in Florida for the break, and we would drive there, stopping in Kentucky so Caitlin could see the Horse Museum, going to Marineland, Disney World, and Universal Studios. The week before we were to leave I read an article in the *Globe and Mail* about the CRTC hearings for the new tier of channels in early April in Winnipeg. Competition for these last desirable spots was fierce, and one of the tightest races was for the new History Channel. An icy thought formed in my head. The CBC had lost its battle for the channel before it even started, but maybe it would lose the Canadian History Project too. It's so obvious, I thought; why hadn't I realized it before?

Applicants before the CRTC traditionally make extravagant promises about Canadian content and the great contribution they are going to make to Canadian society. Since they are almost all planning to make their money by importing American programming, the more original or theatrical their Canadian ideas sound, the better. Everyone in the production community had a pretty good idea what the History Channel might end up being: a lot of American documentaries bought from A&E and an endless rerunning of *Bridge on the River Kwai*. A ten-minute panel discussion about the movie you've just seen would pass for Canadian content. So what would be a high-profile promise an applicant could make to look as Canadian as possible? Something that would tie in with schools, something that would allow them to get countrywide support from historians, universities, teachers, and historical societies. Something that, although expensive, was one-time and not a permanent drain on the production budget.

I went to Vince Carlin, deputy head of news and current affairs, to be reassured that I was worrying too much. He offered no reassurance. Trina McQueen's company, for example, was one of the applicants for the history licence. "I think it's not only a possibility, it's a probability," he said. "It's especially the kind of project Trina McQueen would like. And if anyone beats us to the punch, we'll be in a very weak position." So, the day before leaving for March break, I called Bob Culbert and told him I had just written him a memo making a pretty outrageous proposal. Would he take it up to Jim Byrd while I was away?

TO: Bob Culbert, Vince Carlin, Norm Bolen
March 7, 1996
As I mentioned to Vince Friday, I've developed an anxiety about the two history channel applications, and it hadn't dawned

on me till this week that they could steal our thunder. Briefly, if you were applying for a History Channel, what's the first thing you would promise to do? And particularly the Labatt's application, with the US History channel, because Trina McQueen has always been a believer in what she called "national treasures" programming, as you might recall.

The application process, I believe, formally goes public in May, but it is usually preceded some time in advance by a flurry of articles about the promises each applicant makes. I'm worried that one of them might announce a mega-Canadian history series, and the CBC might end up in a "me-too" position with all the thunder taken out of us.

I think we should be prepared to announce that the CBC is developing a plan for A People's History of Canada, which will bring together the best historians, the best directors, the best CBC and independent producers across the country to produce it over the next five years. . . . I think we should be poised to take the franchise. . . .

There are months of detail work to be done, discussions with Radio-Canada, NFB, etc. In other words, we're not going to have the full scheme worked out, negotiated, budgeted and ready to announce for months. . . .

In case you need the sketch for an announcement, or a mention in a speech, or a leak to some friendly journalists (if there are any), I leave with this (attached) two-page safety kit. In Emergency, Break Glass and Make Announcement. My advice: Be pre-emptive.

Mark.

Attached was a two-page draft for a press release which began: "CBC Television is developing a production plan for an epic historical documentary series, A People's History of Canada, which would create the first definitive history of our country. The proposed series would be an unprecedented national endeavour which would mobilize production talent and historical expertise across all regions of the country and in both languages."

By the end of the afternoon, Bob Culbert was on the phone.

"I've seen you pull some stunts in your day, Mark," he said, "but do you actually expect them to announce something with no budget, no production plan, no approval, on something that will cost millions?"

"Well, I said it was cheeky," I replied, "but we'd just be announcing that we're developing it."

"I don't think you have much of a chance," he said. "But I'll try. I'll take it to Jim myself next week."

"Will you support it?"

"You know I will," he said.

I had just got a hands-free cellphone system installed in our old maroon Honda Accord, prior to our expedition to Florida. I was quite pleased; it all looked very professional. There was an antenna on the roof and a handset full of twinkling lights right beside the gearshift. The drive down took three days, and the only disappointment was that no one, absolutely no one, called us on my cellphone. I would have settled for a wrong number – I just wanted to hear it work. Since it was a weekend, I couldn't even invent a reason for my office to call us. That's the trouble with cellphones: either they drive you crazy, or they become constant, twenty-four-hour affirmations that no one on earth wants to talk to you.

Eventually we made it to the bungalow we'd rented on Sanibel Island. The four doors of the car were open and the family was unloading the suitcases when electronic pulses boomed out of the speakers in each open door. The sound filled the neighbourhood, and it took me a second to realize it was the speakerphone. I didn't know how to answer it, or where to speak. Finally, I pushed the "send" button, and that seemed to make the phone receive.

"Is that Mark Starowicz?" the Honda's four open doors asked.

"Yes, it is," I replied, speaking to the steering wheel, since I didn't know where the microphone was. The kids just kept noisily unloading bags, looking at me with irritation as I motioned them away.

"This is Bridget in Jim Byrd's office, Mark. Please hold for Jim."

The vice-president of English Television calling could only mean some disaster had occurred with *Witness*. I kept waving the kids away, and they finally rolled their eyes and went into the bungalow. Jim came on – from his voice, obviously on a speakerphone himself.

"Mark? Bob Culbert gave me your history memo with the emergency press release." He was audible a block away. I couldn't find any volume settings on the handset and wasn't about to hang up on him accidentally by trying.

"Have you consulted with the National Film Board?" he asked.

"No."

"The French network?"

"Well, no, I didn't feel I had the authority to. We just can't wait," I said. "Negotiating with everyone will take months."

There was a long pause, and I remember taking in the vegetation around the bungalow for the first time as I waited, including the sign that said "Alligator Pond."

Finally, he said: "I agree. Let's take out references to both languages until we can get the French to come on board. Take out twenty hours in case that changes. And let's move up the millennium project angle. I'm going to add that the development stage will determine the feasibility of the project, with CBC seeking financing from Canadian foundations, institutions, and corporations. That sound OK to you?"

The last addition was tactically good. After all, how could the CBC mount such a large project when it was complaining it was being bled to death by the cuts? Byrd had turned the problem around by saying the CBC was going to raise the money from outside. But even with all the cautions he had written in, he knew that the headlines would read "CBC to Make History of Canada," not "CBC to Develop Proposal and Examine Financial Feasibility of. . . ." He had agreed to set a chain of events in motion which he knew would be irreversible. I went into the bungalow. "You won't believe what just happened. We're doing the history of Canada."

That evening, watching TV in the bungalow, I fell asleep and woke up to a sports show that was discussing football. I don't follow football, so I was about to shut it off when I heard one of the panellists talking about the Hail Mary pass, which originated with the Notre Dame university football squad. It is used by a team only as a last resort, at the end of the game, when they're behind in the score. The quarterback falls back and throws a long, desperate pass to the receivers, praying that one of them will catch it. Fifteen per cent of the time, the pass is caught and wins the game. After that, I called the history project the CBC's Hail Mary pass.

Two weeks later, when I came into my office Monday morning, I was met by a stack of newspaper clippings on my desk. Almost all of them said something like "It's about time." In the mail were the first applications to work on the project from former CBCers, from students, young historians, cameramen, and researchers. As I opened some envelopes, black and white pictures fell out; Canadians had started to send in the stories of their fathers at war, photocopies of letters, and even their grandparents' diaries. There is a moment in the torturous process of giving a project life when you get an inexplicable feeling of lightness, as if you've slipped the bonds of gravity and just become airborne. It's a feeling I've had no more than four or five times in my life. That Monday morning, I felt it again. We had liftoff. I pulled Gene Allen, my colleague on *Dawn of the Eye*, into my office and let the clippings drift from my palms onto the desk. I kept stuffing applications and letters into his hands as he stood grinning and shaking his head.

"Can you believe it?" I said. "A two-page memo, one simple press release – and *this!*"

"There must be a law against this," he said, going through the applications and letters.

"There probably is. Nevertheless, it looks like you have yourself the history of Canada."

Gene Allen is a rare combination of journalist and academic, son of the legendary war correspondent and magazine editor Ralph Allen. Tall with a broad bald dome, he looks the part of a professor, but his soul is still more in the press room than in the faculty lounge.

He had been foreign editor of the *Globe and Mail* and also had a PhD in Canadian history, but for some reason he succumbed to the lure of television. He left newspapers to join CBC-TV News, then CBC Radio, then drifted into our documentary unit, becoming entangled in *Dawn of the Eye*. Every time we screened early footage of Canada for that series, he became enthused at the dim and distant hope that we would someday make a history of Canada. "The things we could do, Mark," he'd say, "it's such an incredible story" – and he'd launch into the telling of one dramatic tale or another. Suddenly, to our own amazement, it was no longer a dim and distant glimmer. It was a glaring headlight of a train that was roaring down the track right at us, and Gene Allen was about to have the ride of his life.

Three weeks later, we received a call from the National Film Board in Montreal, asking if we'd be available to meet the government film commissioner, Sandra Macdonald, and the head of the English program at the NFB, Barbara Janes. The formality of this approach meant something significant was up, since Sandra and I were friends and she could have just rung me up. A few days later, Sandra arrived in my office wearing a wide-brimmed straw hat and flower-patterned dress and accompanied by her more sombre-looking deputy, Barbara. Sandra came to the point immediately: "The National Film Board cannot afford to have the CBC do the history of Canada by itself. It could be politically fatal to us. Your press release says you want partners. We want to be your partners."

Don Richardson, deputy head of the documentary unit, was with me and asked, "Partners to what extent?"

Sandra replied, "That's the point. Fifty-fifty. We want to be full, equal partners. We're not interested in just subsidizing the CBC. In all the horror that we are going through at the NFB, I want something vibrant, something being born, and something that gives people hope for the future. I also think the CBC's and the NFB's futures are tied together. Is a full, equal partnership acceptable to you?"

Don and I exchanged glances and communicated wordlessly. "We can't think of a more elegant partnership than between the two largest cultural production institutions in the country," I replied.

Don asked how much the NFB was prepared to commit. Sandra was suitably cautious, saying it depended on the final budget, but given the scope of what we proposed, she was prepared to start off by putting $7.5 million on the table.

The meeting lasted two hours while we developed plans to tell the same story in French and English Canada, to recruit an extraordinary binational team, and perhaps build a bridge between the CBC and the NFB that would change the very nature of our institutions. Exciting stuff. It felt great to have the clear financial commitment; it felt even better to have a partner who believed in the same principles. We agreed to meet in Montreal in two weeks to start hammering out a deal.

The next day, Don and I met with Jim Byrd and Perrin Beatty, who happened to be in town. The NFB offer had cheered us all, but we had a problem. I couldn't go to the Montreal negotiations without a penny in my pocket while Sandra had committed $7.5 million to start – she was in for half of whatever final budget we would jointly develop. "I need to go to Montreal with a commitment of $10 million from the CBC," I said. Don Richardson obligingly devised a plan, with Jim Byrd, whereby the $10 million could be gotten without breaking the English network. It would mean running the series over two years. The two organizations, each with two language services, could absorb the cost if it were spread over two years without crippling anyone. Five million dollars a year was just the price of two Sunday-night movies. That was the breakthrough, and by the end of the week, I had the commitment from English Television. The next step would not be so easy: French Television.

Radio-Canada was boxed in to some degree. The English network had announced that it would make the history of Canada its millennium project, and it would be awkward if the French network left it all to the English or, worse, didn't run it at all. After all, General Wolfe hadn't even arrived on these shores until after 150 years of New France, and you couldn't have the English do the history of New France, the 1837 Rebellions, the Riel Rebellion – or any part of Canadian history – without the French. No, they would have to participate. Our concern was that Radio-Canada might choose to participate in a token fashion by attaching an adviser or two and eventually just run a dubbed and translated version. That approach, however, would risk raising a lot of questions: Why didn't your two services collaborate more? Why is Montcalm an English actor dubbed into French? There is little doubt that Radio-Canada, at its highest levels, had little taste for this project and wished it had never happened because of the Pandora's box it opened. And I'm certain that had the idea gone up through the two networks' normal process of approval at all levels, it never would have seen the light of day. But here it was.

Don Richardson and I flew to Montreal to discuss the project with Claude Saint-Laurent, Radio-Canada's director of news and current affairs, the equivalent of Bob Culbert in the French network. Claude is a large, red-haired, blunt, and colourful newsman right out of *The Front Page*. Our business lunch lasted eight hours and has entered the folklore of CBC and Radio-Canada, both for the endurance of the parties involved and for what it achieved. The deal was done in a fog of nicotine and sealed with a barrel or so of wine. I liked Claude a lot, and I trusted him.

Claude was politically savvy enough to know he had to get involved, but he had restrained enthusiasm for getting into a vague project based on old engravings, not to mention a partnership with the NFB. Newsmen like Claude considered NFB directors to be self-obsessed "auteurs," and NFB directors undoubtedly considered Radio-Canada newsmen the cinematic equivalents of paving contractors.

I built my pitch by comparing what we'd do to Ric and Ken Burns's series *The Civil War*, partly to establish that photos don't have to be boring but mainly to emphasize that every word, every quote, every character would be true. Nothing would be made up. To illustrate this approach, I started reciting from memory the opening script of *The Civil War*: "By the summer of 1861, Wilmer McLean had had enough. Two great armies were converging on his farm. And what would be the first major battle of the civil war, Manassas, would soon rage over the aging Virginian's farm, a shell going so far as to

explode in his summer kitchen. Now McLean moved his family away
from Manassas, far south and west of Richmond out of harm's way,
he prayed, to a dusty little crossroads called Appomattox Junction."
Saint-Laurent came to life as if struck by an adrenaline dart, and
stunned me by completing the passage from memory too: "And it is
there, in his living room, that Lee surrendered to Grant. So Wilmer
McLean could rightly say that the Civil War 'began in my summer
kitchen and ended in my front parlour.'" Saint-Laurent was a Civil
War buff, in the last place in North America I expected to find one.
Finally he took in a big breath and said: "I thought that series was
brilliant. So are you saying this series will be like that?"

"Yes," I said, "that's our model. Except we'll have to use actors
before the age of photography." He fixed his eyes on me and underscored each word with his index finger thumping the table: "But
every quote will be completely accurate?" I nodded, and I continued,
"And drawn from their letters and diaries – there will be no composite characters."

"So this is a work of journalism," he said. "I thought it was some
kind of half-drama." No, I said, this would be produced by journalists and historians, to the same standard as all our other journalism.

Claude got more excited at the thought of applying the same
approach as *The Civil War* to the Battle of the Plains of Abraham, to
the 1837 Rebellions, to the conscription crisis. By now the lunch
crowd had disappeared, and the waiters were standing around dis-
consolately. Every hour or so, Claude sent them out for another
pack of cigarettes. Hours later, the supper crowd started to come in,
and we had come down to discussing the French versus the English
version. I knew that certain episodes and characters had more
importance in Quebec than in English Canada. I suggested that
those chapters could have a longer version for the French audience,
and the same would be true for some English characters and events.
In my mind, at least, I knew I'd have to concede some significant
differences in the two versions – not in interpretation but in elabo-
ration. Claude pulled himself up again and, with his index finger
thumping on the table once more, transformed the project with a

statement that was breathtakingly bold, especially in the politically charged post-referendum air.

"No," he said. "Thank you for offering two versions, but no. For once, let's tell the same story to both language groups at the same time." I had not expected this. Only a Quebecker could make this offer, because the decision would be quite controversial in Quebec. As if that move weren't audacious enough, he had another: "And we need one team, both French and English combined, working together, fighting together. I think this is the most important idea I have heard. It must have a CBC executive producer and a Radio-Canada executive producer" – my heart started sinking, imagining the dilemma of two chiefs – but he was saying, "and therefore, Mark, how would you like to be an executive producer for Radio-Canada? Because you're my choice for the job. You come from here, you understand the dynamic."

By the end of the evening we had a deal. Don and I had to help each other onto the plane to Toronto. Something of historic importance had occurred in Montreal that day. A single English-French team of journalists and historians would try to report honestly, warts and all, on every controversial event and issue in Canadian history. And Saint-Laurent's backing, I knew, could make it happen.

The next meeting with Sandra and Barbara at the NFB went well. It produced a letter of intent which estimated the cost of the series at $20.5 million, but the NFB found this low. They thought $25 million would be closer to the actual cost. The CBC would take the lead in running the television production, while the NFB, which was interested in developing new media, would take the lead in all publishing, videos, CDs, DVDs, and new-media production. The staff would be half CBC/Radio-Canada and half NFB, English and French divisions.

We had a long way to go in drawing up a co-production agreement, but we had made very satisfying progress in a short time. We toasted each other with our cups of coffee, and I said, "This could be the beginning of an extraordinary production."

Barbara Janes added, as we clinked cups: "Or *Waterworld.*"

In the next few days back in Toronto, I got a call from Perrin Beatty. He had been at a function where the governor general, Roméo LeBlanc, had come up to him. Beatty said, "He saw the press report about the history project, and he is very excited. I don't know if you know that he wants to make the focus of his tenure as governor general the improvement of the teaching and knowledge of Canadian history. He wants to meet you."

It's a modest thrill to climb into a cab at the Ottawa airport on a nice spring day and say, "Rideau Hall, please." His Excellency was affable, welcoming, and very down-to-earth. He and his gold-braided navy aide met us at a side door and beckoned Beatty and me down a hall to the octagonal room rich in panelling and bookshelves that was his office. I paused at the door, to let him enter first, and he said: "No, no, the RCMP says I cannot go in first, in case there is a bomb. After you."

LeBlanc was several things. He was a battle-hardened cabinet minister from the Trudeau years, known to be in the left wing of the cabinet. He was also a former journalist whom I remembered from my newspaper days, and he conveyed the ease of an old warrior. As an Acadian, also, his hospitality was flawless and his speech direct.

"I think this is the most important project I have seen, with a possibly fundamental impact on the country," he said. "Nobody knows their history, we leave it buried in myths. The myths and prejudices are so deep, people don't even know how to talk to one another; no one understands where the other parties are coming from. How can I help you make this a success?"

Our problem, Beatty explained, would be funding the project. "We need to find several major corporate sponsors who will put significant money into this, so that it doesn't drain the CBC coffers."

"Tell me whom to call, and I will use whatever influence this office has to encourage that corporation or foundation to help you," the governor general replied. "If you want to have a fundraising event, use this place," he said, his outstretched arm taking in the mansion and the grounds, "and tell me what you'd like me to do." In the short time between March break in Florida and this June afternoon in Rideau Hall, I had gone from despair to the biggest run of good fortune in my life, and to the excitement of an epic series. In a few days, that fortune would take a sadder turn but also profoundly shape my view of the series.

Soon after I got back home, my mother, who had been hospitalized for two years, her body and her mind ravaged by diabetes and strokes that left her completely incapacitated, was rushed to Toronto General with another stroke. I was told she would die within three days. Instead she lived for sixteen more days, which were an anguish for both her and her family. During this time her wartime friends came to pay their respects. They told me about her role during the Warsaw Uprising and in history's first female prisoner-of-war camp. It was a revelation. I had known the outline of the heroic uprising against the Germans, but I had never heard stories about my mother smuggling guns past German lines, forging documents, and delivering messages through Warsaw's sewer system.

The veterans who came to my mother's bedside all had grandchildren now, all over the continent, Québécois, Americans, Albertans, Mohawks, married to Catholics and Jews and Hindus; in the fifty years since they were interned at the Oberlangen POW camp, they had become woven into the fabric of the New World. During those late nights at the hospital and at our house, so many human stories unfolded against the background of titanic events that I didn't need to refer to *The Civil War* any more. I understood how we must do the history of Canada: we had to follow a thousand threads, a thousand stories of people caught in the web of history.

The morning of the funeral service a courier delivered a completely unexpected envelope with the Canadian coat of arms embossed in gold. It was from Rideau Hall and was signed by Governor General Roméo LeBlanc. The letter spoke of my father's and my mother's records in the war, and of the Poles who fought under the Canadian flag. It ended: "Barbara Starowicz is a daughter of the Polish nation and of the Canadian nation. In recognition of that common battle and that joint legacy, we would be honoured if, alongside the Polish flag, Barbara Starowicz would rest under the Canadian flag." She did.

That summer went by in a hurricane of activity finishing the three versions of *Dawn of the Eye*, which meant writing six hours of scripts and getting permission to use thousands of photographs and films from the century of cinema. The program director of the History Channel came up from New York and loved what he saw, which meant that we had a $1-million deal with them, on top of the $1.5 million we got from the BBC. The British side of the co-production, however, was maddening, because both executive producers, the BBC's Glynn Jones and I, had equal authority over the series, and this was consuming literally hours a day on the phone. I was reminded by someone of Napoleon's adage: "Better one mediocre general than two brilliant ones." I would remember that for the history project.

In August, Perrin Beatty and I were to meet the governor general again, but Beatty had to back out at the last minute, and at one in the afternoon I found myself alone at Rideau Hall with Roméo LeBlanc. He was concerned about the continuing troubles at the CBC, and I spent at least two hours telling him how I thought it was being destroyed, and how the national broadcasting policy was doing radical damage to Canada's future. We talked about the Internet, convergence, the thousand-channel universe – he was well-read on everything, and hungry to know more.

LeBlanc is a remarkable raconteur, and he told me stories of battles in cabinet meetings, anecdotes about Trudeau and about life as an Acadian. "My father worked for the railway, and he believed in precision," he said. "He hated how Montrealers always assumed they were at the centre of the world and wouldn't even recognize that some French communities lived in other time zones. He always fumed when the French network would give the time. He'd pull out his watch and point to it. 'Six o'clock! It's not six. It's seven! Who the hell do those Montrealers think they are?'"

The vibrant, self-contained cultures that make up this country have always fascinated me, but none more than the Acadians. I have always wondered why the Acadians, who had survived far greater tribulation at the hands of the English than Quebec ever had, didn't nurture the same feeling of being victims as their Quebec cousins. Most Acadians were federalist.

"Oh, we've had two centuries to digest it," LeBlanc said, "but I think we have a better understanding of what really happened, and who our enemies were. It's not the British that wanted us out – it wasn't Pitt in London who was obsessed about some tiny people in North America. When you go looking for the answers, you'll find them in the Boston board of trade." At the time, I just found his answer puzzling. In a year, when I started to research the episode called "Battle for a Continent," I would realize what he meant, and just how little I knew about the drama of this continent's history.

By now, he had brought out a bottle of Scotch, and we were almost halfway through it as the afternoon turned to evening. He talked about his interest in aboriginal education and his travels around the world as governor general, but the conversation invariably returned to history and his conviction that we were becoming a nation without a memory. He didn't mean history as something patriotic or "feel-good," he meant it as a function of the Canadian society and psyche. "If we don't know what shaped the differing regional and national perspectives," he said, "how can you ever hope to have an intelligent dialogue, or negotiate a modus vivendi?" The naval attaché came in two or three times to remind His Excellency that I was booked on the 6:00 plane, and then, when we had my reservation moved, to remind him it was time for me to leave to catch the 8:00. Each time, engrossed in conversation, LeBlanc politely waved him off. Sandwiches carried us through supper, and we continued with one of the most delightful, candid, and thought-provoking conversations I have ever had.

"You know, Your Excellency," I said, "this is not going to be a rose-coloured, feel-good history of Canada. A lot of it is going to be pretty ugly, and not only the episode on the Acadian Deportation. This is a history of racism, religious persecution, massacres, anti-Semitism, as well as heroics. This series will bring up every toxin and poison from the Manitoba Schools Question to anti-Asian riots in British Columbia."

"I wouldn't expect any less from you," he said. "Honesty in confronting the past will not sink this country. But complete ignorance and silence will."

As the long summer evening finally turned to dusk, the aide came in one last time: "Your Excellency, the last plane out of Ottawa for Toronto is leaving in forty minutes." This time I had to leave. LeBlanc called up his official private car and driver and bundled me in, and he and his aide stood at the entrance waving as the car turned around. He shouted, "Don't worry, we pay the speeding tickets." And with that, in a black car bristling with cellphones, radios, and whip antennas, I was raced to Uplands airport.

Claude Saint-Laurent at Radio-Canada was very uneasy when I reported my conversation with the governor general. "I like him, he's a terrific guy, but this could be fatal to our credibility in Quebec," he said. "In English Canada the office is seen as being above political partisan affairs. In Quebec, it's not, you know that." I did know that, but we were talking strictly about the governor general helping us open doors to corporations and institutions, I said, where a phone call or a letter from him could make a world of difference. "Editorially it makes no difference," he replied. "You know there are a lot of interests which will take one straw like this and distort the whole story, try to paint us as some federal 'Save Canada' initiative. Our editorial integrity is everything. That's why I wanted you." He was right about the danger of the Bloc Québécois or the press distorting any contact with LeBlanc. But I thought accepting his offer of initiating corporate contacts was not only defendable but critical to the scale of money we would need. And second, this project – so far – was just a press release; it could still blow away like a feather in the wind with everything that was happening at the CBC. Sandra Macdonald's commitment at the NFB had brought the project one step nearer to reality but it hadn't made it solid. But Roméo LeBlanc's conviction that this project was critical for the conduct of a civil debate in the country was the strongest card I had against any backsliding by the

CBC, and a powerful card in opening corporate doors. The faster we got a couple of major corporate sponsors, the faster we'd have unstoppable momentum.

I e-mailed Beatty to report on both the conversation with the governor general and Saint-Laurent's deep concern. Beatty didn't understand Claude's view, saying, "The governor general is a non-political office," but I reiterated that that was not the way Quebec saw it. We could not have a big sponsorship dinner or event at Rideau Hall, but we might well accept LeBlanc's offer to help us make strategic corporate contacts. Beatty thought I was being too cautious but conceded that I now reported to Saint-Laurent as well as the English network, and left it to me. Still, the thought flitted through my mind a few times that this must be one of the few major countries in the world where having an encounter with the head of state was something to keep quiet.

The next time I met LeBlanc was in the fall. He was coming to Toronto to open the horse show at the Royal Winter Fair, and he invited me to dine with him afterwards in the governor general's suite at the Royal York Hotel. On the day, when I got off the elevator, I was met by two RCMP plainclothesmen, who glanced nervously at the box I was carrying. "It's the PBS series about the Civil War," I muttered. "A present for His Excellency."

We dined at a table for two, and he told me about a world gathering of the Acadian community in Louisiana he had recently attended. The experience had moved him deeply. Because all the family names were the same as in Canada he felt a tremendous connection. When they learned of his role in Canada, Acadians from all over the world treated him as if he were the elder statesman of their people. While we talked, I could see the shoes of the RCMP security men through the crack under the door as they paced constantly back and forth. Later, his son and some of his friends joined us briefly, and I got the sense of a large, warm extended family.

When we were alone again, I screwed up my courage and told him about Claude's concerns, and how we probably couldn't use Rideau Hall as a venue for launching the fundraising. Would he be offended if we accepted his offer to open corporate doors for us on a more private basis instead? He agreed, though I could see he was wearied by being treated as a foreign entity in Quebec. He told me how he insisted on using the governor general's other official residence at the Citadel in Quebec City, to make the point that his office was not just an English-Canadian institution.

Then he pulled a file folder out of his briefcase which contained an alphabetical listing, prepared by his staff, of every major corporate leader in the country from Asper to Zimmerman. "As you can see," he said as he passed a copy over, "I've been doing my homework. Now, whom can we go for?" We went down the list, debating the likelihood of Conrad Black participating as a sponsor, how to approach the banks or the transportation sector, and how to describe the series. I felt a bit sheepish giving the governor general of Canada tips and phrases about how to describe the project, and advice on what to avoid, but he dutifully wrote it all down like a diligent researcher. "I'll be at an event with the Bombardier people soon," he said, "and I'll see what I can do." It was impossible not to like him more with every encounter.

But I had a problem when it came to fundraising: it was, technically, none of my business. Yes, the president of the CBC had welcomed the governor general's offer of help and had left the rest up to me, but I had no authority in the business of commercial sponsorship, which was one of the worst muddles in the CBC. We didn't even know what form of sponsorship we wanted. Would the series carry commercials, or would it have the kind of "soft" corporate sponsorship that PBS had with *Masterpiece Theatre*? I thought it would be unconscionable to run commercials in the history of Canada, and I told Beatty and Jim Byrd that "we can't have a Red Lobster commercial popping up in the middle of the Acadian Deportation." But at a time when $200 million more was being slashed from the CBC budget, no one was prepared to guarantee a non-commercial series. Then there was the sales department, or rather the two sales departments – of the CBC and Radio-Canada – which reported to separate vice-presidents and which, I soon learned, loathed each other. There had been some battle royal recently about Olympic sponsorship, which left a trail of bad blood and which I neither understood nor wanted to. To make matters worse, the CBC was thinking of privatizing its sales department as part of the avalanche of reorganizations that the consultants had been encouraging. So there was really no one to negotiate with. I was also getting the distinct impression that the history project was as welcome to the sales departments of both networks as smallpox.

I didn't quite grasp this until a friend in the department explained, "The series is at least twenty hours each on two networks in the millennium year. Unless it's declared fully commercial – that is, twelve minutes an hour that we can sell – then you represent twenty prime-time Sunday-night hours that these guys can't sell at market rates. Don't forget, they make a lot of their income on a percentage of their sales." No wonder the sales department wasn't hot on the series.

The problem remained: how could I answer the governor general's questions about how much money we were looking for from each corporation if I didn't know whether we were selling air time by the minute or were looking for the prestige "sponsorship" of a non-commercial series? It was the difference between selling a plaque on a church pew and renting space to a hot dog cart in front of the church. It was impossible, without reordering the entire sales and sponsorship theory and structure of the CBC and Radio-Canada, to get a clear decision. I had to stall.

That autumn there were even more unsettling signs that things were out of control in the CBC – at the highest reaches and in the strangest places. The CBC had carried the Summer Olympics in Atlanta in August, and the CBC chair, Guylaine Saucier, had gone down with some other board members, ostensibly to see the games and cheer the CBC Sports crew on. Then rumours started to circulate that the main purpose of the trip to Atlanta was something else: that Saucier and the board members wanted to have a confidential meeting with Sheila Copps, the minister responsible for the CBC. Their objective, the rumour went, was to unseat Perrin Beatty. Many board members felt the appointments of the chair and the president made the previous year by the PMO had everything backwards, and that Guylaine Saucier should have been made president, because she had a strong corporate background, and Beatty should have been made chair, since he had a policy background. Several board members regarded Perrin Beatty as likeable but ineffective and weak, and their dissatisfaction with him had evolved from grumbling to active conspiracy.

It transpired that Perrin Beatty and his supporters on the board got wind of the hidden agenda of the trip and hastily booked themselves to Atlanta so they could inhibit the other board faction from seeing Sheila Copps alone. I learned later that this led to a modest standoff between Saucier and Beatty, and some tentative division of powers. None of this, however, was particularly inspirational to the troops, who were dejectedly waiting to be decimated in the next wave of cuts. It certainly gave me little confidence about the viability of the history project. The CBC felt more like a corridor in the Kremlin these days, and I never knew if the person I was negotiating with would be there in a month's time.

Christmas came, and with it more bad news. My colleague Brian McKenna called me from Montreal to tell me that Nick Auf der Maur, the closest friend I had on earth, had just been diagnosed with cancer. This was unbearable. In seven years I had lost my father, Stanislaw, then Barbara Frum, then a program that was almost my family, then my mother; and now the man who for thirty years had virtually been my elder brother was facing death. The news devastated hundreds of us, a generation of Montreal journalists. If Nick, the colourful buccaneer who had cut such a swath through Quebec journalism, wasn't invincible, then neither were we.

Dawn of the Eye went to air the first week of January 1997. In Canada the series was met with almost universal acclaim from the critics, with the *Globe and Mail* calling it "the magisterial work of a generation of very talented and caring journalists." While it was on the air, the CBC started laying off the same journalists the press was lauding, the people I was counting on to produce the history series. I had thought the documentary unit was safe from cutbacks, since it

actually generated money, attracting investment from Telefilm and
bringing co-production money from the BBC. So I hadn't worried
about losing our team. I should have. I had forgotten that two of our
best directors, Alan Mendelsohn and Bill Cobban, both veterans of
The Journal's documentary team, were technically on the news
department's books. They had been seconded to us, and we repaid
the news department their salaries while they worked for the project.
In January Alan and Bill were summoned by the head of news.
Mendelsohn remembers being told that *The National Magazine* was
being reorganized, and being handed a notice that his position in the
news department was being eliminated. He had been laid off. "I was
completely shocked. I felt I had been hit on the head by a baseball
bat," Mendelsohn says. He had been at the CBC for twenty-two years
and had been one of the central people at *As It Happens*, and later
one of *The Journal*'s best documentary field producers, producing
many award-winning films. "I was an easy cut, because I was out of
sight while I was working for *Dawn of the Eye*," he says. "Also, I was
definitely part of the old *Journal* guard, and they were being picked
off like flies." Cobban was called in just after Mendelsohn. He was a
little more sanguine about it because he knew he had a future outside
the CBC. He had taken a leave of absence the year before to produce
a documentary for an independent production company, a film shot
in India documenting the selling of children into the prostitution
trade. It had just been broadcast to considerable acclaim. Still, it was
ironic that the CBC laid him off just after running his film. A few
weeks later, it won an Emmy in New York.

Laine Drewery had left the CBC a few years earlier and was an
independent working on contract. The layoffs didn't affect him but
they confirmed for him that he had done the right thing in leaving
years earlier and that there was no future for serious documentary
production inside the CBC. These were three of the brightest producers of their generation. The common denominator among the
three producers now was that the CBC had no interest in any of
them. It's not that they were costing the news department money
(we were paying for them), it's that each department had to come

up with a body count for Ottawa. And these people were more valuable to the CBC as layoff statistics than as producers.

In a few months, as soon as we had finished the American edition of *Dawn of the Eye*, the CBC would have no jobs for Cobban, Mendelsohn, Drewery, and Gene Allen, nor for Michael Sweeney, the cameraman, Murray Green, the editor, nor Ron Krant, the visual researcher. All the talent, skills, and synergy that I had hoped to turn into a documentary unit would be gone – unless I could nail down the history project, which right now was just a mountain of good intentions. There was no appetite in the CBC for capitalizing on this collection of talent, and no comprehension that it was a team, an asset, that should be repurposed. To divest ourselves of them was the equivalent of a Silicon Valley company laying off its software designers.

The hope of scoring a big sponsor fast, with the governor general's help, was mired at the CBC. The only other hope for making the project real was Sandra Macdonald at the National Film Board, but she was running into problems within her own institution. The NFB is as sharply divided between French and English "programs" as the CBC is between its two networks. The head of the NFB's French program didn't like the draft memorandum of understanding Sandra had drawn up with us and wanted more editorial and staff control. I flew back and forth to Montreal, dividing my time between meetings at the NFB with the French program and Sandra, and seeing Nick Auf der Maur. Brian McKenna and Stephen Phizicky, two of my oldest friends, had organized people to shop for him and to take him to Montreal General for chemotherapy. I joined the team for those days I was in town, and Nick and I would find ourselves in the basement of the General, early in the morning, with about fifty other patients, waiting his turn. He had bravely decided to write about his diagnosis in his *Gazette* column, so the entire English community in Montreal knew about it and was rooting for him. I could see people glancing up from their papers at him while we sat in the clinic. As soon as he was called in and was out of sight, the room would burst into excited murmuring that the star cancer patient of Montreal was here. "They say he always wears a Donald Duck tie," I heard one woman say, as if she were talking about the Lone Ranger's mask. It was true, Nick had the world's greatest collection of Donald Duck ties and other memorabilia – a childhood thing. I stayed with him the nights I was in Montreal, and we'd talk long hours about the history project, and in particular our experiences in recent Quebec history.

In the mornings when I was in town, I'd drive him to the clinic and then go to the film board, where I'd work with the executive producer I had hoped the NFB would assign to the series, Adam Symansky. Adam, who has a close-cropped beard and an easy manner, had worked with Donald Brittain, loved the NFB as much as I loved the CBC, and was just as dismayed about what cuts were doing to his institution. He took me through a giant studio, which seemed the size of a football field, and gestured to the high lights and the giant scrims, saying, "These days are over forever." We'd discuss possible directors, then spent hours trying to arrive at a common vision of how to use actors.

What became clear were the big cultural differences between our institutions. The National Film Board had a "director's" culture, a climate that encouraged filmmakers like Jacques Godbout to produce intensely personal cinematic visions. They regarded the CBC as a "factory" that trampled individual vision. But I was convinced that a team that would research, write, and produce the history of Canada could not be an "auteur" team. It would be hard to mesh the two cultures, but if we could bridge these mutual suspicions, we might be able to revitalize both embattled institutions. One late afternoon, as I was leaving to see Nick, Adam introduced me to a producer who wished us good luck with the series. As we walked away, she shouted after us, "Above all, do not produce a boring history of Canada!" I forgot her name, but not her warning.

The next time I was with Nick at the General, he came out of chemo and we were walking to my car when he did a pirouette in the snow. "The tumour has disappeared!" he declared. "They say it's gone!" That evening, I missed my plane home because of the partying at Nick's two hangouts on Crescent Street, Winnie's and Ziggy's.

Back in Toronto, not only had the sales and sponsorship clouds not cleared, but I discovered entirely by accident that the CBC, through its movies and mini-series department, had agreed to co-fund a giant, multi-million-dollar drama on the Battle of the Plains of Abraham, which had been developed by an independent produc-tion company. I went storming up to the new program director, Slawko Klymkiw, and could barely control my anger.

"How many Battles of the Plains of Abraham are we going to have?" I demanded. "It is the centrepiece of one of our episodes in the history series!"

Slawko hadn't been involved in the other project so was caught off guard. "Well," he said, trying to be even-handed, "why can't we have both – one is a drama, the other is history."

"How do you think that's going to look in Parliament!" I stam-mered. "We're pleading that we've been cut to the bone, then we finance two entirely separate Battles of the Plains of Abraham! One entirely in English, while the other is in two languages. Neither Radio-Canada nor Sandra at the NFB knows anything about this, and we're going to look duplicitous, because no one's going to believe I didn't know anything about it. And most of all – how come one side of the CBC is negotiating with an independent company and Telefilm, while we on the documentary side don't even know a word about it?" It wasn't as if our project was a secret; it had been a year since it was announced in every paper in the country.

Slawko told me to calm down and promised he'd try to sort it out. What he found out was that the script for the drama had been written a long time ago by an independent producer, and the CBC drama department had always wanted to produce it, long before our history project. The movies and mini-series people assumed our series would be mostly narration and engravings. No duplicity had been intended. Months later, the private production company failed to put together enough financing, and the potential disaster was averted.

The negotiations with Sandra Macdonald were finally coming together. She had to shuttle between her French and English pro-grams, trying to come up with suitable language for a deal, while I commuted between Montreal and Toronto, trying to negotiate the allocation of edit suites, cameramen, and budgets between the French and English networks. We were both working toward having everything in place by June, when all the parties would be at the Banff Television Festival.

As soon as we arrived in Banff, Sandra and I holed up in a sandwich and soup parlour, with our laptops, spreadsheets, and documents, hammering out the final clauses that would please the CBC English, the NFB English, the CBC French, and the NFB French. At one point, Sandra looked up from the mess of papers and sighed: "Give me something simple to resolve. Like Bosnia!"

As soon as we had completed our drafts, we rushed them to Jim Byrd, who crunched the numbers into CBC categories. He spent the night going from room to room in the Banff Springs Hotel with scribbled figures on graph paper, conferring with Michèle Fortin of the French network, Perrin Beatty, and the Head Office finance people. He took any changes back to Sandra, who faxed them to both the French and English programs at the NFB in Montreal.

Thursday was barbecue night at the Banff festival. Hundreds of people descended on an outdoor arena full of towering bonfires, with wild fiddle music and rock and roll reverberating in the various dance areas, and started to drink far too much. This is where Danish and Korean program directors in cowboy hats can let go and learn square dancing, just as we Canadians do every day in our offices. It can be quite surreal, with two-metre flames licking the sky, illuminating uncomprehending Taiwan television delegates as the speakers blare out "Barrett's Privateers."

Here, at nine o'clock at night in the middle of June, the president of the CBC, wearing a straw cowboy hat, formally shook hands with the government film commissioner, also sporting a straw cowboy hat, and the deal was consummated. We talked about making a joint announcement in Old Montreal, and I actually square-danced that night.

On Monday, back in Toronto, I told the unit the good news: we had a deal and they had jobs. But the next day, everything fell apart. In a three-hour phone call with Adam Symansky, I found out that there had been nobody at the NFB receiving any of the faxes from Banff. Now he had read them and he didn't like the deal; the French didn't like the deal. I was at my wits' end. "Doesn't the government film commissioner represent the NFB? I feel like we've been negotiating with poltergeists for a year," I said.

Adam did not like the decision that there would be just one executive producer, namely me. He felt he had been sold out to the CBC. I think, however, that we had established enough mutual respect that he would still have gone for the deal, understanding I would be the executive tie-breaker, not dictator. But what killed the partnership in my mind was when he said, "Mark, they are already assigning directors to it in the French program. Without checking with you or me. How am I going to walk into an NFB edit suite, in our culture of directorial independence, and tell someone that what they are doing about the Acadian Deportation is unacceptable – to me, or worse, to some guy in Toronto? This whole apparatus won't work. Never mind whether or not you and I will get along, I think we will. But Mark, we'll have no authority." Adam had verbalized a major concern I had been suppressing. By not emphasizing that the entire project had to have one leader, we were virtually guaranteeing years of strife between our two institutions. This project was now more complex than Canada itself, with *two* English teams (CBC and NFB) and *two* French teams (ditto). If Adam didn't think it would work, it wouldn't work. When I heard that directors were being named at the NFB without any consultation with us at CBC, or even with Adam, it just confirmed for me that this was a mare's nest.

That night I took Gene out for supper at the Kit-Kat restaurant on King Street and told him the whole story. "Well," he said, "Adam is angry because he wasn't kept in the loop. He will come around."

I said, "The problem is he's absolutely right. Shooting the history of Canada is going to be hard enough without bridging two institutions, two cinematic cultures, and four separate interest groups. You and I are going to be running around trying to please sixteen different interests and visions and egos. This is mathematically and empirically impossible."

To this day I believe that factions within the National Film Board undermined Sandra Macdonald, rejecting her vision of a history of Canada and a strategic alliance with the CBC and Radio-Canada. I know that what happened hurt her very deeply, although she's far too diplomatic to say it publicly. An innovative collaboration between the Canadian broadcasting and cinematic communities was subverted by internal division and turf protection.

Later, she recalled how it all collapsed. "I had a choice to make; I could push ahead and make a deal which NFB staff felt was not an equal partnership (because the vision for the series was going to be the CBC's) and face a revolt at a very emotional time in all our layoffs and departures, or I could swallow the bitterest pill of my tenure there and put internal peace ahead of something I really believed in. I'm still not sure I made the right decision."

A week later, in a conference call with all "stakeholders" in the project, including Beatty, Byrd, and Saint-Laurent, I told them what had happened. "This is the third memorandum of understanding negotiated between us and the NFB in twelve months. Each one is turned down, and the concessions we made in the last one become the baseline for negotiating the next one. In the end, there is no deal possible with the NFB, because the government film commissioner is not in control of the NFB. Nobody is. They have now terminated three handshake deals, without any counter-offers. We're supposed to be on the air in two and a half years, and we have only two winters left to shoot the history of Canada. I recommend we do not go back. I'd rather kill the project."

It had been a year of late-night flights, missed evenings with my family, sterile rage, and institutional helplessness. I would have happily cancelled the whole history project, except I had deluded at least a dozen people into passing up private-sector job offers for a pig in a poke. I was even evading phone calls from Rideau Hall, because I was too ashamed to tell the governor general what paralysis there was about sponsorship.

In the latest round of downsizing, the *Undercurrents* unit was arbitrarily split in half by management – without any consultation with the executive producer – and half the staff was laid off, including my wife, Anne Wright-Howard, who had knocked herself out for that program. As if that news weren't bad enough, I found out that Nick Auf der Maur's tumour had returned, and only radical surgery held remote hope. Jim Burt, the head of movies and mini-series, on whom I was depending as an adviser in reconstructing two hundred years of Canadian history, collapsed in a management meeting that summer, and an ambulance had to be called. Later he would be diagnosed with an inoperable brain tumour.

Out of this debris strode an old friend from radio days, the man who was once my deputy in the years when I was executive producer of *As It Happens*. Mike McEwen was tall, handsome, eternally diplomatic, and political, and he was now the CBC president's second-in-command. McEwen trusted me, and I trusted him, although you could not have asked for two more different personalities and backgrounds. We had encountered each other in a hallway at the Broadcast Centre a month before, and went off for a beer and a hamburger. I told him the whole madcap scheme to do the history of Canada, and McEwen, a strong Alberta nationalist, seized on the idea. "This place is a zoo, Mark," he said. "It's not like the old days. If you need an ally on this project, you can count on me."

So, with the NFB deal in ashes and the project effectively dead, I called McEwen, the only person in Head Office management who actually had experience in broadcasting and had worked to a deadline in a studio. I told him the sad saga of the twelve months since the press release. I was calling in twenty-five years worth of chips. He asked a lot of pointed questions and ended with the only phrase a dispirited man wants to hear: "Leave it to me."

On July 22, 1997, McEwen assembled all managers involved in the project, from the president to the sales department, in the big boardroom on the seventh floor of the Broadcast Centre. It was a long meeting, but eventually it was agreed that the CBC would replace the funding gap the NFB left behind – how, God only knew. Perhaps from corporate sponsorship. I was asked directly how much I needed, and I said $25 million, which was the estimate the CBC and the NFB had jointly arrived at. I was asked if I could do it for $20.5 million. I said, "Only if it is accompanied by a total mobilization of all the CBC management and its departments, with no more bureaucratic foot-dragging, and everything being put on an emergency footing. Just remember, at normal business speed, the real price is $25 million."

By the end of the meeting, McEwen had persuaded everyone to sign off on a base of $20.5 million. Before we left the room, Perrin Beatty took a lot of dramatic space to look everyone in the eye and say, "If there is any doubt, or any question, let this be understood. This is the single largest and most fundamental programming priority of the CBC and Radio-Canada. Does everyone understand that?"

Downstairs, on the sixth floor, the team in the embryonic history project were working, unaware that the unit's existence had been in question until this meeting ended at four o'clock in the afternoon. They had been planning our first shoot in Newfoundland, which was going to happen in a few days. I had never told them about the collapse of the NFB deal or the meeting in the seventh-floor boardroom – what good would it have done except to weaken what little morale they had left?

Only Gene Allen knew the whole story. He was dumbfounded when I told him about the meeting. "This is like Lazarus rising from the dead," he said. "So this is now a CBC project through and through?"

"Yes," I said. "Just don't ask me how we're going to get it on the air in only two years."

3

Misadventures at Sea

Sixteen months after the CBC's dramatic press release, in July of 1997, the Canadian History Project was nothing but a growing pile of paper, almost all of it memos about failed negotiations. Since finishing *Dawn of the Eye*, I'd done little but negotiate endlessly over everything from office space to computers and cameras, which, in an extraordinary departure from the norm, Head Office finance wanted the project itself to pay for. After almost two years of trying to describe the project, we hadn't succeeded in getting people to visualize it. How would we do two language versions? Would it just be old paintings and engravings? How could we use actors? How could we reconcile two totally different points of view? We were trying to convince people with pieces of paper and our fatigued enthusiasm. It wasn't enough to sharpen support. "Even I'm sick of hearing us talking," I said to Gene. "We've got to capture people's imagination. All they hear are the three deadliest words in television: 'Canadian,' 'history,' and 'documentary.' Then we say 'sweeping' and they hear 'long and deadly.' Our problem is that Canadians think our history is a snore. We've got to produce a powerful short film that shows them what we're going to do and brings them to their feet cheering and opening their chequebooks. It's got to be epic."

Gene didn't like the sound of this at all. "We've lost a year negotiating with the film board, we don't have any scripts, we haven't recruited our directors, the timeline for the series is already suicidal, and we don't need to divert effort to produce something which won't even get on the air. We need scripts."

We've got to follow both tracks, I argued. "Yes, we desperately need scripts and storylines, but they will take months to produce. In the meantime we've got to start shooting landscapes and scenes that we know will be in the final script. Quebec was bombarded. That will be in the script. Why wait? Furthermore, we have to get shots of the caribou migrations, the spring breakup of the ice, voyageur canoes on the Saguenay in autumn now, because there are only two autumns and two springs left. And we use those images in our promo, because if we don't produce a film which can galvanize the board of directors and open some corporate pocketbooks, there will be no series."

Gene and I went back and forth on this all autumn and most of the winter, getting pretty testy at times. As senior producer, Gene was facing a daunting task: "I've got to organize research into five hundred years of history and find personal quotes and testimony to describe everything. Guess what? They're not there! Most history books are not descriptive and don't quote ordinary people. I need to get people digging out primary documents – letters and wills. I don't want them chasing caribou now." We sawed off on this compromise: no scenes would be shot unless they were guaranteed to be in the final series.

There was one shoot we did agree on that was coming up in days. The replica of the *Matthew*, the ship on which John Cabot had crossed the Atlantic in 1497 and landed somewhere in Newfoundland or Labrador, was sailing across the Atlantic. The crossing had seized the popular imagination, and there were reams of television coverage. As far as we knew, this was the only floating replica of any fifteenth-century ship, and if we didn't shoot it right away, we'd never get an opportunity again. When it landed in Bonavista, it was greeted by twenty thousand people, and it was hopelessly surrounded by tourist boats everywhere it went as it circumnavigated the island of Newfoundland. So we had to find a stretch of coast and ocean so isolated that we could film the *Matthew* alone, against an uninhabited coast, with no power lines and away from flight paths and the possibility of white vapour trails in the sky. The answer was to shoot the ship while it was in the Strait of Belle Isle, between Newfoundland and Labrador. Gene quickly arranged permission with the organizers of the *Matthew*'s voyage. And so it came to be that a project that was virtually dead before the July 22 meeting was going to embark on its first shoot five days later.

The first problem was to find a boat. Gene called the CBC station in Corner Brook and spoke to someone who knew someone who had an old twelve-metre cabin cruiser that he had restored. This appealed to Gene's parsimony, which had already endeared him to our business department.

We had a boat; now we had to get a camera. For months we had lusted after the Sony 700, a digital video camera that had the capacity to shoot wide-screen. It was prohibitively expensive to use film, so we knew we'd be shooting video, but it was also pointless to shoot the series on standard video cameras. First, the picture on these video cameras was too low-resolution; second, the images degraded after a few years. This series had to be shot to archival standard – which meant digital video. We also felt there was no point in shooting the series to fit conventional TV screens. The next generation of TV sets was going to be digital and wide-screen – "letterbox" – and we could not afford to shoot the series in a format that would be outdated in a few years. But there were no digital wide-screen cameras anywhere in the CBC. The only way we could get one was to borrow it from Sony, which agreed to let us "test" one. So, with a borrowed $100,000 camera, we prepared for the project's maiden shoot.

I was really excited. Finally, after almost two years in meeting rooms, I'd be in the field again. I wanted to bring my daughters. My younger, Madeleine, was at camp, but I had enough frequent-flyer miles to bring Caitlin, who was thirteen, on this maritime adventure.

We went to the Mountain Equipment Co-op and bought sleeping bags, rain gear, pocket flashlights, whistles, and more paraphernalia than we'd ever need.

On the evening of July 25, Caitlin and I met the others in the dining room of the lodge in Corner Brook: Gene Allen, Mike Sweeney, Keith Bonnell, who had flown in from St. John's, and Louis Martin from Montreal. Louis was an institution in Quebec French journalism, a bit like Nick was on the English side: a fiercely independent journalist. He was in his sixties, a bon vivant, connoisseur of fine wine and beautiful women, and slightly eccentric with an absent-minded, dreamy, and disputatious intellect. He was greatly respected by Quebec nationalists for his grasp of provincial history and politics, as well as for his integrity – that's why Claude Saint-Laurent wanted him in the project as editorial adviser.

We had a good supper, though Louis was a little pained by the wine, and we toasted the adventure before us. The next morning was bright and sunny, and we spent it buying basic supplies, after which we set out to locate the boat, the cc. We found her tied up on an isolated stretch of harbour near a muddy road. The sight of her gave us pause. There would be no danger of anyone suggesting we were being profligate with public money. The cc looked like a floating plywood box that had seen better days. The captain was affable and introduced his two crew members. As we loaded gear on board, he told us he had gotten the cc as a bit of a "handyman special." He had just finished painting her and installing a motor out of an eighteen-wheel truck in her. He took us below to show us the bunks he had just built for us out of two-by-fours. He said he was very eager about the trip because we were his first charter. None of this comforted us, and out of the crew's hearing, Gene kept saying defensively, "Look, it's a reasonable rate, a guy at the local station suggested her, and what the heck, she's a forty-footer, she'll be fine." Louis had the same look he had while tasting the previous night's wine.

The maiden voyage of the Canadian History Project and, it appears, of the cc began at two in the afternoon, with blue skies and moderate winds, as we motored along the bay to rendezvous with the *Matthew* in the Strait of Belle Isle. The crew had brought a bucket of lobsters, and we sat on the stern deck, on a brilliant day, watching the shore recede as the bay widened, feeling that our luck had finally turned.

The *Matthew* was about fifty nautical miles up the strait, about six hours' sail away. As soon as we cleared the bay and hit open water, any illusion of a pleasant sail was dispelled, as the CC crashed through the waves. Within an hour, the captain had more news for us. There was a storm forming directly in front of us, about two hours away.

For a couple of hours, sailing was an adventure. But then the sky darkened and the wind rose and the CC started pitching and plunging. The first to get sick was the first mate, which was not encouraging, then one by one, each of us except me, which was astonishing as I could get seasick on the Toronto Islands ferry. By the time Louis Martin had crawled outside to throw up, the sea had become so rough that the stern deck was being swept by crashing waves. As Louis lay on his stomach vomiting over the stern, we had to hold onto him by his ankles lest he be pulled into the sea. Then he crawled back inside to join Mike Sweeney, Keith Bonnell, and the first mate, who passed out in the bunks by the camera cases. Caitlin clung to a rail in the wheelhouse, being sick out the window. Gene and I were still alert enough to argue about what to do next – an exchange which had to be shouted over the din of the storm.

"This is crazy," Gene yelled. "We have to get out of this storm."

"If we pull out now," I yelled back, "we'll lose the rendezvous with the *Matthew* and the whole bloody shoot."

"There's no one here in any shape to do anything if we do find her," Gene shouted. "We can't spend the night at sea in this."

We lurched to the wheel position and the captain tried to unroll a chart. "There's no port along here" – his finger moved along the grids of the shoreline – "but we could make it into Cow Head. It's a sheltered cove where we could wait out the storm if you wanted to. But we'll never catch up with the *Matthew* if we do."

It took us another awful hour to pull into this isolated cove. It was so dark and windy and rainy that we couldn't see anything, but we felt the welcome calm as the captain tied up in the lee. Caitlin and I went below and unrolled our sleeping bags onto narrow benches in the bow, falling asleep to the sound of water trickling from seams in the deck above.

The next morning, Gene greeted me with good news. He had just got off the radio. "We haven't lost the *Matthew*," he said. "It was too dangerous for her to move under tow in the storm, so they sat it out in the middle of the Strait. She's only four hours ahead of us. We can catch her by late afternoon if we move fast, and get our sunset shots."

Everybody grinned. We had all recovered, it was a bright day, and the adventure was back on. But we had to move quickly. The *Matthew* had to make up for lost time too, because she had to get to Red Bay, on the Labrador coast, to pick up the premier of Newfoundland, Brian Tobin, and several cabinet ministers, before rounding the northern tip of Newfoundland and sailing to St. Anthony's, where thousands were gathering to watch her enter the harbour. She couldn't wait for us or slow down. We gunned the CC's engines and the race was on.

It was four in the afternoon before we spotted the *Matthew* and the *Groswater Bay*, the sleek Coast Guard vessel that was towing her at the end of a sixty-metre line. Viewed from the dock in St. John's, the *Matthew* had looked small, even quaint, but seeing her from the water, with the vast expanse of an ocean around her, I had a glimpse of what it must have felt like to lay eyes on such a vessel five hundred years ago. I felt as though we were approaching some apparition from another world. In her time that's exactly what she would have seemed to the Beothuk who lived here. Europe was not another continent but an unknown world.

I shook off these thoughts and pitched in to get the shoot ready. By the time we started shooting, we had two hours left before sunset, and the *Matthew* had her sails down, since she was under tow. Within an hour, the crew of the *Groswater Bay* had undone the tow, the crew of the *Matthew* had laboriously raised her sails, and we had erected a huge gimbel on the stern deck of the CC. A gimbel is a black iron tripod-like structure that looks like a tool of the Inquisition. It stands about one and a half metres tall, with a heavy iron counterweight like a clock pendulum, and smoothes out the movement of the boat. Shooting from one boat to another is one of the most difficult things in motion photography, as the two vessels rise and fall about two metres with each wave, but never in unison. To make room for the gimbel on the stern deck, we moved the inflatable lifeboat canister, the size of a barrel, to the top deck.

For over an hour we shot the *Matthew* from every angle, as her sails billowed and her bow cut through the water. Her crew had donned period clothing, and Mike Sweeney made the CC circle her a dozen times as he shot close-ups of the tiller, the bowsprit coming right at us, the banner of St. George framed between the mainsails, and finally, the critical shot of the *Matthew* framed against the sun sinking on the horizon – the trickiest shot of all. As the light faded after the sunset, the *Matthew* lowered her sails, the *Groswater Bay* hove into view again and tied the long tow line, and they both sailed to Red Bay.

We packed up our gear and followed from a distance while debating whether we should also go to Red Bay. There were reportedly impressive shores there with primeval scenery and whale bones on beaches that could prove very useful to the series. I had run out of film for my Nikon and asked Caitlin to go down to the forward section to get some out of my backpack. She started down the steps, then called out: "Hey, it's full of water down there." She wasn't exaggerating. There was close to half a metre of water sloshing around. Paper plates, sleeping bags, shirts, film canisters, knapsacks were floating and colliding with every swell.

The captain rushed to the hatch in the centre of the wheelhouse and hurled it open. "I can hear water!" he said with sharp alarm. "Shine a light down here." As he descended the ladder, we heard his hollow voice: "There's tons of water here!"

Mike Sweeney moved to the hatch with an auxiliary light and looked below. "It was just boiling with water down there," he says. "When the captain got to the bottom, the water was above his waist. He looked for where the hole was and eventually dived completely underwater searching for it. All I could see was a vast churning pool of water, with the top of the engine steaming out of it. It was still running."

The captain surfaced and rushed up the ladder, shouting, "It's rising very fast," and clambered to the wheelhouse deck. As he stumbled to the wheel, I looked below, and the water seemed to be just a metre below where we stood. And where we stood was at least three metres above the water! It meant that the water inside the boat was higher than the water level of the sea. "She's pumping water in!" someone shouted, as we hurriedly battened down the hatch.

The captain's hands flew over the instruments and switches, he pressed the distress button on the Global Positioning System, and then I heard, disbelievingly, "Mayday. Mayday. Mayday." He gave the CC's position and then all the lights went out in the wheelhouse. There was a crack and hiss of electrical circuits frying, and the cabin began to fill with smoke.

"What's burning?" I heard a voice say. "It's electrical, I think. I can't see an open flame." It was ink black.

The captain, who was only an arm's length ahead of me at the wheel, turned around in the smoke and spoke loudly but calmly: "Did the mayday get out before the electricals failed?"

"Yes, just," I shouted.

"Everyone put on your life jackets immediately," the captain ordered. "Life jackets immediately! Then get out on deck until we see if we have an open flame. This boat is loaded with fuel. On deck!"

There was confusion as we helped each other with life jackets, trying to train flashlights onto buckles and snaps. I grabbed a full-body orange life suit and tried to help Caitlin put it on. It was a tangle of sleeves and zippers, and very quickly we saw that it was too large.

"I'll put on a life vest," she said. "You put that on." I watched her slip hers on and then help Louis Martin with his. As she fastened the straps around him, I had that first flashing insight that my daughter was no longer a child.

We were still afraid that the CC might blow up at any second, since the wheelhouse was billowing smoke like a volcano. Even if the fire was electrical – and it smelled like electrical smoke – it could burst into an open flame. And all the CC comprised was an engine, plywood, and hundreds of litres of fuel. The captain told us to move to the far edges of the boat, away from the wheelhouse. Caitlin, Mike, Keith Bonnell, and I moved to the foredeck, Gene and the others to the stern. The sea was now lapping at the main deck, occasionally dousing my shoes as the deck rocked in a swell.

Voices in the stern were talking about the main life raft. It was in the barrel we had moved to the upper deck to make room for the gimbel during the shoot. The barrel was connected to an anchored rope. When you throw the container overboard, the rope tightens and triggers a carbon dioxide canister that explodes the container open and immediately inflates the huge raft. But the container was on the top deck, and if thrown from there, the life raft would inflate over the smoking wheelhouse. Useless. The captain decided to release a smaller life raft instead, and to postpone trying to launch the tangled main raft till the CC sank lower. Everyone agreed that Louis, as the elder on board, should get in, and they helped him into the perilously bobbing rubber raft.

"Bonnell can't swim," I heard someone shout, "put him in next." As I saw Keith clambering in, I said to Caitlin, "You're in next."

She looked at the tiny raft, rising and falling by a metre or so relative to the deck with each wave, and said calmly but decisively: "No way."

From the wheelhouse, the captain shouted the welcome news that there was no flame, and the smoke was dying down.

Then, to everyone's shock, the CC lurched and the submerged engine inexplicably gunned into life. We all grabbed what we could to steady ourselves. Louis and Keith fell backward in the life raft as the CC shot through the water for what seemed like sixty metres before groaning to a halt. None of us, to this day, have any idea how that engine started up. Louis and Keith were totally soaked and shaken, and the people at the stern reached to grab their wrists and pull them back aboard from the heaving raft.

"That, in retrospect, was the most dangerous moment," says Gene Allen, "dragging Louis and Keith at high speed, nearly foundering the raft. It's amazingly lucky that we didn't lose either of them. In fact, the engine dying again was the best thing that happened to us."

We didn't know at the time that while the engine was running, its cooling system was pumping water into the engine room, not through the engine and out the rear water exhaust but right into the hull itself, because the intake pipe had ruptured. Had the engine kept going, we would have sunk within minutes. This is the moment when Keith shouted to us never to jump into the water, because we wouldn't survive.

For the next hour, there was darkness and mostly silence, and we were alone with our thoughts and, worse, our imaginations. Every few minutes, Gene would cup his hands and cry "Help." I blew three short, three long, and three short bursts on the tin whistle, and then he would cry help again. I also flickered a Morse code SOS on my flashlight toward the distant shore where we could see a twinkle of lights. Before blowing the whistle I turned to Caitlin and asked: "How does it go? Three short, three long, three short? Or three long first?"

All this time I had been looking at her for panic or tears. Instead, her calmness and focus had been completely intact. Now I realized that her teenager's conviction that her father was a ditz was also intact, as she responded dryly, in the only moment of comedy aboard the CC. "If you think about it, Dad, after you start the sequence, it doesn't matter." This was the moment I realized that this kid, if I ever got her to shore, would do just fine in life.

The only comfort for the next hour was that the boat seemed to have stopped sinking. We kept our gaze focused on a small ribbon of about ten lights far off on the Newfoundland shore. At the time of the mayday, the captain had estimated that we were three nautical miles off someplace called Anchor Point. If anyone had heard our mayday, one of those lights should have started moving toward us. None did, and we stood in silence for an hour. I did another roll call, and everyone responded. There was nothing to do. The silliest thoughts went through our minds.

"All I could think about was Sony," says Mike Sweeney. "We had a $100,000 camera. I stood on the gunwales, worrying that the water level below had reached the camera and the tapes we had just shot."

"I looked up at the stars," Gene Allen remembers, "wondering if we were going to die. Then I thought, If we don't die, what are we going to tell Sony about the camera?"

Images of my daughter drowning, and both of us in the water, with me out of breath and unable to reach her, pulled at the edges of my mind. To block them, I thought about my Nikon. I had been everywhere with that camera – Africa, Borneo, China. "I guess the camera's screwed," I said to Caitlin between whistles. "And my favourite alarm clock," she replied. What else was there to say? All I could think of was a line I always used in our family whenever we were in a weird place: "So," I said, to Caitlin, "you come here often?" She smiled at me.

Then there was a flurry of exclamations. Three of the lights along the distant shore seemed to have detached themselves from the ribbon. I kept flashing three short, three long, three short, and whistling, as Gene shouted "Help" for the next half-hour. The lights grew larger, then wandered in the wrong direction, then finally directly toward us. All of us started shouting and waving at the approaching lights, more out of excitement than for any practical purpose.

"What was coming toward us looked like something out of science fiction," Gene remembers. "It was big. It looked like a hotel, a thirteen-storey building, but the lights were high above the water, as if they were only on the thirteenth floor and the sixth floor. We were looking up at it."

It looked like a spaceship hovering many metres above the water, not floating on the sea at all. When it loomed into view, we could see it was a huge commercial trawler, and the lights were mounted on the ends of the poles that hold the nets up. I gave Caitlin a bear hug: "We're going to be OK."

The next few minutes were a bustle of shouts and ropes flying across our deck as the trawler tied the CC to her port side, the two vessels bobbing up and down in different rhythms. We reached for hands extended from the trawler and were pulled up over the chasm between the two decks. On the rescue vessel, we sat exhausted on the rope coils, and the crew brought out blankets to wrap around each of us. We had been rescued by the scallop trawler MV *Cape Anchor*, out of Anchor Point, captained by Bruce Genge.

Then the captain of the CC, Mike, and Keith climbed back onto the sinking boat to see what could be salvaged. Our film gear alone was twenty-two cases, plus videocassettes of the *Matthew*, all in the rear cabin where the water was thigh deep. Mike went directly for the camera, which was on one of the bunks. "She's still dry!" he shouted. For half an hour, a human bucket brigade passed the gear across the treacherous gap, then the knapsacks and duffel bags. All of those, containing our clothes, books, and personal cameras, had been floating in the foredeck and were totally waterlogged.

The two captains decided that the *Cape Anchor* would try to pull the CC in, hoping she wouldn't sink totally; if she did, they'd have to cut her loose. Captain Genge radioed the rescue station that we had been saved. The crew told us they had our general coordinates from the mayday, but hadn't known exactly where we were until they spotted the blinking flashlight. I felt vindicated about my Mountain Equipment Co-op extravagances.

The two crews lashed the CC to the *Cape Anchor*, like the carcass of a whale, and a moment later, the loudspeakers crackled with a message to all shipping in the Strait of Belle Isle: "This is Air Sea Rescue Station Corner Brook. Attention all marine traffic in the Strait of Belle Isle. With respect to mayday issued at 10:30, this mayday is cancelled. Attention all shipping, mayday is cancelled. All souls on board have been saved. Repeat. All souls on board have been saved."

We looked at one another gravely. I didn't know they still said things like "All souls on board." There was something magnificent about that moment. As lonely as we had felt on the CC, it turned out that we had been surrounded by life, that all shipping in the Strait of Belle Isle had been searching for us.

The engines of the *Cape Anchor* roared into life, the tow lines pulling the CC groaned, and we sat mutely on piles of coiled rope under a starry sky, saying nothing as the radio loudspeakers broadcast the chronicles of the night of July 27, 1997, in the Strait of Belle Isle.

The MV *Cape Anchor* pulled into the tiniest cove imaginable, just a small arm of rocks protecting a minute harbour that was bathed in the light of many headlights from the high ground above it. As the giant trawler tied up, teams of men with ropes pulled the CC into the shallows, where she settled at a 45-degree angle, the water lapping through her wheelhouse windows. Within a minute, we were surrounded by men, women, and even children with blankets and Thermoses of hot coffee and soup, asking us in a tumult of thick Newfoundland accents if anyone was injured, if anyone was in pain. Caitlin was now invisible, surrounded by women smothering her with blankets and comforting her with soup.

I think the whole little outport of Anchor Point had been on the shore, waiting for over an hour. The air was alive with the sound of running pickups and dozens of voices calling out, "Yes, there's a girl that was out there, but she seems all right," and "They said it didn't sink, but a couple of them are real wet," and "You get their stuff on Jason's truck, Jane will take the girl in her van." I could barely see the faces except when they crossed in front of a headlight, as each of us was adopted by a different group, led to a vehicle, and gently bundled in. Caitlin and I were in a van with a woman who told us that another party had gone ahead to open up the motel at the St. Barbe's ferry, about fifteen kilometres away, which was where she was taking us.

Louis Martin, whom I had lost track of half an hour earlier, was being similarly cared for with cups of coffee and blankets in a car with three men, but with no concept of what was happening. "I couldn't understand a word anybody said because of the accent," he said, "but I didn't want to offend anyone when they asked me questions, so I muttered what I could. One of the men in the car was one of the Newfoundland crew members on the CC, and I whispered to him, 'What are they saying?' He whispered back, 'I have no idea, I come from a different area.' Then a moose came onto the road, and we had to put the brakes on hard. This moose stood there and looked at us for a long time. Actually, everyone in the car was enchanted by this moose, and we sat there for at least five minutes."

When I saw him at the motel, Louis, still soaked from the disaster on the dinghy, was remarkably tranquil, given that he had almost died. I think he was invigorated by being back on a journalistic adventure – or misadventure – after years in bureaucracy. He clearly liked what little he had seen of Newfoundlanders, though he was puzzled by their admiration of moose. "They're not rare here, I believe," he commented. Indeed not, Keith told him: every second road sign in the interior is a moose-crossing sign. "It's been an interesting trip," Louis said later that night. "Do you think they have any wine here?"

An advance party from Anchor Point had fired up the motel kitchen and set the tables for us, complete with menus. The men and women who had driven us then poured fresh coffee and tea, and asked us what we would like to eat, perhaps a chicken sandwich, some hot soup, or a hamburger. It dawned on me then that there was no staff in this abandoned motel. These were the people of Anchor Point, with their own lives and jobs, who at three o'clock in the morning were now jotting down "club sandwich" or "hamburger." Caitlin gazed at the menu, undecided, then looked up and asked, "I dunno, do you have fries and gravy?" I kicked her under the table and whispered, "This is not a restaurant, don't put these people to more trouble," but she glowered at me, and indeed they had terrific fries and gravy.

As we gratefully wolfed down our food, our hosts joined us to hear our stories of the storm, the *Matthew*, and the Canadian History Project. They were pleased that the first scenes of the history of Canada had been shot in their waters, even if we had made a huge botch of it.

I began to realize how one small event could affect dozens of communities and crews at sea. When I told them how dramatic it had been to hear "All souls have been saved," they told me that it was seagoing tradition – indeed maritime law – that anyone hearing a mayday immediately abandon their plans and steer for the last known coordinates of the distressed vessel.

"For example," one of the men added, "the Coast Guard ship that was towing the *Matthew* dropped her tow lines and headed out to your last known position." I froze.

"You mean the *Matthew* is somewhere out there in the strait, bobbing in the sea?"

"I expect," the man said, "it'd be a couple of hours before the Coast Guard ship could get back to her, since they were pretty near to Anchor Point when we found you. But the *Matthew* will be fine. She has engines if she gets into trouble."

I knew the *Matthew* would be fine, she had just crossed the Atlantic. But the premier of Newfoundland and half the cabinet at Red Bay had been expecting her by morning, to take them to St. Anthony. Twenty thousand people, live television crews, flotillas of boats, historical societies, boy scout and church groups from all over Newfoundland, as well as foreign dignitaries from Italy, Britain, and France were waiting to greet them, to mark the great moment when two worlds met, and which the CBC and its idiotic history project had just scuttled by obliging the Coast Guard to abandon the *Matthew* on the high sea, after disrupting all shipping in the Strait of Belle Isle.

That night I slept between fresh sheets for the first time in days. But before I drifted off, my brain was on fire with imagined *Globe and Mail* headlines that would make us pariahs in Newfoundland. This would not look good to the board of directors.

In the morning, an RCMP constable wrote down what we had to tell him about the incident, while we found rental cars and stuffed our still sodden knapsacks into them. We bought a bottle of Scotch for Captain Genge of the *Cape Anchor*, but he had gone out fishing at four in the morning, so we left it with his family. Gene set out to find the name and address of the woman who had heard our mayday and alerted Bruce Genge; Gene learned she was Dulcie Way, who lived with her husband, Llwelyn, in Savage Cove, sixteen kilometres farther up the rocky coast.

Down in the tiny harbour, the tide had gone out, leaving the CC beached. The captain was trying to save the engine by washing it. I climbed in to find my camera and other belongings. The Nikon was already rusting from the sea water, and Caitlin's CD player and alarm clock were useless, but we gathered what we could. The captain held up a twisted plastic pipe: "Here's the villain." The 7.5-centimetre-diameter pipe was the intake for sea water to cool the engine. It had melted and burst open, so the pump was filling the hull instead of feeding the engine. That explained why the water inside the CC had been higher than the waterline. The captain's theory was that, during our manoeuvres around the *Matthew*, perhaps a plastic bag floating in the ocean had clogged the intake, or a floating log had shattered it, and the pipe had ruptured. Gene paid him the $2,000 we had agreed, which was a relief to the captain, and we said farewell to the CC. Then we bought a bouquet of flowers and drove to Savage Cove.

The two-lane highway between Anchor Point and Savage Cove hugs a rocky, almost treeless shore. The landscape is flat and grey, the ocean silver, and the sky wide and leaden. Jacques Cartier called the strait "la baie des châteaux," the bay of castles, because of the titanic, cathedral-like icebergs that he encountered there in 1534. Across the strait, on the coast of Labrador, is the oldest ceremonial burial site yet found in Canada, the grave of a twelve-year-old child buried seven thousand years ago, before the pyramids were even built in Egypt. The coast we were driving along was once settled by the French. The first Englishman to settle on the French coast over two hundred years ago was a man named Genge, and it was his descendant who had rescued us.

Savage Cove was much like Anchor Point, a huddle of low bungalows around a small natural harbour. We knocked on Dulcie Way's door, and a voice invited us in. We were seven, so it took a while to file in, the first of us feeling a bit awkward while we waited for the rest of our group. Dulcie Way, a short, grey-haired woman, stood at the other end of a living room adorned with pictures of children and grandchildren in grade school and in graduation caps and gowns. Caitlin was the last to enter the room, very shyly. The awkwardness was broken instantly. Dulcie Way threw her arms out, rushed to Caitlin, and engulfed her in a hug, exclaiming in a beautiful Newfoundland lilt: "Darlin', if I'd known it was you out there, I'd have swum out for you myself!" The teapot came out, and we were introduced to Dulcie's husband, Llwelyn, a man in his seventies, with a finger missing on one of his large, strong hands. He had been a fisherman all his life, retiring twelve years ago. On the table, a small marine radio crackled all the time we were there.

"We keep it on all day and night," Dulcie Way said. "We like to keep in touch with the comings and goings. I heard your mayday at 10:30, and didn't know what to do since I didn't know you. But then I remembered that Bruce Genge had a trawler up in Anchor Point, but I didn't know how to reach him. Of course everyone in Anchor Point is a Genge, so I kept dialling till I got someone who went down to his house and roused him. What were youse doing out there?"

We told her we were from the CBC and Radio-Canada, and we were following the *Matthew* because we were making a history of Canada for television.

"Well," she said, "it's about time."

After an hour of tea, stories, and many group portraits with the Ways, we set off in our two cars for the long journey to St. Anthony. I drove and Louis Martin sat beside me pensively. Finally he said: "Twelve years since he's been a fisherman. And every night they listen to the voices of the sea. . . ."

Our destination was St. Anthony, but our objective – as responsible journalists – was to completely cover up what had happened. If the Toronto or Montreal papers found out that the vaunted Canadian History Project had distinguished itself, on its first day of shooting, by nearly drowning and losing a $100,000 borrowed camera, we'd be the laughingstock of the industry. If they found out we were responsible for the abandonment of the *Matthew*, by now the most celebrated ship in Canadian waters, the stranding of the premier of Newfoundland in Red Bay, and the disappointment of twenty thousand people in St. Anthony's . . . Well, the story wasn't going to get out, that's all. Before leaving the motel in St. Barbe's that morning, we had lined up at the one pay phone and called home, having agreed that we'd play down what happened, "so as not to alarm our families." To the documentary unit office, we made no mention of boats sinking, or of maydays; we referred only to mechanical problems that had changed our itinerary. In short, we lied. I had no trouble telling my wife we had had a bump or two on the way, which seemed preferable to telling her I had almost drowned our first-born. The flaw in the plan, as Gene reported with his newspaperman's eye, was the RCMP report that would soon be filed. In Gene's and my day, junior reporters were required to phone every police station, every outpost, every three hours to harvest every incident report, every accident, in case there was a good story. "Don't worry," I said, "no newsroom's that efficient any more."

Our subterfuge quickly collapsed. Over the car radio we heard CBC Newfoundland report that a CBC crew from Toronto had been rescued after sinking in the Strait of Belle Isle. I pulled over, signalling Gene to stop so that we could confer on this unpleasant development. If CBC Radio in St. John's reached us, we agreed, we couldn't lie, but we didn't have to go into details about borrowed cameras or be too graphic in describing our maritime plight. And the *Matthew*? Well, after all, it was second-hand knowledge, and it wasn't up to us to report she had been abandoned, and Tobin stranded.

"At all costs," I said, "we can't let this story get off the island of Newfoundland."

"Maybe we'll be lucky and the Toronto newsroom won't check," Gene said.

As a precaution, we shut our cellphones off.

Hours later, we entered the outskirts of St. Anthony, which was teeming with people. When we pulled up to our motel, we were mortified to find out we were already celebrities at the front desk, in the restaurant, and, worse, in the laundromat downstairs where Caitlin and I washed every article of clothing to get rid of the salt. Person after person came down with their laundry and said, "Hey, you must be those CBC people from Toronto who almost drowned last night." The next day I was woken by a producer with the CBC

Radio morning show out of St. John's, which was proving far too enterprising for my taste. I stammered my way through an interview, thanking the people of Anchor Point. By ten, the whole province knew who we were. Later that day, we played our notoriety to advantage. St. Anthony was so crowded it was hard to get into a restaurant or past many police traffic cordons. We just had to mention who we were to be admitted everywhere out of pity.

We found out from the organization in St. John's that was tracking the *Matthew*'s journey by radio that the celebrated vessel was going to arrive on schedule, because her captain had decided to forget Red Bay, abandon the premier and his ministers, and head right for St. Anthony. This was uplifting news, until we realized that we might be the only ones in St. Anthony who knew that when the *Matthew* arrived, she would not be carrying the premier. Assuming that the Newfoundland media would become curious about the absence of the premier from the most important arrival ceremony since the *Matthew* had landed in St. John's, we decided to get out of town. We would film at L'Anse aux Meadows, the site where Vikings had wintered nine hundred years ago, an hour's drive out of St. Anthony. To catch the morning light, and incidentally avoid unwelcome media attention from St. John's, we left in convoy at five the next morning.

L'Anse aux Meadows is a mystical place, made all the more haunting by how casually you encounter it, in a cove, next to a farmhouse, with only one sign pointing to the site of the oldest European settlement on the North American continent. Here were grassy mounds barely perceptible on the landscape, and a reconstructed wooden perimeter and low sod huts. The story of that legendary settlement became an epic poem that read more like a Tolkien invention, complete with "red people who hissed like geese," the Beothuks.

Gene had arranged to make radio contact with the *Matthew* at four o'clock as she approached St. Anthony so that we could get some shots of her from land, again in an isolated setting. So, after filming at L'Anse aux Meadows, we lugged our equipment to a high cliff between two promontories, about eight kilometres west of the

St. Anthony harbour, and a CBC transmitter engineer joined us to make radio contact with the *Matthew*. Below us was a breathtaking vista of swirling currents and reefs, with nothing modern to spoil the shot.

It took about an hour before our signal was picked up by the *Matthew*; then while Gene exchanged coordinates, Mike Sweeney mounted the camera on a portable jib – a three-metre-long, Canadarm-like metal pole that allows a camera to be raised and lowered in fluid motions, and which almost broke my back as I helped him carry it up the cliff. He trained his lens between two distant high rocks and waited. A few minutes later, the flag of St. George appeared between the high rocks, and the *Matthew* materialized mystically from the rocks and surf. It was a stunning shot.

For the next half-hour, as the *Matthew* sailed back and forth through churning sea and reefs for us, we filmed cinematic gold. Then, by radio, the *Matthew* told us to stand by, as she raised more sail and headed into a stronger current to try to achieve her greatest speed. These would be the highest winds she had encountered, in the most turbulent waters she had sailed – it would be the most magnificent shot of all. Then, suddenly, a huge yellow double-rotor helicopter buzzed into camera range and hovered over the *Matthew*, totally ruining the shot. It was a search and rescue helicopter, and obviously the crew were enjoying a close look at the replica of Cabot's ship, oblivious to the fact that they were ruining one of the great maritime shots of all time, or so we thought.

Then, finally, came evidence that God watches public television. The yellow helicopter shot up dramatically, banked sharply, and disappeared from view, just as the *Matthew* rounded the point. The next five minutes of footage are breathtaking, as the tall ship, all banners snapping in the wind, its sails straining, bobs and dips through white surf and twisting currents against an endless seascape and a vast sky. Sweeney followed her steadily with the camera, muttering, "Good. Perfect. Fantastic." In those five minutes, the *Matthew* reached the highest speed she had ever attained, ten knots, and the footage has since become the signature of the series. It was a $100,000 shot, literally. That's what it would have cost to stage it from scratch. Then the *Groswater Bay* appeared again, tied the tow line, and pulled the *Matthew* into St. Anthony.

On my way back from Newfoundland, I stopped in Halifax to meet with one of the senior producers I had just persuaded to join the series, Sally Reardon. Sally had shared with me the most turbulent times at *The Journal*. Now she was senior producer of the Halifax supper-hour program. I had been determined to get her on the history project for her writing skill, her wit, and her political judgment.

At her farm two hours outside Halifax, I unwound from our seagoing adventures while she described what she had arranged for our next shoot. "I've booked the whole Fortress at Louisbourg, a dozen thirty-two-pounder cannon and enough powder to sink the British fleet, the Compagnie Franche de la Marine in full uniform, fifes, drummers, regimental flags, and a twenty-metre crane, with a generator truck I loosely borrowed from the Halifax plant." Sally's father had been a Canadian general in the Second World War, and her mother an American army nurse, so she came by her love of big military operations honestly. I had asked her to come up with a location where we could film the bombardment of Quebec for our promotional video, with cannons spewing smoke and re-enactors in period-correct uniforms. She knew we needed epic, wide-screen shots to counteract the impression that Canadian history was boring. She had clearly outdone herself. "And," she ended with a flourish, "I got the local ladies' church auxiliary to make egg salad sandwiches for us. We're going to be the biggest boon to the local economy after the tourist season."

Cheered by this news, I flew to Montreal and then on to Toronto to recruit the leadership of the unit. With the NFB out of the picture, and $20.5 million finally authorized, I knew what the composition and scale of the unit could be. The escapade in Newfoundland had been fun, or parts of it had, but going on shoots was not my job. We were supposed to be on the air in just over two years, and all we had was footage of the *Matthew* and a borrowed camera. We had no edit suites, hardly any staff, and just two winters in which to shoot every single winter scene in five hundred years of Canadian history.

I had my work cut out for me.

4

"The Empire Strikes Back"

First, I had to recruit the most critical position in the project: a senior producer to run the Montreal operation. Since the collapse of the NFB deal, our Montreal office was going to be a whole lot bigger than we'd envisioned, with camera operators, edit suites, archivists, and directors who would otherwise have come from the film board. Louis Martin would be the editorial overseer, but he had never produced a television program. The person I needed would have to be an expert producer, perfectly bilingual, politically shrewd, and a skilled diplomat, because this job would sit right on the fault line between the English and French versions of Canadian history. I knew exactly the person.

I met Hubert Gendron in 1965, when I was a copy clerk at the *Gazette* and he had just returned from teaching in Africa to start as a junior reporter. He'd made an instant impression on me by collapsing on the floor and being rushed to hospital by ambulance. It turned out to be a malarial attack. In our time together at the *Gazette* we had lived through FLQ bombings and the de Gaulle visit, so we had a common reference base. He is one of those rare, flawlessly bilingual people who are equally comfortable in either culture.

After the *Gazette*, our careers had gone in different directions, until I had recruited him to run *The Journal*'s Montreal bureau. What an assignment that turned out to be: the constitutional crisis, Meech Lake, the defection of Bouchard and the birth of the Bloc Québécois, the Oka crisis, and the massacre of women at the Université de Montréal. When *The Journal* was killed, he moved from the English network to work for *The Journal*'s French equivalent, *Le Point*. He is slightly older than me, with close-cropped white hair and a short grey beard. His father had been a navy gunnery officer on merchant convoys in the North Atlantic during the war; like Sally, he had the genes of a commander, and he thrived on crisis.

After I'd bombarded him for two hours with enticement, the promise of adventure, and the prospect of immortality, he told me he was flattered but couldn't do it. "It's hard to work on the family album when the house is burning," he said. The shock waves of the 1995 referendum were still being felt, and the possibility of Quebec becoming sovereign in the immediate future still seemed quite vivid. Still, I wouldn't take no for an answer and kept calling him, taking him on long nighttime walks around Dominion Square whenever I was in Montreal, trying to wear down his resistance. Eventually, I resorted to more clandestine strategies. He was close to my friend Stephen Phizicky, who had worked with him in *The Journal*'s Montreal bureau. If I could prevail upon Stephen to keep at Hubert between my visits from Toronto, I thought he could win him over.

I called Stephen at Nick Auf der Maur's and tried to persuade him that he had a duty to give Hubert a push. "Let's see," he said. "It's an impossibly large project, with a ridiculously short timeline, a guaranteed fight between two networks, and the endless grief of working with you. It's not like Hubert to turn that down. Let me see what I can do."

There was another concern holding Hubert back: would the French consider him French enough to back him? Hubert didn't know. "I crossed over to work for the French in 1994, after a lifetime of working in English outfits like the *Gazette*, the *Montreal Star*, and the CBC. Does the French net want me to be its point man? I'm not sure. My roots in Radio-Canada are shallow. I don't want to go back out on the cultural tightrope that I walked all through my journalistic career until 1994, being a Franco trying to interpret the French for the Anglos. Can Radio-Canada afford to entrust the project to - someone who could be 'tarred' as a closet Anglo? That's not for me to answer."

I went to my good friend Jean Pelletier, head of French Television news, son of Gérard Pelletier, one of the "three wise men" who came to Ottawa in the 1960s, along with Pierre Trudeau and Jean Marchand. "I know it's cheeky to ask your help in raiding one of our own deputies," I said, "but I need you to persuade Hubert that he carries the confidence of his French colleagues." Jean hates ethnic clannishness. He agreed to help me, saying, "Hubert knows French Canada better than most people in this building, and for the French network's sake, he has to work on this project." I had a long lunch with Louis Martin, whose credentials in defending the French language and French rights were impeccable, and suggested that Hubert would be moved if Louis asked him to join the history project on the French network's behalf, which Louis was delighted to do.

This gives just a hint of the complex currents in which this project would be navigating. I prayed my manoeuvring would pay off, because there was no other person in Montreal with Hubert's profile and experience. I was counting on Phizicky's persuasive skills, and on Hubert's family ghosts. His ancestors were Patriotes in the 1837 Rebellion, and he descends directly from the Chevalier de Lorimier, the hero of the Patriotes who was hanged by the British. Hubert is also a distant relative of Sir John A. Macdonald, and he confessed to me on one of our walks that his full name is Macdonald Walter Lucien Hubert Gendron. "No wonder you're always arguing with yourself," I said.

Back in Toronto, I was after the project manager from hell. Producing a series that was at least twenty hours, in two languages, with producers from two networks, in a paralyzed corporation was going to be a crushing load. I needed someone who understood pro-duction and whom crews and producers respected. This person also had to be trusted by the director of finance in Toronto and the vice-president. There was only one person who fit that profile, and the problem was that she was now working for Slawko Klymkiw, the network's program director. Stealing her from Klymkiw would not be a way to endear us to him, but there was no choice. I had to have Anne Emin.

Anne dresses stylishly and in public she is demure, even shy; but behind closed doors she can raise blisters on a concrete wall. She had been the business manager of *The Journal* until it was taken over, and she was now the director of business and administration for the entire English network – in other words, the only person who knew what every program cost and the financial consequences of any pro-duction decision. At *The Journal* she and I squabbled publicly at every morning editorial meeting. Visitors would be comforted later by staffers telling them, "Oh, pay no attention to them, they're like an old married couple, they actually like each other." She gave me a stern lecture every time I submitted a cab chit or bought a book for research – "Couldn't you have borrowed it from the public library?" – but when it came to getting a story or supporting our units in a war zone, she became obsessed with overcoming all obstacles.

"This network needs her more than you do," Slawko Klymkiw said when he called to protest my wooing her. "You know, Slawko," I said, "if I tell her you went behind her back to get me to lay off, she'll be furious, and you'll be in deep shit with her. You know that she thinks whom she works for is none of our business." He paused, and I could see him imagining Anne's wrath. "You're right," he said. "Forget I called." Finally, Anne agreed to work for both of us and told everyone that she worked "for the two biggest madmen in the CBC."

She had two conditions: one was that I had to get Casey Kollontay back from Dome Productions, a private company where the former facilities co-ordinator of *The Journal* now worked. Kollontay was an island of calm and patience, and the only person Anne would trust as production manager. "And Wilma Alexander will be business manager, take it or leave it." Wilma had worked for her at *The Journal*, where she'd watched every penny as if it were the last one on earth. She hums in her office, chews on carrot sticks, and is always looking for a better deal. But like Anne's, her ruthlessness was directed at making sure great programming was done, and not a penny wasted on anything but what the viewers saw on their screens.

After these assignments became public, Kelly Crichton, who was head of the news department and a friend of Anne's and mine, told me, "With so many *Journal* veterans together again on one project, the nickname of the history series in the rest of the building has become *The Empire Strikes Back*."

For senior producer in charge of the Toronto team, I wanted Gordon Henderson, who ran one of the most successful independent production houses in Toronto, 90th Parallel. I had worked with him on many projects and found him to be one of the most reliable and talented producers in Toronto, always delivering on budget and on time. He was also an amateur historian and had written a popular book for young people on Canada's prime ministers. He was, like Gene, passionate about Canadian history. Directors trusted him, because he always erred on the side of the better story rather than just the bottom line. I thought we needed a hard-headed private producer in charge here, someone with little patience for CBC bureaucracy. I also wanted to gain the trust of directors in the independent industry and send out a message that this series was not an exclusive CBC club. The trouble was that I would be asking Henderson to put a perfectly lucrative independent business on ice for at least two or three years. Like Hubert, who might be his opposite number in Montreal, he demurred. But I could sense hesitation: the romance of the history of Canada was gnawing at him. He was already envisioning the series in his mind: "I want people to *experience* our history, to wonder what it was like to be a pioneer during the first winter. What was it like to cross that portage? To stare at those mountains for the first time? I want people to imagine the unimaginable, to share the horror of war, the desperation of winter, the thrill of achievement. Let's not be afraid of *passion*." When Gordon was in Grade 7 in

Ottawa, he delivered a speech about the great explorer David Thompson, and he still had the trophy in his home. I was certain that he couldn't resist the challenge of the series.

As senior visual researcher, we had Ron Krant, the thin, taciturn, chain-smoking film detective who had scoured the world for *Dawn of the Eye* footage, and who spent his spare time painting wild expressionistic canvases. We, of course, had ribbed him endlessly about his new-found art career, until he sold a painting for $14,000 and became known as one of Canada's hottest "outsider" artists. "Why do you still come to work?" I asked him. "Actually, I get a lot of my ideas from the images that I see here," he told me. "Here" was two rooms choked with filing cabinets and bookcases full of photos, slides, film cans, videotapes, and reference books.

The picture genius I hired for the project was Murray Green, the senior editor who would weave all the elements together into symphonic structure. Video editors seem like computer geeks, but they lead rich internal lives of complete madness. Murray maintained, "We editors meet once a week, in a secret coven at the CBC, to invent terms like 'multiple frame buffer' and 'frame synchronicity,' simply to confuse producers like you."

A good producer's or film director's reputation for excellence is often based on his or her alliance with one editor. The person you marry will be the most important decision in a producer's life. The editor you ally with will be the second most important, and the relationship is likely to last longer. Now Murray would be in charge of recruiting the editors who'd make the history of Canada.

The editorial team comprised both *Journal* veterans and newcomers. Julia Bennett, who had been my producer when we did a documentary in China, would be working on Wolfe, Montcalm, and the invasion of Canada. Tall with curly long jet-black hair, she is a fireball of energy and dedication. Like Gene Allen, she is a devoted cheapskate who booked such cheap accommodations for *Dawn of the Eye* shoots that the first underground rules of the history series were: Never stay in a hotel booked by Julia Bennett, and never board any means of transportation booked by Gene Allen (a reference to the CC). Julia also has the distinction of having the loudest sneeze anyone has ever heard in a human being, which disqualified her from any delicate nature shoots.

Wayne Chong, an experienced field producer at *The Journal* and *The National Magazine*, was researching the Loyalists episode for the series. Early on, he and I gave a presentation about the project to a Loyalist society in Toronto. The audience seemed not the least distracted by the fact that two people named Chong and Starowicz were telling them how the CBC was portraying their history. I took this as a sign of national maturity. Fiona McHugh, an elegant lady with an Irish accent, was an inspired addition: she was a producer but also a writer who had adapted episodes of *Anne of Green Gables*. Rachel Brown, a young, perfectly bilingual graduate of McGill and Laval Universities, was hired as my assistant. Red-haired and energetic to the point of exhausting everyone around her, Rachel Rollerbladed to and from work, right though the CBC corridors, leaving protesting security guards waving after her. Wilma, Anne and Sally Reardon had vetted a hundred applications before settling on Rachel, impressed that she had run tree-planting teams in the Quebec bush in a previous job. "We thought she'd survive working with you," Sally said.

While I was recruiting the senior producers and directors, Gene Allen was recruiting the historical battalions. His first target was Ramsay Cook, one of the most respected historians in Canada, author of *Canada and the French-Canadian Question*, which was *de rigueur* reading when I was at McGill. Most important of all, since 1989 he has been co-editor of the *Dictionary of Canadian Biography*, the magisterial fourteen-volume collection of biographies of Canadian historical figures. He needed us like a hole in the head, I thought, but I subsequently learned that he believed historians had to reach out through the modern communications media. Gene courted him with many phone calls and finally brought us together at a Portuguese restaurant on College Street.

Our proposal had a few weaknesses, we thought, when it came to attracting the best historians. Unlike *The Civil War*, where historians appear on screen, our series would use no historians on the air, because we wanted to stay "in the period." We wanted to write it as if all the incertitude of the moment were still alive, with the audience having no idea how things would turn out. So there was no on-camera time to tempt historians. Neither was the money enticing. They were all being offered modest honorariums, and any specific time spent vetting scripts would be billed by the hour. This was no way to pay off the mortgage. In exchange, we wanted to be able to call them any time, night or day, with any question, large or small. They would have to read every draft, screen every rough cut, and attend planning meetings. Finally, they would not have any veto over decisions. There was a sound reason for this: we wanted to recruit a spectrum of political and social opinion, and the Canadian historical profession is radically polarized between the "social historians," who study areas such as labour, women's studies, and native studies, and the "political historians," who stress the grand narrative of political, diplomatic, and military events. We wanted to be able to involve both schools and did not want to set up a central committee that could agree on only the blandest compromises. And not least, we did not intend to give up our authority to make our series both popular and narrative. So the historians were told: "You will be consulted on every major planning decision. You will see every outline, every draft of the episode script, all the rough cuts, and your views will be treated with the utmost respect. But in the end, we are responsible for the final product; there is no veto. You have the right to remove your name or, if you wish, criticize the series publicly."

At the restaurant Ramsay Cook told us that he had been worrying about the decline in knowledge about Canadian history. "An electorate that has no context for its decisions will make the wrong ones," he said. "This may be the most important history of Canada ever done. I'd be pleased to help you." I'm pretty certain that if Gene Allen hadn't been the one asking, given his doctorate in Canadian history and the respect historians had for him, we would not have recruited Ramsay Cook, nor any of the others Gene set out to woo next.

At the annual general meeting of the Canadian Historical Association in St. John's, Newfoundland, Gene and Louis Martin spread
the word about the history series, to prepare the ground for when our
researchers would call. They particularly wanted to recruit Jean-
Claude Robert, the tall, distinguished chair of the history department
at the Université du Québec à Montréal and former president of the
Canadian Historical Association. Robert was impressed by the daring
of the project and agreed to be an adviser – which was communicated
to the rest of us in Toronto with great excitement. Now we had two
of the very best historians in Canada. Gene also wanted to recruit
specialists in social and regional history, and at the convention he
badgered Greg Kealey, one of Canada's top labour historians, until he
agreed to join. Later he also recruited Veronica Strong-Boag, a specialist in Canadian women's history, Judith Fingard, whose specialty
was the Atlantic region, and Gerald Friesen, the leading historian of
the prairies.

One of the major differences between this history and earlier
general histories of Canada in books was going to be the weight given
to the story of Canada's aboriginal peoples. Gene flew to Ottawa to
recruit Olive Dickason, the former journalist and author of the pre-
eminent history of Canada's First Nations. With Dickason, Cook, and
Robert, we had the three great currents of Canadian history covered.

Meanwhile, I was still waiting to see if Gordon Henderson
would be willing to leave his company for three years, and if Hubert
Gendron would take on the prickliest assignment of his life. Nor was
I doing well in recruiting the directors for each two-hour episode.
Alan Mendelsohn was shaken by his layoff and bitter about the CBC.
He needed a full-time job – so he joined an independent production
company. Bill Cobban couldn't wait for the project's funding to
come through and took on a history of the RCMP for the National
Film Board. And Laine Drewery, disturbed by the meltdown he was
seeing at the CBC, wanted to establish his credentials as an independent producer for the future. I tried all summer and fall to persuade them to come aboard, because they were the producers I

trusted most. Together, we had screened virtually every historical documentary and film of note and had spent hours at the Acme Bar and Grill debating techniques.

At this point, the fall of 1997, we may not have had any cameras, but we did have three of the greatest cameramen in Canada. Mike Sweeney, whom we had almost drowned in Newfoundland, had agreed to be the director of photography, the person who sets the whole visual style and grammar for the series. In Halifax, Sally persuaded the head of the local CBC to let us have Derek Kennedy, one of the original *Journal* cameramen with Sweeney, and a genius at lighting and mood. We also succeeded in getting Maurice Chabot, known as "the Prince of Darkness," because he was a genius at shooting where there was almost no light. Maurice was a militant sovereignist and was eternally squabbling with his frequent collaborator on news assignments, Stephen Phizicky. You would not want to be in the same van with them on the way to a shoot at the time of the referendum. I was hoping Phizicky had been badgering Hubert Gendron with similar vigour about joining the history project. "I think he's weakening," he reported. "When I walk around the block with him he's arguing with himself. And you know Hubert, that can take a long time, since he'll always use two thousand words where twenty will do."

Gordon Henderson finally called: "How can I resist a series on Canadian history? How could I look my history profs – guys like Michiel Horn and Irving Abella – straight in the eye? In this series I can work in an editorial landscape I love, because I do love this stuff. I believe this series will matter. My wife, Pam, also told me I would regret it for the rest of my life if I didn't jump on board. She's right."

Henderson's willingness to take a chance on the series meant that we had a second shot at Mendelsohn, Drewery, and Cobban. The most respected independent producer in Toronto – no CBC apparatchik – had tossed his lot in with the series, at considerable risk to his own company, and this meant the Canadian History Project was more than a CBC in-house production. He immediately set about recruiting the stars I couldn't land. He was unable to make Alan Mendelsohn change his mind, but Laine Drewery came on board and Bill Cobban finally agreed to direct the first episode of the second series, about the Northwest Rebellion, a year later. Gordon and I sometimes had different convictions about style and methodology. But the best lesson I ever learned from Peter Herrndorf was not to hire people who agree with you. The series would have been totally impossible without Gordon Henderson, his respect for the human story, and his sense of wonder at Canadian history.

Then Hubert Gendron called me in October, a few days after our latest late-night meeting in the lobby bar at the Sheraton: "Mark, on Saturday, I was sitting at home enjoying the sunshine and thinking about how I would do this scene or that scene which we had discussed. And it suddenly dawned on me that if I was going to spend a glorious Saturday worrying about your project, I might as well get paid for it." That phone call calmed more circuits in my brain than a shipload of Demerara rum. Gendron's participation was the icing on the cake. Now we had the absolutely drop-dead elite production corps.

That week, three of the seven cameras we had had to fight with Ottawa to get finally arrived from Sony, cameras so beautiful and so intricate it took a week to program their settings. We stared at them, with their switches and settings, as if marvelling at newborn triplets. After a week, we were able to resume shooting for the promotional video I was determined to make, the one that had led us to grief in the Strait of Belle Isle. The location this time was the Fortress of Louisbourg on Cape Breton, where we would film the bombardment of Quebec. Sally Reardon had reserved the entire fortress for us and made herself an expert on cannon.

With considerable excitement, I flew to Sydney, Nova Scotia, to meet Sally and Derek Kennedy, and joined their convoy of crane, generator truck, and camera vehicle. Maurice Chabot flew in from Ottawa to be the second unit's cameraman, and Louis Martin and Hubert Gendron came to mark the moment. It was December 19, and bitterly cold. At the hotel in Sydney, we once again toasted the beginning of a great enterprise, promising one another we would not board any boats.

Louisbourg looms out of the Cape Breton mist like a castle in *The Count of Monte Cristo*. It is a whole city, reconstructed according to the plans and on the foundations of the great city-fortress France built in 1713 to guard the approaches to New France. I walked through its streets, storehouses, and battlements in amazement and excitement. "We can shoot half the series here!" I declared. There was everything we needed: dining halls, barracks, kitchens, and ballrooms, period gowns and uniforms, flags, lanterns, carts. Everything down to the slightest detail was correct for the period, including the horses, sheep, and chickens, the vegetables in the gardens, and the glass in the windows, which was bought from the same factory that had made the original panes more than 250 years before. Here we had almost everything, ancient and modern, that we needed for the first six episodes, including power outlets, a fire station, and armaments and explosives experts on site. During the off-season, when it wasn't being used by movie companies as a location, it was at our disposal – an entire city with dozens of gigantic cannon. When I rejoined Sally, she said: "You have a megalomaniac look in your eye."

Sally had assembled two uniformed drummers, a company of men in artillery uniforms to fire the cannon, and several infantrymen, and had commandeered two majestic regimental silk flags. She had also booked a mobile construction crane, which groaned its way up the embankment looking like a giant yellow crab. All of the shooting was planned for that night, since you could see the flash of the cannon only in darkness. The crane's job was to hold an artificial moon, a round six-thousand-watt light, which would diffuse enough ambient lighting to allow the cameramen to show faces in the darkness. A technician had to stand on the narrow platform, twenty metres in the air, to adjust the huge light and brace it in the wind.

Finally night fell, the crane was raised, the battlement lit, and a cold, wet fog drifted in. It made the barrels of the cannon glisten, but soon everybody was numb with cold. The poor drummers and fife player – local teenagers – were freezing by the time we started rolling, and we had to retake a dozen scenes with them as their numbed hands and lips missed a beat or a note. But finally they were finished and dispatched to the sandwich and hot-coffee table set up in the powder room, while we turned our attention to the cannon. There we encountered another dilemma. To fire the battery of cannon, men rushed through a complex drill of aiming, loading, and priming, to the shouted commands of the artillery officer. It was now so cold that their breath was visible. This was visually dramatic but historically wrong. The attack on Quebec City was in July. A huddled conference finally persuaded the artillery officer to mouth his commands while sucking his breath in, and the soldiers to breathe in while they strained to load the cannonballs. We would dub the voices in later. This was not as easy as it sounded, and it took us an hour to get the first shot fired. "That's one for the blooper reel," Sally observed after it was done.

Then came the problem of filming the cannon from the other side of the battlement, to show the flame and smoke spit out of their mouths. It took several firings to find the right amount of powder to get a long plume effect. By the time we got it, the wind had shifted and was blowing at the cannon, flattening the plume and dispersing it instantly. By this time everyone was so cold that all of us, soldiers and CBC, retired to the powder room, eating egg salad sandwiches and sipping coffee from trembling hands, until someone said, "Where's the Man on the Moon?" Jack, who had been manning the artificial moon for the past several hours in the frigid wind and fog, was missing. Derek Kennedy tried to raise him on the walkie-talkie but got no response. Alarmed, we all rushed out and shouted "Jack!" at the sky, and after a few moments we heard a weak "Here" drift down through the mist. The crane was lowered slowly, and ghostlike Jack appeared, dusted in frost. He was given a cup of coffee and raised back into the sky as we made one last attempt to fire the cannon. Finally, after mixing more concoctions of gunpowder, and with Jack steadying the moon, the wind abated just long enough for us to fire off a deeply satisfying, earth-shaking, and billowy cannonade. "It's going to be very hard to go back to normal documentaries," Sally observed. "You can get hooked on this."

In the basements of the CBC in Toronto, there are vast carpentry shops that we documentary producers had never had the need to visit until now. The department was doomed by the cuts, and the CBC had announced it was negotiating to lease the basement levels to a company that would flood them and turn them into a giant sea aquarium. For now, the Canadian History Project was the principal customer for this decimated department, which was milling wooden cannon barrels for us and assembling old carts and period furniture. On one side of the vast carpentry shop they were building a wall out of Styrofoam, for a scene where a British cannonball devastates a street in Quebec City. The accuracy was impressive: a photo of a surviving eighteenth-century wall from Quebec had been enlarged and pinned to a large corkboard, and each stone was moulded out of Styrofoam and placed in a six-metre replica. Some of the "stones" were inserted loosely, so that an explosive charge would send them flying. Elsewhere in the shop, a period-correct wooden wall and roof were being constructed to be blown up and set ablaze at the same time.

But the most impressive of all was the ship. Six metres long, with masts and sails, this quarter-scale replica of a French vessel was being built for the sole purpose of being blown up during the episode on the invasion of Canada by the British. The carpenters bought a derelict metal boat for $800, then painted it to look like a wooden vessel and constructed a superstructure with masts and sails. When the British fleet arrived off Quebec City in July 1759, the French had a surprise ready. About a hundred ships and rafts had been loaded with gunpowder, pitch, and other combustibles and chained together into a deadly necklace a kilometre and a half wide, with one man on each boat. The plan was for each man to ignite his vessel on a signal and jump into the river, and the necklace of fire would be carried by the strong current into the British fleet. The graphics department assured us that if we blew up one boat and shot it from various angles simultaneously, they could reconstruct the exploding-boats sequence for us. All this destruction was scheduled to take place soon in a stretch of Lake Ontario in east-end Toronto, with the freelance director John Hudecki in charge.

On a bitterly cold January night, the ghost ship (as we called the model being built in the basement) was wheeled out on a trailer onto John Street, to the amazement of passing motorists who found an impossibly tall, fully rigged eighteenth-century ship moving in the traffic beside them toward Clarke Beach, at the foot of Cherry Street. Mounting this shot had become a military operation in itself, requiring coordination with the harbourmaster, the Toronto Police Emergency Task Force, to supervise our use of explosives, and the Toronto Harbour Police, to keep other boats away. Three cameras were set up on the beach – including one on scaffolding and another on a dolly and tracks – to get three different angles of the ghost ship, since it would blow up only once. Two rafts full of explosives were tied alongside the boat as well, to multiply the explosions, and the ship itself was loaded with bags and barrels of powder. Its masts also had small explosive charges rigged at breakaway points to shatter them. The special effects team leader, Tim McElcheran, using a panel of radio remote-control switches, would discharge all the explosions. As the special effects crew lowered it into the water at the Outer Harbour Marina on the Leslie Street Spit across the bay, Hudecki was on the beach with the camera crews. Then he got a message on his walkie-talkie.

The boat was sinking. Caitlin was with me, along with several friends she had invited to see her father's impressive film shoot. She finally looked at me, saying, "We just don't seem to have any luck with boats, do we, Dad?" I responded with a phrase that I'd use often during filming: "Thank God the *Globe and Mail* isn't here."

"Well," said Hudecki, "the race is on to see if we can get the shot before our permit to explode charges runs out." While Wilma Alexander was desperately calling the Toronto Film Office on her cellphone, Tim McElcheran's team rapidly repaired the boat. Wilma got the permit extended till 2:00 A.M., but not a minute later, and at one the walkie-talkies came alive with the excited news that the ghost ship was in the water and floating toward us from the marina. The special effects team soaked it in gasoline as John went out in a dinghy to shoot some close-ups, then returned for the finale. John took the megaphone and shouted "Fire!" The sky itself seemed to ignite, and fire climbed up the masts, the rafts burst into flames, the masts split, barrels flew through the air.

The sleeping residents of Leslieville who were woken by the blast would have had no idea what their taxpayers' dollars were doing that night, and we certainly were not going to try to explain. It took three hours to clean the beach and the water, but the special effects people were able to report a week later that they managed to sell the metal hull for $1,000, which was $200 more than we had paid for it. More immediately, the next day we had to blow up Quebec City on the Leslie Street Spit, where the Toronto Police usually explode suspected package bombs. I had persuaded Hubert Gendron to come to Toronto to watch the shoot, feeling he needed a boost, and the next night we watched Tim McElcheran's team set up the Styrofoam wall and, near it, the wall and roof of the wooden house. Once again the detonations went into the night, as pieces of wall flew impressively, without any of yesterday's mishaps. Hubert did observe, however, "Your idea of cheering me up is to bring me to watch my ancestral capital blown up?"

5

Adrift Again

It was becoming clear by the fall of 1997 that the darkest rumours about Head Office were true: it was a civil war zone. Tensions between Perrin Beatty and the chair of the CBC board, Guylaine Saucier, had reached the extent that Saucier would roll her eyes and shake her head whenever Beatty spoke at board meetings. Head Office was split into warring camps, one behind the president, one behind the chair, and everyone else was either playing both ends or ducking for cover. About the only thing the two camps could agree on was distrust of the English television network in Toronto, which the Head Office finance department considered financially reckless.

For the Head Office, desperate to meet the government-ordered cuts, English Television, the largest single unit in the CBC, was the obvious target. The other media lines – English Radio, French Television, and French Radio – were happy to point a finger at English Television and portray it as bloated and overstaffed, in order to ward off any cuts to themselves. Many a scandal or embarrass-ment that found its way into the papers was leaked by someone in the other divisions. At the best of times, senior CBC and Radio-Canada management politics resemble warlord-era China, and this was the worst of times. We had confused authority at the top, with two contending chiefs, neither of whom had any CBC experience and who were thereby susceptible to whispered rumours. The senior vice-president of resources, Louise Tremblay, had no production experience either, but in this atmosphere she held the reins of power. This was not an atmosphere that engendered creativity. "As a programmer," Slawko Klymkiw said, "I feel like we're working for forensic auditors." Any middle managers trying to push anything through the system, like cameras or edit suites, were likely to attract the unwelcome attention of Tremblay's department. And the Canadian History Project would work only if a dozen managers went out of their way to make things happen, particularly since there was no precedent for such a French-English collaboration.

My only entree to the inner councils in Ottawa was Michael McEwen. "If you don't have someone in Ottawa pulling things together for you," he had warned me, "you'll just get crushed between the two networks." He was right. So many departments needed to be coordinated – sales, publicity, engineering, design, new media, archives – that unless someone with overriding authority could knock heads, there was a good chance everything would get bogged down. The president couldn't do it, the work was too detailed; and besides, I couldn't go running to the president with every blocked purchase order. I needed a day-to-day friend in court, and McEwen was the man. Until he fell afoul of Guylaine Saucier.

McEwen was loyal to Beatty and was effectively acting as his executive vice-president, the position that runs the CBC from day to day. Beatty was ineffective and naive in many things, but he had an endearing manner. Most of all, as an old-guard Conservative, he was a strong nationalist and a fervent believer in public broadcasting. McEwen was the only senior executive in Ottawa who had run a network. Everyone around him in Head Office not only came from outside the CBC but came from outside the broadcasting industry, which was an unhappy state of affairs. McEwen inevitably found himself defending the operations in Toronto to this new Head Office, and this quickly earned him the reputation as an apologist for the status quo. Beatty had wanted to make him executive vice-president two years earlier, but the board rejected his nomination. Saucier had determined to fill the position with a "businessman." McEwen found himself neutralized by Saucier and the board, and finally he announced he would leave the CBC at the end of 1997, after more than twenty-five years of service.

"I feel really sad," he told me. "The CBC was never a job, it was a mission, a passion, a way of doing public service in the tradition of the 1960s. We had updated the management and slashed costs, but the money didn't go back into programming, it went into government coffers. The corporation I love can no longer deliver on its core mandate." The shabby manner of his departure was more evidence to me that the CBC was losing its soul. And for the Canadian History Project, not having McEwen around was politically disastrous. Beatty had asked Michael to be the guardian angel of the project because they both thought it was key to the CBC's future. Now we were adrift again, in waters so treacherous they made the Strait of Belle Isle a placid memory.

Guylaine Saucier found her man in the person of James McCoubrey, a heavy-set man in his late fifties who came from decades in the advertising world. Most recently he had worked for Telemedia, the company that published *TV Guide* and ran a string of very commercial radio sports and music stations like "The Fan." His reputation was of a hard-headed bottom-line manager, accustomed to wielding the hatchet. The appointment appalled most people at the CBC.

By the end of 1997, the history project's mood had turned gloomy again. The excitement of getting Hubert and Gordon, of blasting cannon into the Atlantic night, was being replaced by dread. It was clear that there would be no edit suites available in January in Toronto, and the Montreal unit was an empty shell, with no office space, much less edit suites and cameras. Despite Claude Saint-Laurent's support, the Radio-Canada management above him was manifestly indifferent to the project. Toronto management, except

for Jim Byrd, was not much more enthusiastic. The program director, Slawko Klymkiw, was openly saying the proposed series was too
long and too expensive, that it would gobble up the resources of
English Television, and that he didn't know where he could schedule
"this monster." Some of his fears were real: who, after all, was footing
the multi-million-dollar bill? If it was going to be foisted on the
English network entirely, it would paralyze Slawko's capacity to commission other productions. Ottawa had appeared brave in replacing
the NFB's portion last July, but it seemed Head Office was being brave
with other people's money. It was not committing any Head Office
funds, believing the money would come from sponsorship. The piece
of paper guaranteeing at least $20.5 million had been signed by
someone who had just been purged, and with him went the understanding that the budget was more likely to be $25 million. In fact,
while Perrin Beatty supported the project, others at Head Office
seemed determined to scuttle it. The finance department at CBC
Ottawa had sent another memo asking for justification for our
capital request for the remaining cameras and edit suites, which we
had already provided half a dozen times, with the full endorsement
of Toronto plant engineers and Toronto finance. The sales department had made no move to line up corporate sponsorship, and its
head, Peter Kretz, made it clear he wanted no part of it. Toronto had
half the office space it needed, and that was scattered over three
floors. I was hiring people, persuading them to leave solid jobs, for a
project that might evaporate in days.

A cold fear was forming inside me as we approached January
1998 – two years before broadcast. It was the anticipation of massive
failure. "I'm terrified of going down in the CBC annals as the man
who screwed up the history of Canada," I told Hubert. "That is something you wear the rest of your life. Worse, it is something your
children wear."

Christmas Eve dinner was muted that year at our house. It was
the second Polish dinner we were cooking after my mother's death,
and it had been poignant to go to all the Polish stores she frequented
to buy the ingredients. In Montreal, Nick Auf der Maur was getting

weaker and thinner, and the latest prognoses from Stephen Phizicky and Brian McKenna, who were in weekly contact with his doctor, were grim. Everyone and everything seemed to be slipping away. Even receiving a Christmas card from Rideau Hall depressed me, as it was evidence of another front I couldn't act on because of the paralysis surrounding the project. In the days between Christmas and New Year I was a cloud of gloom in our house, staying up late each night, pacing. I couldn't think of a move.

Sometimes, in a logjam, it's best to provoke some action – any action – that will at least dislodge the jam. The danger is that you might not like where some of the pieces fall. Although I was far from confident that it was the right thing to do, I decided that I had to meet with McCoubrey, to try to read where he stood on the project. But it had to be an unofficial, private, and off-the-record meeting, because I had no business, bureaucratically, involving myself in Head Office politics.

Dokie Koorenhof was the secretary to the executive suite in the Broadcast Centre, where Beatty, Saucier, and McCoubrey worked whenever they were in Toronto. Dokie was a smoker like me, so we were often out in front of the building chatting (I've picked up more intelligence in the butt-strewn entrance on Front Street than in a dozen executive meetings). I drove down to the CBC, knowing exactly where to find her. "He'll be in his office alone all day on the 31st," she said as we froze in the wind. "You'll be guaranteed no interruptions, and the building will be deserted." She put me in the appointment book for 10:00 A.M.

The meeting began badly. At ten, McCoubrey was on the phone to his broker, making transactions, it being the last day of the year, and I had to pace in the hallway outside his office for thirty minutes. McCoubrey had an impassive face with a thin smile, and he rocked in his swivel chair as he talked, never meeting my gaze. The conversation was not easy, since he talked only in short, compressed sentences. There was a tenseness about him, and I felt as though a police inspector were interviewing me. We had been at McGill together, and he had been president of the student union shortly before I became editor of the *McGill Daily*, so I brought up that subject. His response was to ask, "What happened to Sandy Gage?" who had been an earlier editor. I told him I didn't know. "He was a weirdo," he said, and that ended our college reunion.

"You know, your program director isn't very happy with your project," he said, opening the business at hand.

"Well," I replied testily, "the president, the vice-president of the English network, and the executive directors of news and current affairs of both the English and French networks are quite happy with it."

"He'd be happier if it was shorter," he said. "Can't you do it in ten hours?"

"I can do it in one hour if you want, but that's not the point. It's been almost two years since we announced the biggest television project in our history, and we seem to be still debating it."

"Why does it have to be so expensive?" he asked. "I mean, it's just a documentary, as I understand, which means photos and paintings."

"Just a documentary" was my red flag, but I tried not to show my irritation. I was getting the sinking feeling that things were every bit as bad as I had feared, or worse. Even the basics seemed to be at issue. I told him it wasn't a matter of some paintings and some snoring academics. I then tried to paint the picture of the style – the exploding boats, the diaries, the dispossessed. He remained impassive. He was one of those people who, I could see, aren't listening when you talk, but are thinking of their next point, and come in with it at mid-sentence.

"He's also concerned this isn't likely to get good ratings." Now I wasn't even sure if McCoubrey was quoting Slawko or voicing his own views.

"For the first time in CBC history we have a French-English co-production, a binational team, which goes against all the gravitational laws of this corporation," I said. "Instead of support from a management that's looking for efficiencies, we find ourselves in an eternal debating society with only token cameras and no edit suites, and we're on the air in two years. This winter will be wasted, leaving us one winter to shoot every single winter scene in five hundred years of Canadian history. Now, I deduce from this conversation, the length of the series and maybe its budget are still in debate."

Nothing I said seemed to have any effect. There was no "Tell me about the team you've assembled," which I would have heard from Peter Herrndorf. No sense that we were some kind of Delta Force going into combat, as I had with *The Journal*. No sense of the corporation I once knew. At 11:30, he had to attend to some personal matters, and I walked out feeling like a dismissed child. I just kept repeating to myself, "Keep your cool, show no emotion." He had ended the meeting by remarking, "You must have taken this meeting very seriously to wear a navy blue suit on New Year's Eve." I told him every suit in my closet was blue, but yes, I took this matter very seriously.

As I walked down the empty corridor, I heard him call out: "I'll do everything I can to help you. I honestly will." What did this mean? Was his impassiveness just his way of listening? But his comments about length, cost, and "photos and paintings" kept rolling in my head as I drove home.

That night, New Year's Eve, my wife, Anne, and I went to supper with Bernie Zukerman and Danny Finkleman, and I wasn't very good company. "Lighten up, Starowicz," Bernie said, "it's only a bloody television program!" I welcomed 1998 with the thought that I had, through my own arrogance, made the biggest mistake of my life, and I was dragging a dozen people who genuinely trusted me into a quagmire and the biggest television humiliation ever. There was no way we could pull this off. I had finally run out of buttons to push, out of patrons who had always defended me. I wanted desperately to get out of this nightmare project, but what would I say to the dozen people I had press-ganged into joining it?

The New Year brought a perverse ray of hope in Montreal. We finally had space allotted to us, right on the first floor of Radio-Canada, and pretty good real estate at that, with windows fronting on the main terrace. But there was a catch. It was the space that had been set aside for the much-awaited daycare centre for the children of CBC employees. Hubert told me that we had to keep this very secret before we were accused of having scuttled the daycare facility. In fact, the daycare was to be located just a little farther down the hall, but no one knew that yet, and by the end of the week our people in Montreal were being ribbed in the corridors as "the baby-killers." Whatever. At least we could move our people into their own space and get down to serious recruiting.

Three days later, the worst ice storm in a century devastated Montreal and cut off all power. Richard Fortin, the only researcher we had in Montreal, was trying to get home in a cab when a police cruiser smashed into his taxi, crushing his hand and landing him in the emergency ward. Nick Auf der Maur's neighbour, a close friend, died of a heart attack carrying wood into his freezing home, and Nick had to attend his funeral, knowing his own was probably imminent. Hubert, whose house was freezing, checked his family into a hotel to get some heat and food – then the power went in the hotel.

"It was exhausting," he said, "a city the size of Montreal blacked out. No trains leaving. People couldn't even get off the island for days, and we almost lost our drinking water. It was an otherworldly experience, streets littered with debris. Everything was so cold and so dark you couldn't wash, you couldn't cook, there was a run on food – it was psychologically exhausting just doing the basics of life."

By the time it was over, we had lost a month in Montreal, and the infant unit moved into its new offices, as Hubert put it, "extremely tired, worried how far behind we were, isolated, and panicked." To make up for lost time, Toronto and Montreal went into manic activity. Hubert recruited candidates for directors, researchers, and production assistants, and I'd fly to Montreal to be part of every interview. Gene and Gord were organizing the options for how many episodes we'd need and what would go into them; since we now had an active Radio-Canada unit, the French-English negotiations could begin. And separately, John Hudecki and Murray Green and Ron Krant were assembling the shots and sequences for the thirteen-minute video that I still thought might save our skins.

I'd meet Nick and Phizicky and Brian McKenna at Winnie's every lunchtime when I was in Montreal. One day in February, Nick came in and took the seat next to me at the bar. Margo, the bartender, poured him a fruit juice. "I just came back from the doctor," Nick said without emotion. "I have six months to live." His ex-wife, Linda Gaboriau, who had joined us, took his arm and said, "Then we're all going to make them the greatest six months of your life."

The next two weeks at the history project were all-consuming, which was a mercy under the circumstances. The council of senior producers met for an intense two days in Toronto, to tackle the daunting task of dividing twenty thousand years of Canadian history into approximately twenty-four hours. Hubert and Gordon hadn't been part of our preliminary discussions. It was an almost impossible task. What would we leave out, and by what criteria and guidelines? After three days it was clear that there was no way to do a chronological history of Canada in twenty-four hours if it was going to have any room for the voices and stories of the men and women who lived the history. We could do great moments in Canadian history, or turning points in Canadian history, but a chronological evolution of Canada – at least, one with any narrative dimension – would be dense as porridge if reduced to twenty-four hours. The Acadian Deportation, for example, would have to be done in four minutes, the Riel Rebellions in fifteen, the Second World War in thirty minutes, and so on.

The discussions got tense. "I'll be damned if we squeeze the entire history of New France into sixty minutes," Hubert fumed, and Gordon Henderson countered with, "That means we have to reduce the entire exploration and opening of the west, the whole fur trade, Radisson, Thompson, the Hudson's Bay Company into one hour." Sheets and sheets of flip-chart paper were ending up crumpled on the floor, and every whiteboard on the walls was covered in undecipherable multicoloured scribbles. There was no other way to do it than to build it from the ground up, to virtually build a scale model of the entire series, stand back and look at it, and see what it added up to.

We agreed on the themes that would govern our choices and run through every episode. First, the aboriginal story would run right through. Second, so would the English-French dynamic. Third, the continental dynamic of Canada and the United States. Fourth, the immigrant waves that shaped Canada. Finally, there would be an emphasis on the role of women, labour, class, and regions – this was a social history. In so doing, we understood what the weaknesses would have to be: the series would not be as strong on diplomatic, business, scientific, or cultural history, because that would require a "survey" approach. We were opting for a "narrative" approach, one that would be built on the stories of several characters who lived in that particular time, and unless Alexander Graham Bell or Banting and Best were some of those "through characters," then the invention of the telephone or the discovery of insulin would not be a chapter. There had to be a focus, and our focus was the human experience.

The title of the series really should have been *A Narrative History of Canada*, but this wouldn't work, we thought, because narrative history is a particular subset of historiography and few viewers would understand the term. *The Civil War* was based heavily on Shelby Foote's *A Narrative History of the Civil War*. History, as an academic discipline, is largely an analytical field, studying demographic and economic and political context and trends. It has its subdivisions, such as military, diplomatic, and scientific history. Narrative history is not analytical but descriptive, and it leans heavily on the eyewitness accounts of individuals who lived through it, unaware of the bigger trends and forces. Often it is a microcosm, such as *The Return of Martin Guerre*, or an epic, such as Allan Nevins's nine-volume *The Ordeal of the Union*.

There has always been a rift between the narrative historians and the analytical ones, and it continues today. Narrative history is often written by non-academics like Pierre Berton, who are sometimes dismissed as "popularizers" by the academic historians. I was shocked to hear one professor, at a history conference in Toronto, boast that he "would never dream of letting a Pierre Berton book in my class" and be applauded.

Since "narrative history" was too technical a term – or so we thought – we called it at first *A People's History of Canada*. But some people, including Perrin Beatty, thought this sounded a little Marxist, so we did the Canadian thing and shifted the words around – *Canada: A People's History* – and everybody was happy. Except for our huddled group of senior editors, who, after one week of exhaustive brainstorming and negotiations between Toronto and Montreal, came up with . . . thirty-two hours!

"There's no way!" I said, throwing up my hands. "The program director is openly saying he prefers sixteen hours, and the French network would prefer sixteen minutes! We're committing suicide here. We have to cut."

It was tense when we started weighing the value of one historical topic against another: Port Royal versus Newfoundland, Maritime history versus western history. Comments flew like "We can't bloody do a chapter on one isolated fur trade post and drop a hundred years of Newfoundland history" and "Screw Franklin, it was a British expedition, not Canadian history!" It was exhausting, and bruised feelings lingered for days. But we got it down to twenty-eight hours. Later, it went back up to thirty.

The whole project was changing as a result of the French-English co-production. Up to now, there had been no French unit to negotiate with, so the initial outlines were deficient. If you are doing a history of English Canada, or at least one which leans on the experience of anglophones, the Boer War becomes big and the nineteenth-century exodus of a million French Canadians to the United States looking for jobs is a minor story. If you are doing a history for a French audience, the reverse is true: everyone has a relative who moved to the States and lost his language, hardly anyone has a relative who died in South Africa. Both events happened, but both do not occupy the same space in the social memory bank. We were doing four histories, really – French, English, aboriginal, and immigrant – because we had decided that the historical memory and experience of each would be given equal weight in this narrative.

We would argue for the next three years that we were, first of all, definitely not doing *the* history of Canada. It was *a* history, the product of a specific group of people, of a specific generation, a specific sensibility, in a specific time. But more than that, we'd try to shake off any suggestion that we were coming up with an overarching "reconciliation" of Canadian history, or some amalgam. By deciding to follow four points of view, we were not attempting to arrive at one. We were going to tell all four simultaneously. There is a big difference. A single history attempts to resolve contradictions into one version. We, on the other hand, were going to illustrate contradictory perspectives of the same events and try to leave the viewer with an understanding of why people felt and acted as they did, in their time and place.

Once we had the editorial architecture, which now filled pages, we had to break everything down by detailed costs. This is like building a miniature model of a city in order to count every window, the number of street lights, the acres of parkland, and projected water consumption. It took days with Wilma Alexander standing at the whiteboard asking questions like, "Champlain departs into interior. How many canoes? How many extras? How do they get to the location? Do they need hair and makeup on location and can they be predressed? Costumes? Location fees? What unions are involved? Can we avoid overnight motels? Any animals involved? Closest power source?" Anne Emin would sit there with her calculator and periodically slam her pencil down and say, "You ran out of money forty minutes into the episode. This isn't *Gone with the Wind!*" Then we'd start again with one canoe, which the graphics team could clone into ten, and somebody who knew somebody who had a river near his farm. Finally we had it down to just over $25 million.

"I've only got authority to go to $20.5," I said. "And McEwen is gone."

Anne was furious: "There's never been anyone who believes this can be done for $20.5. Everybody's been told time and time again it's at least $25 million, right from Sandra Macdonald and the film board down. They know it as well as you, but no one wants to bite the bullet. They're not going to just hand it to you. Your job is to go get it."

The board was going to be in Toronto for a major meeting at the end of March. A report on the state of the history project was on the agenda. Until now, board members knew little more about the project than what they had read in the paper. I was counting on this critical meeting to turn the tide of our fortunes. Having the president's support had not been enough to pull us out of the doldrums. My meeting with McCoubrey hadn't had any discernible effect. Jim Byrd couldn't blast the logjam in Head Office finance. There was only one level of power left which might push us over the hump: the board as a whole.

If we could get the video edited in time, I was sure the sweep and the scale of the story would galvanize the board. Our secret weapon was that people had very conservative expectations of what "Canadian history" would look like. They supported the idea intellectually but expected it to be worthy and academic. They weren't expecting what we were concocting. If we could get enough momentum going in this board meeting, then we might escape the gravitational field of corporate inertia. If every manager got the message that the series was a top corporate priority, the debate would be over.

The history project was critical for the board as a model of the English and French networks working together. In the middle of crippling cuts and clear hostility from the government, this high-profile experiment in cross-cultural production was essential. As far as the board was concerned, everything was going fine, since none of our troubles had been reported in the papers. If the board knew how bogged down we were at Head Office, there would be hell to pay. It was unthinkable for an executive producer to go directly to the board with a problem. It violated the reporting lines and would have done severe damage to Perrin Beatty, who was our ally. On the other hand, if I gave the board a sunny status report in person at this meeting, I could be accused months later of complicity in misleading the board.

Anne Emin had been telling everyone for months that this project was at least a $25-million project. Costs of space, travel, and the sheer complications of working in two languages were not being factored in by Ottawa in its $20.5-million budget. Furthermore, the later it got, the more expensive it got. If we had to simultaneously edit all the episodes in the first wave, as we called it, we would need nine edit suites. We had planned four in Toronto, because some episodes would start earlier, finish earlier, and allow more episodes to be edited in the same suite. But with no edit suites and only three cameras, we were getting perilously close to the edit-all-at-once scenario, which would make the costs soar. In effect, then, we would be the ones to bear the financial consequences for the foot-dragging in other departments.

So I asked for one more council of the project's senior producers and the business and production managers. I asked every section head to give me the paper trail on every delay. For a whole day, in my office, we constructed the whole sequence of events and omissions. Then I started writing.

I went to my boss, Bob Culbert, and outlined the trap we were in. If I said aloud that the emperor had no clothes, then I could turn a potential disaster into a real one, burning some of our best allies. Saucier might use it against Beatty, and I didn't know how McCoubrey was aligning, or how Tremblay's finance department in Ottawa would behave. If I kept quiet, I would be complicit, and in a few months it would be too late to produce the series.

"This is a dysfunctional administration which is having an internal civil war," Bob said. "It's not your job to get involved in it any more than you have to. The only people you have a responsibility to report the whole picture to are the ones you report to – and that's me and Claude Saint-Laurent."

I told him I was glad he felt that way, because here was our plan: We were compiling a chapter-and-verse report which detailed all the inertia and delay. And we wanted the fact that this report was being written to be known – just the fact of our collecting all the memo traffic would make it clear what we were doing.

"I'll submit a completely candid report to you and Claude," I said. "It will have all the financial projections, and a complete assessment of where we stand. You, I know, will have to pass it up the chain. If the cameras and the edit suites aren't cleared in time for the board meeting on March 16, and Ottawa is still arguing over capital allocation, then I'll tell the board the project is now unachievable for the year 2000. What do you think?"

Bob knew that you didn't have to broadcast a memo for it to have an effect. The fact that enough people know it is all being written down is sufficient, sometimes, to get results. "I don't think you have any choice," he said. "Besides, it just may be the piece of ammunition Jim Byrd needs."

"Is there anything in there that will damage Jim with Ottawa?" he asked.

I shook my head. "Not unless supporting a production unit is a crime these days."

"I'll fill Jim in," he offered, "and I'll spread the word."

For three days I went through draft after draft of a seven-page, single-spaced memo, with an attachment of four pages of tables and cost options. For someone who had fancied himself writing epic history, writing memos that only a few people would read was dispiriting enough. Writing one you hope *nobody* would read was truly perverse. Here it is, in part.

TO: Bob Culbert, Executive Director, News, Current Affairs and Newsworld, CBC; Claude Saint-Laurent, Directeur-Général, Information, Radio-Canada, Montreal.
FROM: Mark Starowicz, Toronto.
10 March 1998.
Confidential

Dear Bob and Claude,

Attached is the proposed episode division options requested at the meeting of February 13, plus revised cost estimates, and an assessment of the situation we find ourselves in. Thank you for your generous help and support over this process.

The video, both French and English, will be ready by Sunday night. Hard copies of this report, and this attachment, are in the overnight courier shipment.
Best regards,
Mark Starowicz.

Report on Status and Options
Canadian History Project

At this writing, the capital debate is unresolved. We have only three cameras, two cameramen. No editing equipment – except one aging Avid suite in Toronto which has been diverted from the Documentary Unit till the end of the month to edit the video. No edit equipment in Montreal; no sound equipment. The snow is melting, the winter is almost gone. . . . Last July I stressed we would need a corporate mobilization to make this happen on time. The President asked if we could deliver on budget and on time. I answered that we could do it only if the resources of CBC/Radio-Canada mobilized in task force energy. This mobilization has not happened. . . . I have spent the winter writing memos instead of history.

The problem is that this project does not fit our normal operations. It is not something we are geared to do through our normal working patterns. It is in two languages, in a collaboration between two networks, on a subject which is a matter of great passion to our founding cultures. In the editorial group, we have to learn to think differently. On the management level, this project has to be constantly reinforced, and constantly supported, precisely because the natural laws of corporate gravity are being violated. . . . The most dramatic, but by no means the only example, has been the capital debate. Whatever proprieties were in dispute, the propriety of leaving a production team stranded on a beach with three cameras, two English cameramen, and a diverted edit suite, till we are within two weeks of the end of the fiscal year, is a textbook study in corporate inertia. I could use stronger words. No program has ever been required to buy its own cameras, tripods, Avids. Weeks – precious weeks – have been wasted on a sterile debate about equipment. Montreal and Toronto are equal in *owning not one edit suite.*

The production plan envisions the first episode completed in 13 months. The second in fourteen. Edited where? Shot how? To delay picture-lock from April to June requires nine suites at peak loading, not six as budgeted – do we go to another budget revision to increase editing?

Many other dimensions are hanging in the air. Publishers want to discuss publishing series books. . . . They will have to assign writers this spring to meet their own deadlines. But with the incertitude described above we cannot give them hard facts, much less start negotiating. . . . These fronts have to move now, or there will be no book, no CD-ROM, no music CDs.

Can we still do it? I hope so. With pro-active management intervention – not just letting the laws of corporate gravity prevail. With real mobilization and support, instead of sterile debate about capital, with equipment ordered and with urgent construction of suites.

We believe – I'm tempted to write "hope" instead – that we can deliver the attached plans on time, on the budget outlined ($25 million), by dint of extraordinary work, without vacations, God willing with no strikes or disasters, and no ice storms, no illnesses, and with proper corporate support. . . . There are no margins left.

I am not prepared, unless we get the tools ordered immediately, to stand in front of the Board of Directors on Monday and say that this series is attainable in January of 2000. It is a privilege that we may, as the video says, produce the first History of Canada in the Television Age. That is a considerable honour, worth the risk and the sacrifice. It is, however, a nightmare to contemplate that we may be the people to wear the consequences of corporate inertia, and be responsible for screwing up the opportunity of a generation.

We will not deliver a mediocre History of Canada. We are at the margins of fiscal conservatism, technical capacity, and common sense.

I don't know how many copies ended up where, and who put it to what use. I don't even have any evidence that it was pivotal. The rumour that it was being written was probably more important than

anything in it, but I can't even be sure of that. We were now in the
realm of pure drama. Anne Emin, Casey Kollontay, and Bob Culbert
kept spreading the word that I would speak out at the board meeting
if the hurdles weren't cleared by Monday, that we had no choice: we
weren't going to take the rap for a disaster not of our making.

There were no real villains in middle and upper management
in Toronto or Montreal. I think there were in Ottawa, but not in
Television or Radio. An atmosphere of such fear and recrimination
had been created by the slash-and-burn policies of the past two years
that it was dangerous for anyone to stick their necks out, clear a work
order, take responsibility for something that wasn't in quadruplicate.
I suspect that the fear of a board inquiry into what had gone wrong
suddenly made it possible for people to process a whole array of
routine requisitions they otherwise would have been reluctant to deal
with – not out of malice but for fear of not having their asses covered.

On the Friday before Monday's meeting, as the board members
were on their way to Toronto, Casey reported that all the cameras
would be delivered, all the edit suites would be constructed by May 18.

That Friday night, the few of us left in the office watched the first
mix of the Canadian history video. Then we went out to a bar and
drank far too much, behaving like teenagers on March break. It had
been deeply satisfying to see all the elements come together. It looked
like it would work. We'd have to see it on the big screen. That night I
had the first deep sleep in weeks.

6

Thirteen Minutes

I spent that weekend in the large sound-mixing suites on the seventh floor, balancing the music and sound tracks, making them surge at the right punctuation points – a process as complex as mixing a rock video. I had booked the eighth-floor theatre for Sunday night, Casey had had all the projecting and surround-sound equipment tweaked by the engineers, and we sat down to watch our video for the first time on a wide screen. No matter how much you've laboured over a film, no matter how much you've stitched every word and frame, cursing it over the months, even though you know everyone is an actor, every sound an artifact – if you've done it right, it still transports you. It shapes your emotions, takes over your breathing, even your pulse and the hair on the back of your head. The whole piece, as it is in music, is infinitely larger than the sum of its keystrokes. The conjunction of motion and colour, sound and music – when it works – is like a symphony, but even more powerful. Something that never existed before is born before your eyes. It is a feeling so profound that it is no wonder men and women go to the extremes they do to create a cinematic work.

Ours lasted just thirteen minutes, after which we sat there speechless, glazed like opium smokers, knowing that somehow we had captured what we wanted to say about the birth of this country, in a way that could never be written on paper. This short film persuaded even us that the series was possible, that whatever grief we were living would be worth it. I drove Murray Green home that night, as we lived in the same neighbourhood, and we were silent most of the way. He got out of the car in front of his house, and as he closed the door he said: "Now we know it can be done. I didn't want to say anything before, but I wasn't so sure up to now."

"Me neither," I said.

The board was meeting at 12:30 the next day, Monday. We spent the morning fussing in the eighth-floor theatre, testing everything and then testing it again. Then we got word that the chair did not want to have the screening upstairs. The board was meeting in the third-floor conference room and coming up to the eighth floor was too far for them to go; they were running late, and we would have to come down. This was a disastrous prospect. The conference room was a sterile, fluorescent-lit space, with no sound system. We protested through secretaries, but the reply was that the chair wanted to see the video on a TV screen, like she would at home. We replied, through the secretarial telegraph, that a huge conference room with thirty people seated at tables did not duplicate the home environment. Finally, Murray saved the day by pointing out that our film was on digital videotape, and it was not playable on any other machine in the building. That settled the issue. I think I lost a couple of kilos that morning.

We set out juices, coffee, tea, and sandwiches of a modest character suited to a budget-conscious era, and thirty copies of a document describing the series. We sent out parties of escorts to guide the board to the screening room and ensure no human losses in the elevators. Slowly, they straggled in, in clumps of three and four, clearly tired and seeming bored at the prospect of this next item, which was screwing up lunch. They talked among themselves about the business of the morning and exhibited little curiosity about the series. It was clear they had limited expectations, which was perfect. Then Jim Byrd came in and took me aside: "Saucier refuses to come up. The PMO has just announced her term is being renewed, and she's giving interviews." I was crestfallen – half the point of this entire effort was to get Saucier on board. "She just refuses," Jim said. "Go ahead without her." We had the board, the president, the vice-presidents of the CBC and Radio-Canada, Bob Culbert, and nervous Claude Saint-Laurent, all balancing sandwiches on their knees as the house lights dimmed.

The dark theatre filled with a threatening grinding of iron wheels on wood, as if some mechanical beast were approaching, and the screen filled with close-ups of ropes groaning through block and tackle. In the darkness and fog on the wide screen, the glistening barrel and mouth of a massive, sinister cannon appeared, lurching forward with every heave on the ropes as it approached the battlement. The mouth of the cannon filled the screen, and the first tense orchestral note was heard as the image dissolved to the words: "The Canadian History Project/Le Groupe Histoire du Canada."

The fuse on top of the cannon was lit, and a roar shook the theatre as the cannon spit a three-metre plume of fire and smoke that seemed to envelop the whole room. The flash illuminated an audience of transfixed eyes and partly open mouths, as the music swelled and the smoke of the cannon dissolved to the giant sails of the *Matthew* filling the screen. We were plunged onto the high seas to the sound of wind and gulls and the crashing bowsprit of the *Matthew*. The sound of a helicopter grew louder, and the screen filled with Niagara Falls looming toward us as we were immersed in deep rumbling and clouds of mists. Then the voice of Kenneth Welsh, sounding like God's stenographer, spoke: "It is the most sweeping and epic documentary series in Canadian television. A series which brings together the best directors, artists, and historians to tell a story that spans the centuries. It is a story of the endurance of the human spirit, a testament of honour and betrayal, war and peace. . . ."

For thirteen minutes, image was piled upon image, sound on sound, while the narrative stitched them together in electrifying tones.

Then came darkness, and a very long silence as the house lights slowly came on. "They were completely stunned," Murray Green remembers. "Some of them had tears in their eyes. No one said anything for a while, then one voice said, "This is wonderful," and another voice said, "This is incredible, I had no idea." And a third voice said, "This is exactly what the CBC is supposed to be doing!" And the room filled with applause.

I was standing at the front, under the screen, and questions and comments started to bubble up. "I thought it was going to be all paintings and sketches," someone said. "You mean all those characters and all their words are true – nothing is made up?" Not a word, I said. Another asked, "I guess, in the French version, you're going to use subtitles?" No, I said. "With your indulgence, I am now going to play this film again, with the exact same music, same images, same script, but you'll see one difference." I knew this would be the clincher. Hubert told me later that Claude Saint-Laurent leaned over and whispered to him, "Is ours as good as this?" "Watch," Hubert said.

The house lights dimmed to play the same film, except with the rich voice of narrator Jacques Godin and with different actors.

It was one of the most satisfying moments in my life, to see a room of Conservatives and Liberals, French and English, westerners and Acadians and Toronto lawyers click onto the same idea at the same time. The second video moved them as much as the first. It just seemed so simple and so obvious.

"What about Riel, and conscription, and all the difficult stuff?"

"You've just watched the destruction of a French city by an invading English fleet, with women and children huddling and crying. I don't think anyone here thinks it was so inflammatory it will provoke a political crisis," I said. "We'll do the rest the same way – journalistically, accurately, showing the emotions of both sides. People will not shrink from that. We don't have to be afraid of history. We'll show the political views of everyone, the passions of both sides, and all the consequences. Why should this be so strange? We do it every single day in this building. We covered the end of Communism, minute by minute. We covered the FLQ crisis and the

War Measures Act. We covered two referendums. We cover explosive and violently divisive issues every day. That's our craft. We do it by the rules of journalism and by the journalistic policy handbook of the CBC. And we will do the past exactly the same way. In real time."

"Why no historians?"

Because, I replied, the participants in those events represent every single point of view for every one of the great crises. We don't need to break out of the past. We are not interested in having a floating Supreme Court of historians passing judgments on events.

The discussion went on for half an hour. Time and again the question was asked: "It will be the same story on both networks at the same time?" Yes. "Same script?" Yes. Perrin Beatty, though clearly delighted, finally voiced one concern. "Where'd you get the pictures of that ship blowing up?" I told him we blew it up ourselves. "You blew up a ship?" he repeated with alarm. I couldn't resist letting him stew for a few seconds, as I imagined he was seeing headlines in the *Globe and Mail.* "That's right, Perrin. It was right here in Toronto Harbour. That's real gunpowder kegs exploding, not computer effects." I think he could see his image of fiscal responsibility sinking with the ship. When I finally told him it was a quarter-scale model, which cost us $800, and that the Toronto Harbour Police and the fire department had supervised the whole thing, he visibly relaxed.

But I took the opportunity to make a point. We would be broadcasting to a generation raised on *Star Wars* and *Titanic.* Their visual grammar is very sophisticated, their video games far more intricate than half our special effects. I repeated what we'd been saying for a year now. "We're tired of the American story being wide-screen with orchestral sound, while ours is three etchings and a piano track. We're not going to engage Canadians, especially Canadian kids, with that. Not in this age." Sitting in the front row, Brian Peckford, the former premier of Newfoundland who now sat on the board, jumped in: "That's absolutely right. Nobody's going to watch the boring old style, these kids are really sophisticated, and we've got to do this properly. It's time we used all the tools at our disposal. I'm with you guys all the way. What did you say this project costs?"

"The current budget is $20.5 million," I said, expecting the night-mare to start.

"Well, if you ask me, that's chicken feed in television in this day and age," he said, turning to everyone behind him, "and if the series is like what I've seen here today, it's worth every penny and more."

That was the end of the discussion about money. One board member was particularly enthusiastic, as if something had dawned on him. He asked, "What are you going to do about the Acadian Deportation?" I replied we'd show it in all its horror, burning villages and people herded onto boats like animals. I didn't know then who he was, but I remembered his excitement after the film. And in a few months, I would come to know Clarence LeBreton's name very well.

Downstairs, the unit was waiting for news from the screening theatre as if it were white smoke at a conclave of cardinals. Rachel phoned down to say that the video had been a big hit, which set everyone cheering. As the board members filed out of the theatre, Jim Byrd came up to me smiling broadly and said, "It's in the bag. You've totally sold them. Until now no one could picture it, and now they can hardly wait. This is the turning point."

When I dropped Murray off at home that evening, he said, "Well, thirteen minutes down. Twenty-nine hours and forty-five minutes to go."

Two days later, Hubert called me to say that Saint-Laurent had told him to change one word in the French version of the video, from "nation" to "pays" (country). If I had needed to be reminded that every adjective and noun in this series would be weighed, then this last-minute substitution would have woken me up to it.

The video had also invigorated the small Montreal team, and Hubert went into hyperdrive. His farewell party from *Le Point* fea-tured Jean Pelletier dressed as Montcalm and the host, Jean-François Lépine, as Wolfe, in full regalia. From that, I picked up the habit of calling him "Monsieur le Général," and in return he called me "Mon-sieur le Maréchal." Now Monsieur le Général Macdonald Walter Lucien Hubert Gendron was in full military flight in Montreal, filling the office with boxes of supplies, interviewing candidates for jobs every two hours. It felt like we were staffing an Antarctic expedition. Hubert had ransacked the props department and pilfered a huge model of D'Iberville's ship, *Le Pélican*, and had placed it in the hallway. With this ship, D'Iberville had ruthlessly devastated the English in Hudson Bay in the 1650s. "No offence to Toronto intended," Hubert said.

The first director we hired was Claude Lortie, an energetic and experienced producer in his fifties who worked on international documentaries for *Le Point*. He would tackle the difficult story of early New France, a period scarce in letters or diaries by ordinary people, since most were illiterate then. We would have to mount an unprecedented effort to find the "voices" of common people, which meant searching court records and letters of parish priests. To do that, Louis Martin had already hired a brilliant young researcher from Radio-Canada, Richard Fortin, who was currently out of action, convalescing after injuring his hand during the ice storm. We urgently appealed to Jean-Claude Robert for a replacement. Claude Berrardelli was one of Robert's star graduates, and he had the temperament of Saint Francis; he would need it. Before he could even find the toilet in the building, Berrardelli was assigned the urgent task of mining for quotes all of Champlain's writings and letters, as well as the Jesuit *Relations*, all fourteen volumes, and all in archaic French. Spring was nearly upon us, and we had to film according to the seasons. Champlain had set out in spring and summer to explore the interior and make his fateful alliances with the Indians; it wouldn't do to shoot those scenes with autumn vegetation.

The next director we hired was a producer from *Enjeu*, the French equivalent of *the fifth estate*. Peter Ingles is a Franco-Ontarian, the son of a Hungarian father and a French mother who insisted their children be educated in French. What persuaded us about him was a piece he had done on a parish in Ontario where the Catholic priest, a generation ago, had made all the French change their names – even on the gravestones – so Roy became King, and Leblanc became White. This was a French Catholic priest forcing his own parishioners to abandon their heritage. Ingles had done the piece with detachment and without preaching, which made the condemnation of this social atrocity all the more powerful. Though the least *pure laine* francophone on the team, he seemed to bear the weight of French-Canadian history personally. However, he would not let ideology colour his work.

Ingles was paired with Frédéric Vanasse, a young man working in Jean Pelletier's newsroom who had the itch to learn documentary production. The head of the Quebec bureau, Michel Cormier, told him: "If you don't learn how to make documentaries with Starowicz's team, you'll never learn documentaries," and Pelletier encouraged him to join us, even though he was losing a good journalist. Within days Vanasse was plunged into the 1837 Rebellions and found himself, in his words, an arms trafficker. "I had to find period British rifles, the Brown Bess, for a scene in the Halifax Citadel, and my colleagues howled with laughter as I negotiated the rental of these firearms on the phone. It was a long way from editing the news."

The Radio-Canada cameramen we seduced into joining us were the equal of anyone. Pierre Mainville had worked for *Enjeu* and had been the cameraman in Moscow for both networks. He worked like a dog, and even better, he had just the eye, as people say of a great cameraman. Gaétan Morisset, older and more deliberate, was the senior cameraman at *Le Point*, which meant you could throw a grenade at him and he would keep rolling – no chaos could faze someone with his experience, and we had plenty of chaos to offer. To begin with, we now had six cameramen – four in Toronto, two in Montreal – and only three cameras.

Sometimes chaos also delivers miracles, and ours came in the form of a woman who had been going crazy on the TV news desk overnight shift and was determined to get into the history project. Gail Boyd was an Acadian from Moncton whose mother's family escaped the Deportation. It was the first but certainly not the last time that I would realize how deep some people's roots are, and how present their past is. "People who escaped the Deportation" was just a casual phrase in New Brunswick, like "travelled in Europe that summer." My fascination with Acadia had begun with Roméo

LeBlanc, but it was Gail who would finally take me there. She immediately became the indispensable liaison between Toronto and Montreal, the final say for any translation, the person who made sure I didn't make an ass of myself in a French interview, and the embodiment of the unit's spirit.

It was good something was being born, because Nick was dying. I spent several evenings in his living room with him, Phizicky, and Nick's daughter Melissa, who was in Courtney Love's band, Hole, and had recently appeared on the cover of *Rolling Stone*.

When Nick was asleep, Phizicky told me that they had discussed his funeral – "He wants it at the basilica" – and related one conversation that will always remain in my mind. "I asked him recently in the car," Phizicky said, "why he didn't seem bitter. He is only fifty-four, after all. He said it is because his cancer was something he has inflicted on himself. 'I've had such a terrific life, I've packed in five lives into one, and I don't feel one bit cheated.'"

In the meantime, I was still head of the documentary unit and responsible for *Witness*, *Life & Times*, and documentary specials. That entailed going in April to the world's major documentary market, MipDoc, in Cannes, France, to screen what other networks around the world have to offer and to try to sell our own productions and those of our independent co-producers. Cannes is nice, though the documentary market is a zoo of hundreds of delegates trying to sell you films you are not remotely interested in, and they will pursue you into the toilets. I had another agenda as well: what if I could sell a condensed version of the Canadian History Project? Perhaps to a French or British network (after all, these were their armies fighting in Canada) or PBS (we would be recreating the War of 1812 and the American Revolution) or the Australians (two children of the same imperial parent, Canada and Australia) or the Germans (they love our documentaries on wolves and the Arctic). If I could snag a partner, it would give the project financial booster rockets.

On the way to Paris, I stopped in Montreal to see Nick but got no answer from knocking. I went to a phone booth a block away, and there was still so much melting ice my shoes were submerged in slush. "He's just been sleeping all the time, Mark," Melissa, who hadn't heard the knocking, said. "There's no point seeing him till you get back."

In Cannes, I failed miserably to sell Canadian history. I knew nobody wanted thirty hours of Canadian history; I was trying to sell off individual episodes, repackaging them overnight in my hotel room into proposals like "Wars of the U.S. Frontier" for the History Channel or "France's American Wars" for Canal Plus in Paris. I even bored two poor Ukrainian broadcasters with the stories of Ukrainian immigrants to Canada, before realizing these broadcasters had even less money than we did. The Germans, it transpired, were very interested in wolves, but not in Canadians. I couldn't really blame them; if some Austrian had come up to me trying to parcel off pieces of a thirty-hour history of the Austro-Hungarian Empire, I would have suddenly remembered an urgent appointment too. The BBC and Channel Four from Britain wouldn't give me the time of day, and besides, they hadn't heard of the War of 1812.

These old international colleagues felt sorry for me because I hadn't moved on to another major international project after *Dawn of the Eye*. They assumed I must have stepped into a bureaucratic cow patty somewhere to be saddled with the Canadian History Project. If I ever needed confirmation that the only way to tell the Canadian story is to pay for it ourselves, and do it for our own people, I had it.

Within hours of my landing in Toronto, Phizicky called me to say that Nick had just died, in his sleep, on the couch where I had last seen him. I can't say I felt any emotion that night beyond a numbing emptiness, and a memory of that inundated phone booth. All I can remember is going into each of my daughters' rooms and watching each of them sleep for a long time. I watched their chests slowly rise and fall, their bodies shift in their beds, a foot kick out, a hand scratching someplace, and thought what a strange, fragile, evanescent thing breathing is.

Nick's funeral drew three thousand mourners of every conceivable nationality to St. Patrick's Basilica, the spiritual centre of Irish Montreal, where D'Arcy McGee's funeral was held over a century before. It was the largest non-state funeral in modern Montreal history. "A generation was gathering," I wrote in his obituary in the *Globe and Mail*, "with the solemnity of Musketeers burying d'Artagnan."

I never would have found myself working on the history of Canada without him. It was Nick, thirty-five years earlier, who had dragged me into the thrill of living history rather than just studying it. He brought me across the Anglo-English divide, introducing me to a world of journalists, artists, activists, and dreamers of all political persuasions, who seemed like bit players then but became part of history itself. Because of him I had, for two decades, a front-row seat in the evolving story of Canada and Quebec, and grew to love its maddening contradictions. The best tribute I could pay him was to try to capture and convey it.

7

How Not to Stalk a Muskox

The first unit out the door was Andy Gregg's Episode 1 team, which had the biggest challenge of all: conveying the twenty-thousand-year history of aboriginal nations that have left virtually no written records. Gregg, the youngest director on the team, has been fascinated by aboriginal history since his childhood and was determined to produce this first episode from a perspective "where the European world would seem to be the strange and inexplicable universe." Climate was driving him even more than the other units, as the migrations of wildlife and the native rituals which accompany them were already happening.

In April, Gregg, his cameraman, Mike Sweeney, and the producer, Gail Gallant, flew by a charter plane into Baker Lake, Nunavut, a settlement built around a trading post, where few elders speak English and everyone hunts. The objective was to shoot as many traditional scenes as possible of the Inuit hunting and making tools and of their daily life on the tundra.

"In order to explain ourselves to the community, we held an impromptu town meeting at the Baker Lake Lodge," Gregg reported.

They wanted the elders' advice on what was possible. "The faces of the women bore deep, crevassed wrinkles," he said. "The men's faces were almost black from the spring hunt. When I asked them if any people still had traditional caribou skin clothing, every hand went up."

The crew set up their camera in a large traditional igloo that some of the young men had built for the school kids. It consisted of three chambers: an entryway, a soot-covered kitchen, and a large sleeping chamber that had an ice lens, which suffused the room with light. It provided some of the most haunting images in the first episode, and Gregg's unit waited there as members of the community, clad in caribou, came in over the ensuing hours and days to demonstrate the traditional ways.

It was everything Gregg had dreamed of since childhood: "Two spry old women named Lucy and Sally came in and showed us how to light a *kudlik*, or lamp, with two stones, some moss, and some caribou fat. They chattered like schoolchildren in Inuktitut as they concentrated on their chore. They hadn't used stones to light anything for years, but they finally did it. Then they cracked open old caribou leg bones and offered me a chunk of the raw marrow. It tasted pretty bland, like a chunk of cold butter going down my throat."

Lucy and Sally were followed by an old woman who sang traditional Inuit songs, then an ancient man who played the sealskin drum. Through the images gathered each day, Sweeney and Gregg were collecting the visual metaphors to illustrate the Inuit creationist legends about the seal, the bear, and the walrus, and the fables of survival in this extreme world. Accuracy of manner, song, and dress was essential, so everything was checked with the elders. But Gregg was determined to get not only accuracy but the community's approval too: "At the end of the day, we screened everything we had shot for some of the community. They looked wistfully at images of their own past. We knew we had captured the right thing."

Back in Toronto, we eagerly awaited reports from our first expeditionary team as if they were an Apollo mission. For the rest of us, the project was still paper and books, so it was exciting to know that Inuit elders, bush pilots, and dogsled teams were now part of our enterprise. At the weekly coordination meeting I got a kick out of saying, "Episode 1 team is leaving Baker Lake today with Inuit hunters in traditional dress to follow the muskoxen." There was a palpable thrill in the room.

Gregg, Sweeney, and the soundman, Chris Davies, travelled by komatik, the traditional Inuit sled, which was lashed together for maximum flexibility. Even so, they found the novelty wore off quickly. "I soon learned that I should have had a chiropractor's appointment already booked for my return to Toronto," said Gregg. "It feels like you are sitting on a board and someone is continually picking it up more than a metre and dropping it on a cement floor." They went nine hours before they saw anything: the tracks of a wolf following two muskoxen. Soon they came upon two bulls, and Sweeney unpacked a powerful 800-mm lens for the camera. It was now ten at night, and the light was dusky yellow. Andy decided to try shooting the hunting scene: "Isaac, one of the elders, and a young hunter named Barney struggled out of their parkas and into their caribou skins, left their hunting rifles with us, and started to crawl on their bellies toward the bulls. Isaac is a traditional craftsman and had made Barney a spear, while he carried a bear-rib bow and an arrow made from bone and antler."

The hunters crawled closer and closer, till they were within twenty metres. "Then Isaac rose up on one knee, directly in front of the bulls, and drew his arrow. As he did, as if on cue, the bulls spun a half-turn and stared him down. Then, finally, they turned and lumbered off. It was exhilarating for Mike Sweeney to film. But Barney said he had never been so scared in his life, and Isaac – sixty years old and the most experienced hunter in Baker Lake – said he had never done anything remotely like that before without a gun. But since Gregg hadn't called him to turn back, he had continued. "He said he just kept going," Gregg said, wincing, "because he thought *I* knew what I was doing."

The first Montreal field shoot departed for the Village Québécois d'Antan, in Drummondville, to shoot scenes of nineteenth-century pioneer life. Since the assignment to all units was to film seasonal activities of the past, Peter Ingles, the director, and Jean-Claude Daoust, the cameraman, arranged to shoot scenes of settlers breaking the land, splitting wood, pulling out log stumps. The scenes would illustrate the hard life of farmers in Lower Canada in the 1830s, farmers who would join the 1837 Rebellion against the British, which was at the centre of Peter's episode. A bucolic settler scene in rural Quebec. What could go wrong?

"We had the location, the tree stump that needed pulling, and the bull," Ingles reported from his first shoot. "But bulls are not what they used to be, according to Séraphin." Séraphin, apparently, was the only man around Drummondville who could still *talk* to bulls, and he didn't have a lot to say about today's bulls. "They are tiny compared with the real working bulls of the nineteenth century," Peter said. "We've seen pictures of the old-time bulls, and they're pretty scary-looking. According to Séraphin, there isn't a bull around today that can pull a tree stump out of the ground, roots and all, like the old bulls."

Peter Ingles resolved to make do with these bulls, however, given that Séraphin had dismissed every other living bull as inadequate to the task. First he had to uproot a stump. Peter called in a huge backhoe, "and we just ripped the sucker out of the ground. . . . Then we put it back in and had the two bulls pull it out for the camera." Even this subterfuge didn't dispel all our problems, however. As the bulls strained on the heavy chain wrapped around the stump, they turned, and Séraphin got caught between the chain and the stump. "We all froze," Peter said. "Then we had a pretty impressive demonstration of Séraphin's voice control over bulls. He shouted 'Whoa!' and the bulls froze – he came out without a scratch."

We were having some close calls with bulls, muskoxen, and other cloven-hoofed extras. Isaac the ox comes to mind. In southwestern Manitoba, the cameraman Derek Kennedy was shooting with Michelle Métivier, the director of the fur trade episode. They had envisioned a brilliant sunset shot of two Red River carts travelling through the tall grass of the open prairie. So Isaac the ox, owned by Dr. Wayne Lees and his wife, Leah, had been brought a considerable distance to the Tall Grass Prairie Reserve near Tolstoi, Manitoba, where he met another younger ox we had procured, called Bucky.

Lees was moving Isaac into position behind Bucky when Isaac suddenly bolted, taking off into the prairie, bucking the cart high into the air. The planned two-cart shot was turned into a one-cart shot, which made it into the series. "Like many performers," Derek concluded, "Isaac didn't like to play second banana." I can't imagine what the finance people in Toronto were thinking as they processed invoices marked "ox rental" or "transportation of ox and cart." They were already dealing with invoices for French sheep, red-tailed hawks, baby beavers, rats, and sled dogs, and now came invoices for one York boat, one piper, one Union Jack, several sacks of period-correct seed, and Scottish sheep for Michelle and Derek's next Manitoba shoot.

The Selkirk settlers were desperately poor people, displaced Scottish crofters, recruited by an idealistic nobleman, the Earl of Selkirk, to cross the Atlantic to Fort Churchill on Hudson Bay and follow the river system south by flat-bottomed boats to the promised land of the Red River. It was a daunting trek, repeated each summer for several years, and it was the Red River Settlement that laid the foundation for Winnipeg. Michelle had obtained a replica of the flat-bottomed York boat and was reconstructing the arrival of the settlers, complete with a dozen re-enactors, period-correct sheep, and a piper. We like to shoot in the "magic hour," just before and after dawn, or before dusk, when the light is soft and golden. So Derek Kennedy was in the water in the pre-dawn light wearing a wetsuit to take a long shot of the York boat being paddled for several hundred metres. Each take would last several minutes, then the boat would be paddled back, the piper would start again, and the actors would paddle toward him once more. After many retakes and being whacked by a paddle as the boat passed too close, Kennedy was finally hauled out of the frigid water. The result was a stunning trademark shot that we would use as one of the major promos for the series.

Kennedy seemed destined to spend half his time on the project under water. On the Bow River, not far from Canmore, Alberta, he had to take a rising shot from beneath an ice embankment, up through a fissure in the ice to reveal David Thompson looking off into the distance for his missing companions. Though he didn't say anything till he got the perfect take, it turned out Kennedy's boots had holes in them, and he was soaking in freezing cold water. There was no time to dry him off. The crew had travelled to the location by helicopter, which was costing a fortune every hour. He was taken directly from the Bow River, his feet still wet, to shoot footage of mountain summits and cliff faces.

Derek and his camera were safely strapped to the inside of the helicopter, but he was actually standing outside, on the landing strut. Now, with frozen feet, he shot numerous lifts up the rock face, being slammed by freezing winds each time they passed the summit. The pilot was not aware that Kennedy was having any difficulty keeping his footing in the high wind, because she was intent on keeping the helicopter blades off the rock face – that's how close they were. Inevitably, as the wind slammed him on one of the rises over the summit, he slipped. A cameraman's reaction is always to save his camera first, so Derek hurled the camera into the helicopter and only then grasped his lifeline and hauled himself back onto the strut. "I was pretty unfazed," he said, "until we landed and I played back the tape. Of course, the camera had kept rolling all the way through the slip, the fall, and being hurled into the helicopter, and I realized how close I'd come to meeting my maker. Then I was terrified." It was typical of a cameraman, we observed cynically, to believe something only when he saw it on film, not in real life. (My theory is that Kennedy's ordeals in frozen water or hanging in mid-air over the Rockies were retribution for forgetting about the lighting man on top of the crane during the Louisbourg shoot.)

While Derek was hanging about in the Rockies, some of us were trying to find period-correct ships. It was a daunting task. Museum models were useful only for stationary shots, and historical vessels moored in ports were of little use because their sails were tied up, and it was impossible to get a clear shot of them without city back-grounds. So we began to track the movements of any replica of any ship built between 1500 and 1950, and when one was heading for open water, we'd try to negotiate a berth for a day or two. Often this was prohibitively expensive, sometimes up to $10,000 a day, since these ships are owned by associations who can maintain them only if they charge such rates to film crews. Another problem was that they would put out to sea for several days and there was no way to get off them after a day or two. HMS *Bounty*, the replica of Captain Bligh's vessel from the movie starring Marlon Brando, was sailing down the St. Lawrence to the U.S. coast, and Andrew Burnstein was assigned the task of getting every conceivable shot of her, with close-ups of her bow crashing through the waves, sails billowing, and flags flying. "I got a lot of great shots," he reported, "but most of them were useless because of other river traffic. I have a classic of her going downriver while she passes a Canadian submarine going upriver. Great shot. Useless to us." Most of the time the *Bounty* sailed under power, with her sails furled, because she had to maintain a schedule. When Burnstein finally persuaded the captain to stop the ship and raise her sails, he was completely frustrated. "It was a calm afternoon with no winds, and the sails barely moved, but we got the captain to turn on his engines and go backwards, which filled the sails."

On a second trip to the Arctic, Gregg and Sweeney were travelling through the fjords of northern Baffin Island, with another hunter and a replica of a sealskin kayak. The object was to film a sequence of an Inuit hunter navigating the brisk water of the North Atlantic. "The komatik trip was cold," Gregg say. "We had been cold before, but this was really cold. It was so cold that all we could concentrate on was how cold we were." Once they left land, they travelled for several more hours over the ice until they found a kilometre-long crack where a group of hunters had congregated, waiting for seals, narwhals, and bowhead whales heading north for the summer.

"The hunters moved back and forth over the blood-stained snow, wearing baseball hats and no gloves, searching for more seal heads bobbing curiously in the purple open water," Gregg says. "We set up the shot with the kayak, asking one hunter to climb in and make like a traditional hunter. He said he knew how to do that, but we found out pretty quickly that he didn't. We got a few shots of the kayak before it started to sink. We didn't need to speak Inuktitut to understand what he was yelling about."

A talkative kid who was out there hunting with his father had taken a shine to Andy Gregg. "He followed me everywhere I went, asking a continual stream of questions about Toronto, like: 'Do you have a car in Toronto?' 'Yes,' I would say. 'Cool,' he would say. 'Do you have cable TV in Toronto?' 'Yes.' 'Cool.' 'Have you been to MuchMusic?' 'Yes.' 'Cool.' This went on until I set up my tent and started cooking dinner. As I watched my water boil, his endless interrogation suddenly stopped with a half-whispered 'Holy . . . !'

"I looked right into the deep black eyes of a young male polar bear a short distance away. He had wandered out of the overturned ice floes, following the smell of the seal blood saturating the ice shelf. Mine was the tent nearest the edge of camp. Just as a warning pang from my bladder informed me that I was about to wet my pants, some hunters moved forward, rifles ready, and the bear took off like a rocket. But he didn't go far. All that evening the camera, with the special 800-mm lens we brought, captured bear after bear on the horizon, their noses sniffing the air. We got a lot of shots we used in the episode."

It was starting to appear that any time anyone in the history project got in a boat, a kayak, or a canoe, chances were better than even that some calamity would ensue. Any time a shoot related to the fur trade was scheduled, Gordon Henderson couldn't stay in the office, partly because he was in despair about some of the canoeing shots.

Gordon remembers, "When we were shooting in Thunder Bay, we had a group of people in costume in a canoe with North West Company markings. In the morning that was fine. They were Nor'Westers paddling west. In the afternoon, though, in different costumes, they were paddling George Simpson around. By Simpson's time, the Nor'Westers had amalgamated with the Hudson's Bay Company, so the canoes were wrong. There was another canoe, but I was told it was tippy. I asked the lead paddler, who had a strong, confident stroke, what he thought. He said they would be OK in a tippy canoe. They got in and within seconds they dumped. In full costume. Not my happiest moment."

For all of us, reading the original accounts of explorations and expeditions was an eye-opener. We were amazed by how much of the real drama of history had been paved over by bad textbooks or boring writing. One of the best examples was the story of Samuel de Champlain's first winter in Quebec in 1608, and his expedition into the interior in the spring. The fur trade was driven entirely by the fashion for exotic hats made out of the felt of shaved beaver fur. (At one point, Hubert observed, correctly, "Do you realize this country was founded entirely on a hat and a rat?") Champlain had earlier established a post in Port-Royal, but he found that rival Basque traders were getting to the local Indians first from their post at Tadoussac, at the mouth of the St. Lawrence. So his plan was to establish a post where he and his men could overwinter and be the first to contact the Indians in the spring. He travelled for hundreds of kilometres upriver until he came to the breathtaking natural gateway to the continent, a promontory of sixty-metre cliffs, with columns of chestnut trees on top. From here, he could not only defend himself but prevent any other ships from going upriver. The Algonquians called it Quebec, "the place where the river narrows."

Champlain's twenty-eight men cleared the chestnut trees and built a strong, multi-storey structure with fireplaces to survive the coming winter, which Champlain knew from experience would last six months. That winter, twenty of his men died from scurvy, and Champlain himself almost succumbed, before spring brought sudden salvation. "It is strange to contemplate that two or three yards' depth of snow and ice on the river can melt in less than twelve days," Champlain wrote. "On June 5, a boat arrived in our settlement bringing me much joy and comfort. Only eight of the original twenty-eight inhabitants remained alive, and even then, half of us were very weak." A Huron chief had told Champlain that to the south, there was a lake, which led to another, then to a river, then to another river that went all the way to Florida. Champlain embarked with his men and the Huron, in a convoy of canoes that would change the course of history.

Hubert looked up from reading this account and said, "Nine men, who barely survive the winter, emerge half-dead and embark on the European discovery of the continent. Those nine men become the foundation of a race of New World people. No portrait exists of Champlain, who is the father of our country, and who left no descendants on this continent. What has Ulysses got on this?"

Only by reading the day-by-day terrors and hopes and adventures of those men, penetrating deep into the continent, does their accomplishment come alive. You finally realize this is our *Iliad*, this is our *Odyssey*. The story has always been there but was never taught to us. Written and even illustrated by Champlain during nights around the campfire, the words seem to describe a galactic exploration of an alien world – which, in its time, it was.

At the time the Huron, who had allied with Champlain, and the Iroquois were enemies. Champlain describes one terrifying night of war dances as the Huron and the Iroquois, who have made camp within sight of each other, prepare to exterminate each other at first light. In the morning, two hundred Iroquois attacked, and Champlain, dressed in full armour, prepared his arquebus, a huge firearm, three times the size of a musket. "Our men called out to me with loud yells, and opened into two bodies to let me through. I stood out in front of them, and I aimed straight at one of the three chiefs and with a single shot two of them dropped dead to the ground. I had put four bullets in my arquebus." It was the first shot fired in the Indian wars that would last more than a century and change the dynamics of the continent forever.

Claude Berrardelli, the Montreal doctoral student hired for five weeks while Richard Fortin was recuperating, thought he was in heaven at Radio-Canada. "I made more in five weeks that I could in five months of picking up odd research assistant and tutoring jobs," he said. "This was a blessing for a father of three young children." It wasn't only the money he loved. It was the research. "There arrives a moment when a profound bond is forged between you and the person you are researching, and you begin to live to the same rhythm of emotions and adventures as his. I was living Champlain's life." And with that, he prepared to return to the Université du Québec.

Then, Berrardelli says, "One day in July, Claude Lortie, who was the episode director, Christian Pagé, the assistant director, and the cameraman, Gaétan Morisset, were meeting to put the final touches on the shoot that would recreate the journey and the battle. Claude asked me what Champlain looked like, and I said there was no portrait of him, but if you read his own description of himself, and statistics about French men in the seventeenth century, we can infer a lot. About 1.6 metres tall, thin, dark, sinewy, high-strung, determined, and having just survived a painful winter.

"In the middle of my description, I saw they were looking at me more and more, then at each other, slight smiles forming on their lips. Then Claude exclaimed, looking at me, 'Good, well, I think we have our Champlain!' I was pleased because I thought he was saying I had given them a good enough picture of him to cast the right actor. So I asked if this brought a particular actor to his mind and Claude replied, 'Yes. You!'"

Berrardelli would be Champlain for the field shots, the journey upriver, and the battle scene, where his face would never be fully shown. It wasn't a speaking part. Nevertheless Berrardelli was ecstatic and told the university his Ph.D. would have to wait. The shoot took place at the splendid historical site of Sainte-Marie Among the Hurons, near the town of Midland, Ontario. Huronia, which this site commemorates, had been a sprawling town of longhouses with more than thirty thousand people. The sight of it shocked the French. They never expected to find such a complex and highly developed civilization.

"I remember our meeting with the Amerindians who would play the roles of Champlain's allies," Berrardelli says. "The first contact was cold, even hostile. They thought we were here just to laugh at them or treat them with no respect. For them, it was just easy money, and they didn't care about what we were filming.

"I tried to explain the historical context of this union between

Champlain and his allies, not only what Champlain wanted but what the Indians wanted out of it. Over a few days, mutual respect began to grow between us and them, and they had suggestions, their points of view – finally, a real friendship developed. Those who had children started bringing their families to the shoot. It was quite emotional for me to see these little girls and boys looking at their fathers or grandfathers, wide-eyed and full of admiration and fascination – and to watch the men realize their children were proud of their ancestral roles. That was something beautiful to behold."

Back in Toronto, our quarters were filling up with the oddest paraphernalia as the weeks went by: whale-bone harpoons and general's swords in Anne Emin's office, rum barrels in the corridor, tomahawks, tricorne hats, muskets piled everywhere. The small boardroom adjoining my office became a storage depot for regimental flags and lances. You never knew who would be visiting the studio or what they would bring. One scene showed how Samuel Hearne, the famous explorer, when he was the factor of Fort Prince of Wales kept a small menagerie of mink, muskrat, geese, and tame beavers – the very animals they were trading in at the Hudson's Bay Company. He fed them plum pudding all winter. A wrangler brought in a hawk, a baby beaver, and a mink for the director, Michelle Métivier, to shoot while an actor portraying Hearne fed them. After shooting each one individually, Michelle wanted all three animals on Hearne's shoulders.

"Your film speed isn't fast enough to capture that shot. This beaver would be a tidy little snack for the hawk," the wrangler told her.

Stumbling over these artifacts and animals was as close as I got to the action that spring and summer, because I was trying to kick-start the search for sponsors. In Ottawa, John Lewis, the director of business development, was doing his best to help. As he put it, "I've been running back and forth down the hall between the president's and the chair's office, trying to break the logjam in seeking corporate sponsorship." But he was getting nowhere.

The governor general had called me in January with the news that Bombardier wouldn't participate. "They say they don't do that

sort of thing." But, he said, he had spoken to John Rae at Power
Corporation and had encouraged him to meet with me. "Call him,"
he said, "and make your best pitch." Well, I didn't know what to pitch.
Were we selling commercials? Were we looking for contributions
without any commercials? Was this like PBS's *Masterpiece Theatre*?
Were the donations tax-deductible? John Lewis couldn't answer any
of these questions for me because he couldn't get any answers from
Beatty and Saucier. But I couldn't just do nothing. Finally I called
Peter Herrndorf, my old mentor and a skilled corporate tactician.
For two hours, we met in a restaurant across from the CBC and
dreamed up a strategy.

"They can't commercialize the history of Canada," he said.
"You've got to look for sponsorship in the PBS sense. I think you have
to strike quickly and surgically. Go to the CEOs of the ten biggest
corporations in the country and ask for a million each. Don't go
through their marketing departments, go right to the top. It's only
at the top that you'll find anybody with the power to make that decision. These men have already won their corporate battles and care
about their place in history. The governor general will get you
through the front door."

Three weeks later, around ten in the morning, I walked into
Power Corporation's unmarked headquarters on Victoria Square in
Montreal to meet John Rae (Bob Rae's brother) and the former president of the CBC, Gérard Veilleux, the man who had killed *The
Journal*. Now he was a vice-president at Power. "Thank you for seeing
me on short notice," I said, shaking hands, and Rae smiled. "The governor general is a pretty good way to get a fast appointment. What
can we do for you?" I had a five-minute promo, nothing like the one
we were preparing back in Toronto, but it would do for now. I
described the series and explained Herrndorf's theory. I ended by
saying, "If you agree, we'd like to have you be one of the ten." To my
amazement and delight, Rae was swift and decisive. "Herrndorf is
right," he said, "move quickly and surgically. I think you can count on
a million dollars from us, and we'd be prepared to encourage other

corporations to come on board. You have to define some standards about what you'll accept. For example, will you take tobacco money, or do you want any corporations related to beer or alcohol involved? But this plan seems sound to me." Veilleux agreed, and I was back on Victoria Square within the hour. Maybe this was going to be a lot easier than I thought.

I called John Lewis, who thought this was probably the break-through we needed. Over the next couple of weeks, we wrestled with a strategy that would allow us to raise $10 million and use the good offices of the governor general but have a clear separation between the project and the fundraising. We would create a fundraising com-mittee of prominent citizens who had no active political affiliation, clearly balanced between regions and languages. Peter Herrndorf, I suggested, could chair and recruit the committee. I would partici-pate only as the person who described the project, but I would not be involved in active solicitation. If any editorial controversies came up, or any suggestion of pressure about content, then Herrndorf and the committee were the arm's-length shield that preserved us from any pressure.

John liked the concept, and I spent a long February evening per-suading Peter to accept the chairmanship, even though I had no real brief or authority to do it. Together, John and I came up with lists of possible committee members, and I approached two prominent people I know, one a retired businessman, another the retired head of a charitable foundation.

Weeks went by, and John was still unable to get a green light for the committee from Ottawa. I was embarrassed to return phone calls from Rideau Hall and the two people I had approached, even from Peter Herrndorf. I kept stalling, believing we'd get clearance any day. John was hearing from Ottawa that we had to check legalities through the legal department, financial mechanisms through the finance people. More ominously, we were hearing reservations from the French and English sales departments: any money the Canadian History Project raised this way could reduce corporate sponsorships for other projects and sporting events. The objection – always expressed indirectly – was that there was only so much money in the corporate marketplace, and the history project might soak it all up to the detriment of our sales targets. The problem with our plan, it appeared, was that it could be successful! Radio-Canada said that Hydro-Québec, for example, might be good for a million dollars; if it went to the history project, it would leave other Radio-Canada projects dry. But these fears were not limited to Montreal. One friend, highly placed in the Toronto sales department, told me bluntly: "You might screw up a lot of commercial deals on which they make their commissions, and they might not meet their annual target."

But John Lewis persevered and developed arguments that responded to all these internal interest groups. He had hired the big Toronto legal firm of Goodman, Phillips and Vineberg to research how we could set up a fundraising entity that could issue charitable donation receipts. Our own legal department could have done it, but John knew Ottawa trusted only private-sector advice.

Finally, John pulled off the impossible, by arranging a meeting where all players were in one room at the same time, or, if they weren't in town, they were on the speakerphone. In the main boardroom for English Television senior management were Perrin Beatty, Jim Byrd, Michèle Fortin by phone, people from the CBC legal and finance departments, the lawyer from Goodman, Phillips and Vineberg, and, it appeared, anyone else above the rank of corporal who could possibly have anything to do with financing this project. Except Guylaine Saucier (who would not normally attend an operational meeting anyway).

A great deal of time was spent discussing the mechanics of how we might set up an arm's-length charitable foundation, which would have the power to issue tax receipts to sponsors. Then the lawyer from Goodman, Phillips and our own legal department dropped the clanger. The CBC already *was* a charitable foundation with the power to issue tax receipts to any donors. People sometimes left us their record collections, photo archives, or antique radios and cameras for our museums, and could thereby claim a tax deduction.

After ninety minutes, I couldn't contain myself and asked: "You mean, all we have to do is go across the street and open a chequing account at the bank?"

"Essentially, yes," said the lawyer. All we had to do was name one, two, or three trustees, if we wanted to, to ensure that the money deposited was spent for the purpose intended.

After two hours, the meeting ended in a heady atmosphere, with me joking that I'd go across the street and open the account. Then Perrin said, "I think this has been a good day's work, but before we commit to this course, I think I should fly this past the chair. It should take only a couple of days."

A couple of days went by, then the entire summer and much of the fall of 1998 went by. Nothing happened. The fundraising strategy had been key to ensuring we'd get the $25 million that the series would really cost. As the silence from Ottawa became deafening, I realized we'd have to proceed without knowing what our final budget would be, nor how many minutes each "hour" of the series would be. The difference between a fully commercialized series and one with minimal corporate sponsorship amounted to *six hours* of content. Twelve minutes times thirty hours. Toronto and Montreal had almost come to blows over cutting *one* hour a few weeks ago. Six hours is not achieved by cutting a chapter here and a chapter there. It requires a different measure of chronology, since you're cutting one-fifth of the airtime.

The silence from Ottawa left us with no choice. We embarked on the largest documentary production in Canadian television history without knowing how long the series would be.

8

Pathways to the Past

It was one thing to proceed with the scale of the project uncertain, but it would have been another if its style and spirit were unclear. I knew what I wanted, but I was only one of many people involved. Even though I had the title "executive producer," no one in this position can just issue a set of directives. Instead, you have to recruit the support of your own senior producers and cameramen to your vision. And you have to be prepared to change your own vision when a better one confronts you. You have to not only express your vision and ideas but also explain how you came by them and justify them every day.

In 1964, when I was in my first year at McGill University, I went one winter evening to a McGill Film Society screening. The film, *Culloden*, was a documentary reconstruction of a battle I had never heard of, by a director hardly anyone in Canada had ever heard of, Peter Watkins. That film and the impact it had on me have shaped all of my journalism and radio-television production.

Culloden was the last battle fought on British soil and one of the most brutal. In 1746, the Scottish Highlanders led by Bonnie Prince

Charlie were defeated by the Duke of Cumberland at Culloden moor outside Inverness. A thousand were killed in battle, mostly by cavalry and devastating artillery, and a thousand prisoners were later summarily executed, earning the duke the sobriquet of "Cumberland the Butcher."

The film is shot as if modern television cameras had been there at the battle. The images, shot with shoulder-mounted cameras, and the chaotic soundtrack make the film both terrifying and powerful. The story is related by a cold, detached narration (Watkins's voice) which leans on precise detail. "Grapeshot," says the narrator as we see ammunition loaded into the mouth of a British cannon. "A cylindrical canvas bag, eight inches in length, packed with musket balls and pieces of jagged iron. This is grapeshot. This is what it does." The muzzle of the cannon explodes in white smoke, and the camera cuts to bodies falling across the screen, splattered tunics, and men lying on the moor groaning and clutching their wounds.

The film humanizes the battle by picking out a series of characters on each side. It pans the faces, then suddenly stops, and we hear: "James Macdonald, taxman, senior officer in a ruthless clan system, who has brought with him onto the moor men whose land he controls. Alisdair McMurrich, subtenant of a taxman, owns one-eighth of an acre of soggy ground and two cows. Alan McCaul, subtenant of a subtenant, owns a half-share in a small potato patch measuring thirty square feet. Angus Macdonald, servant of a subtenant. He owns nothing."

The uniforms are filthy, the light grey and drizzly, and the vérité style of the film conveys a sense of impending doom. It violates almost every canon of filmmaking. The character's eyes look directly into the lens, and the presence of the camera is always acknowledged, a hallmark of Watkins's later films as well. It is impossible, I learned, to ignore a face that fills the television screen, looks directly at you, and speaks.

Culloden stunned everyone in the auditorium that night. The film ended, nobody reached for their coats. The credits rolled to the very end, the film spool ran out, and the auditorium lights came on. No one moved. Five hundred students sat quietly for minutes before they started slowly preparing to leave. It was my first lesson in how powerful the mixture of journalistic fact and cinematic form could be.

Watkins's documentary, I learned, had created such a stir in Britain that it was hotly debated in the British House of Commons. It was the most controversial film ever broadcast on British television. It had enraged everyone: the English by portraying the conduct of British troops as criminal; the Lowland Scots by portraying them as collaborators; and the Highland Scots by showing Bonnie Prince Charlie to be vain and uncaring and the battle itself as a disaster in military planning. However tendentious the script, the historical facts were solid, and the documentary was an adaptation of a book by the highly respected historian John Prebble. Every name, every detail was impeccably correct, and it was journalistically unassailable. It was never shown again on the BBC, and it would be thirty years before it was seen again on British television – on Channel Four, in a series called *Banned*.

Watkins went on to produce another film two years later, *The War Game*, which shows the gruesome effects of a nuclear attack on southern England. It was deemed so frightening that it was banned *before* it was broadcast. It took the technique of juxtaposing interviews with reconstruction and coldly narrated fact to another level beyond *Culloden* and won the Academy Award for best documentary in 1966. Another Watkins documentary was *Edvard Munch*, a portrait of the painter produced for Norwegian television. It is even more striking because we see his techniques used to peel back the hypocrisies of eighteenth-century middle-class life. There is one scene of a family eating dinner where nothing happens, but eyes meeting the camera's gaze and the ambient sound of forks and dishes make the scene exude tension. With his films, Watkins revolutionized the documentary. In the 1960s, documentary style had suffered from a hangover of government propaganda from the Second World War.

I used *Culloden* as one of the main training films when we were putting together the *Journal* team in 1981, and I used it again with everyone who joined the history unit. Among my colleagues, it became a joke. When new recruits spent an uncharacteristically long time behind closed doors in my office, they would be asked as they left, "Poor kid, did he *Culloden* you?"

While *Culloden* and *Edvard Munch* showed how realism could be brought to the documentary, both of them told a single story. We would be telling a thousand stories. Again, there was a documentary series to point the way for us.

The Civil War, the PBS series by Ken and Ric Burns, first aired in 1990 over five consecutive evenings, achieving the largest audience for any series in PBS history. Thirty-nine million Americans found themselves riveted to a story that was eleven hours long, and which was brought to vivid life with only words and photographs and music. The phenomenon was so striking it made the cover of *Time*. *Newsweek* called it "a documentary masterpiece," and the political commentator George Will wrote: "Our *Iliad* has found its Homer.... If better use has ever been made of television, I have not seen it."

There have been dozens if not hundreds of documentaries about the Civil War, but most have been about the mechanics of battles. Few are memorable, and none attained the epic quality of the Burns series. *The Civil War* succeeds because it presents the stories of ordinary men and women elevated to the extraordinary when caught in the churning currents of history and confronted by good and evil, love and hate, honour and betrayal.

A dramatic narrative structure, applied to a true story and conveyed with precise detail, imbues the power of literature with the authority of history. To me, that fusion is more powerful than either by itself. Telling an epic story through the words and actions of individuals who experienced it makes it accessible to the reader or viewer, because all that is required to understand the story is simple humanity.

We arranged for the senior producers of the history project to spend a long evening with Ric Burns. He was impressed by what we were setting out to do: "You're actually doing the history of Canada – of the entire country!" he said. "That's incredible. I don't think that's ever been done anywhere, the history of a country. If you think about it, that says something about the maturity of a place. I don't think you could get away with that here." At the time, nobody had done a multi-part history of any country, so there was no model. We learned later that the BBC would be doing a sixteen-hour history of Britain with the historian Simon Schama, but we would be finished before them.

Burns kept us all engrossed with stories about the making of *The Civil War* and comforted us by describing the chaos in which it was produced and the principles which guided his team. "The human story is everything," he said. "And the word is everything. The picture is the cradle for the word." The key is the writer. This was refreshing to hear, as the current documentary orthodoxy treats the script as a necessary evil which, like acne, should be kept to a nearly invisible minimum – largely, I believe, because most directors can't write. He spoke of "the barker in front of the tent," the device to attract the viewer's interest, and said, "Slap and tickle. Always slap, then tickle," by which he meant always alternate a dark or tragic chapter with a lighter or humorous one. He also advised us to give each episode a predominant focus, a theme. "Just keep asking yourselves every ten minutes, 'What is this chapter about? What is this episode about? What is my story?' Everything that doesn't propel the story, and the point, goes out."

The art of both the Burns brothers rested on photos from the past, diaries and letters, and compelling interview clips from histori-ans. We intended to walk in their footsteps after photography began in the 1850s; but how would we apply the same style, the same narra-tive ethic, to the pre-photographic era? The first episode with pho-tography in *Canada: A People's History* would be Episode 10, "Taking the West," twenty hours into the series.

Ric Burns was steadfastly against any use of actors, either in recre-ations of events or in speaking to camera. "For me," he said, "it just shatters the spell, and becomes manifestly unreal. I've never seen it done well." It was a substantial debate in our own unit. Any good pro-ducer of historical documentaries usually chokes at the thought of using actors, because it almost invariably comes out corny, contrived, and overacted. As head of documentaries for the CBC, I was notorious for gagging at the use of recreations. But now, with all aboriginal history, all of New France, all of the eighteenth and half of the nineteenth century unphotographed, I had no choice.

Back in Toronto and Montreal, I spent hours and days and weeks discussing how to make the re-enactments look authentic with Laine Drewery and Bill Cobban. Alan Mendelsohn, whom I hadn't been able to persuade to join the project, took part in our lively discussions anyway, along with the cameramen Mike Sweeney and Maurice Chabot. There wasn't a historical reconstruction since the invention of cinema that we hadn't viewed and dissected.

The first glimmer of an answer came to me when I was screening some footage Drewery and Chabot had taken at a re-enactment of the attack on Fort Erie in the War of 1812. It was useless footage because of all the tourists and garbage cans and power lines in the shot, not to mention the perfectly mowed park lawn. But there were fragmentary moments here and there when it worked. The British army was marching by, and you could hear the drum in the distance; then Chabot's lens probed the marching line, looking for a face, focusing on a line of marching feet; then it all fell apart; then the lens groped for another face, for the hands of the drummer. I pulled Mike into the screening room and replayed it for him. "Parts work," he agreed, "but only a few seconds here and there."

"I think I know when it works," I said. "It's when the camera doesn't know where it's going – when it's probing, when it's uncertain. It follows the action, but it doesn't know what the next step is going to be. The documentary camera is uncertain, it has no foreknowledge."

Mike wasn't so sure, and we spent about three hours screening rushes already taken by our units and parts of other documentaries, including a couple from the war that was still raging in former Yugoslavia. This became known as "the Vukovar night," because it set off a detailed examination of all the conflict footage we were seeing on the CBC News broadcasts. I had made sure we hired experienced

documentary cameramen and producers because they knew how
to portray reality. Now it was paying off. In the ensuing weeks,
through constant debate and observation, the history project began
to decode "realism."

What seems realistic is determined by what we see on television.
Our images of history are shaped by the images we have of history in
the making. The codes are embedded in our minds by real wars, real
refugee camps, real battle footage. We don't see army patrols as we
would see them in movies. We never see a hand pounding on the
door, followed by a shot of a frightened family from inside, followed
by a boot kicking the door down. That was the "God's-eye view," an
all-knowing access to every private moment. Instead, our understanding of atrocities comes from seeing images of their aftermath
with the camera panning the burned-out home, the children's
broken toys, an old man recounting what happened.

On the occasions when the camera actually caught unfolding
action, like a battle, there was a clear pattern to the footage. There
were shots of the preparations because cameramen on each side of
the conflict were allowed access, but during the conflict, the shots
were distant, confused, and taken from a vantage point of relative
safety. There were no shots of bayonets coming right at the lens. The
aftermath, like the preparation, was usually well documented, since
the danger was over.

This held for other footage too. The reason a documentary re-
enactment of a frowning commander pacing in his tent looked fake
was that it was not a shot a news camera would ever catch; it was
too literal. In the Yugoslavian footage we were studying, there were
no shots of Slobodan Milosevic in his study rubbing his temples
and looking worried while a voice-over said, "Milosevic knows time
is running out and he has limited options." We saw him reviewing a
parade or waving to the cameras as he entered the cabinet room. So we
decided to take no shots of Montcalm looking worried or Champlain
looking visionary as he contemplated the future of the continent.
Literalism was the enemy everywhere: don't show someone drunk
when you're discussing the whisky trade, don't show someone

looking forlorn when you're saying they're lonely. "Never play the result," says an old theatre adage that we took to heart, "imply it indirectly." Allen Ginsberg once advised a young poet: "Don't say someone feels lonely; describe the sound of rain on the hood of a car. There isn't a lonelier sound in the world."

The debates about form and approach went on all summer and well into the next year, inflamed or calmed by someone's experience in the field or some program we saw somewhere else. One such debate was sparked by the movie *Saving Private Ryan*. About ten of us – directors, cameramen, re-enactment advisers – went to see Spielberg's latest film, having read about the reconstruction techniques he had used. The first half-hour, which has since become movie legend, mercilessly portrays the American landing on the Normandy beaches in a way that breaks all rules. In a tavern later, we were all bursting to interpret what we had seen. "There are no sequences!" Sweeney said, as if struck by an epiphany. "It feels real because there are no sequences in the landing scene." A sequence is the basic building block of action. Doorbell rings. Man rises and opens the door. Pizza delivery man hands box over. The box is opened. Cut to pizza slice entering mouth. It tells a visual story. But the beach landing scenes in *Saving Private Ryan* had hardly any sequences. No cameramen at the battle would have had time to take shots of rifles being loaded and aimed, and of soldiers falling. So the movie cameramen and editors had grabbed images and thrown them together. The result was a cauldron of satanic images, where no individual action could be followed and no one knew where the centre was. Sweeney had been right to hesitate, weeks back, when I thought the documentary camera being "uncertain" was the answer. There was more. The documentary camera, in the middle of chaos, cannot shoot a sequence. Only once the chaos calms can the rules of narrative vision return. In a scene that sets up an Acadian family's farm life, it can follow the deliberate rules of set-up and reverse angles, and the face can look at the camera. But if the English squad beating down the door of the home is shot the same way, if the chaos is choreographed, it begins to look fake.

How do you shoot unfolding action? We talked to re-enactors who had taken part in movie shoots, to try to learn what they had found most realistic, and we found one clue that confirmed the direction in which we were heading. One director had preferred to stage an attack two or three times, and shoot it each time on the fly, rather than sequence by sequence. "Unleash the action and shoot it on the fly" proved to be the key to all the large-scale scenes in the series.

The human face talking directly to the camera was another consideration that tied our directors in knots. Many simply found the idea of someone in a costume and wig talking directly to the camera hopelessly fake; they wanted nothing but voice-overs. I'd protest, "Voice over what? We've already used every sunset and waterfall and beaver known to man in one thirteen-minute promo." Gordon agreed, adding, "If we don't use faces, we'll turn this series into a nature film."

It's always been a mystery to me how a human face, speaking to the camera, conveying all the drama and emotion of human expression, is disdained by television as a "talking head" and dismissed as "radio on television." It's a shot you rarely see in documentaries, except in investigative programs like *the fifth estate* and *60 Minutes*. Body language is important, of course, but I'd much rather see a close-up of a face than somebody's torso. The worst shots, I find, are those in interview shows and late-night talk shows, where most of the shot is of the suit or the set and the face occupies only a tiny proportion of the screen. The information is in the face, not the suit or the set.

One group insisted that looking directly at the camera is an unnatural television documentary shot, and they're largely right by today's conventions. But the memory of the eyes staring into the camera in all of Peter Watkins's films convinced me it was the right thing to do. Hubert Gendron finally won the battle for me. He brought in the *National Geographic* cover shot of the Afghan girl with the fierce green eyes looking directly at the camera and said: "Can anyone ignore this face? Try to achieve this."

Then came the issue of what language the person portrayed on camera should speak. This was trickier. There was an argument that everyone, including aboriginal people, should speak their own languages. This was logical within the documentary ethic but completely impractical. Some thirty aboriginal languages were involved, and many of them are not spoken by anyone today. The screen would be cluttered with subtitles everywhere. We would have achieved purity at great difficulty and cost, and at the expense of comprehension.

Finally, I had to invoke closure on a raging debate. Everyone would speak English or French for two reasons. First, our objective was to make history accessible, not arcane. Second, in a country where 27 per cent of the population has difficulty reading normally, why would we even contemplate a series that would be largely subtitled?

The clincher came when our historical adviser Jay Cassel found a letter written in phonetics from the Seven Years War period. The letter was a phonetic capture of French as it was spoken in the eighteenth century. Read aloud, it was totally incomprehensible to the modern French ear. Would we subtitle such arcane English for the English audience, and arcane French for the Radio-Canada audience? The answer was obvious and the debate was settled. That's why, in the series, Tecumseh speaks English – which, incidentally, he did fluently, though he preferred to avoid it.

Language, images, actors were all hotly debated issues, but the real battle was over "story." Hardly an hour would pass in the life of the series when Gordon Henderson or Hubert Gendron or Gene Allen wasn't telling a researcher or a director, "Story. Story. Story. Where's the human story? Where's the human voice?"

In November 1999, I happened to hear a fragment of Robert Fulford's Massey Lecture on CBC Radio, *The Triumph of Narrative*. It argues that the storytelling form has become the dominant narrative of the twentieth and twenty-first centuries and examines how and why this happened. This is the fragment that I heard.

Those who make news into narratives, and those who read or watch or otherwise absorb them, are apparently responding to a human necessity. Mark Turner of the University of Maryland has developed the theory that stories teach us to think. In his book *The Literary Mind*, he argues that telling stories is not a luxury or a pastime but part of developing intelligence. Stories are the building blocks of human thought; they are the way the brain organizes itself. Turner, who works with his university's neuroscience and cognitive-science programs, argues that the mind is essentially literary. Using the neuroscience of Gerald Edelman, he depicts the human mind integrating bits of thought and sensation through overlapping systems or maps, of neurons. We pull together fragments and find meaning by connecting many elements. And the force that sets the neurons firing and makes these connections possible is narrative – in particular, stories that are blended with other stories. When we compare one story we know with another, we are assembling the elements that make our own brains work. Does this account for our *need* to tell stories and listen to them?

I was excited, because narrative has been so bashed about and so dismissed by historians as an immature form of history practised by hacks. And here was an argument that could be made, in a scientific framework, for something any journalist viscerally knows to be true. Fulford quotes Lewis Lapham, the highly regarded editor of *Harper's* magazine, saying, "History is only intelligible as narrative, but narrative today is against university rules."

But why is narrative so compelling, especially in recounting real events through history, biography, and documentary? The first part of the answer, I think, is simple: we are mesmerized by the idea that something extraordinary is actually true. That is ten times more exciting than fiction. The second part of the answer just flits by in Fulford's lecture, but I think he puts his finger on the central reason: "Does the habit of seeing the world as stories make us understand ourselves better? Does it make us better citizens or worse? My experience suggests that it makes us better. Narrative gives us a way to feel empathy for others." Empathy. That's the key. We are capable of empathizing with another person, even if we disagree with them, even if they lived three hundred years ago. We will be capable, I thought, of having empathy for both the Selkirk settlers and the Métis whose way of life they destroyed. If we could tell the story from both points of view in a human scale, we elicit empathy for the reasoning and emotions of ordinary men and women on opposite sides of the conscription crisis.

"Who cares about the crisis of military versus senatorial government in Rome in 60 B.C.?" I argued in a speech at a history conference. "Or the social mores and clan feuds of Verona? But we line up through the ages to watch *Julius Caesar* and *Romeo and Juliet*. Why? Because of empathy. Every life is a drama, every society a struggle, and if you drill to the core of the story, you will find dreamers and lunatics, love and hate, honour and betrayal, and the struggle of the human spirit. It doesn't have to be pretty, saccharine, or elevating. It just has to be real, and bred into every one of us is the capacity to identify with that person and that struggle. In fact, it is irresistible."

You don't have a program idea if it takes you more than a sentence to describe it. We had found ours: "Canada, through the eyes of the people who lived it."

9

Army Wanted, Urgently

There was one episode I was determined to write myself: the British conquest of New France. I had political reasons: this was likely to be the most controversial episode, and I didn't want it out of my sight. If there was going to be a split in the unit, it was likely to come in this episode, and I wanted to be in a position to put out any fires. It was easier, I reasoned, to write the script myself than to spend days and weeks arguing with someone else's script. Besides, if there was going to be a French-English split in the team, it was better to have someone who was of neither French nor English descent arbitrating the content. "We're doing the Polish version of the Conquest" became the unit joke.

I had personal reasons as well. At the centre of the episode would be the Battle of the Plains of Abraham; it would be the largest reconstruction in the series, and potentially the most controversial. After all the years of playing *Culloden* to students and new researchers at the CBC, I wanted to bring everything I had learned from studying Watkins's films to Canada's pivotal battle, partly as a tribute to the man who had revolutionized the documentary form. It was a matter not of copying his cinematic style but of trying to capture his sense of fate and chance. The way to do the Plains of Abraham was to portray the epic stakes and fates that had converged on this abandoned field just outside Quebec City.

The battle is a hornet's nest, and most people have preferred to leave well enough alone. In the French psyche, it endures as a fundamental humiliation and fuels nationalist politics to this day. It is also at the core of English-Canadian mythology. "The Maple Leaf Forever" has fallen into disuse because of the imperial puffery of lines like "In days of yore from Britain's shore, Wolfe the dauntless hero came / And planted firm Britannia's flag on Canada's fair domain." There are plenty of Canadians, however, who still see the battle, and the Conquest, in that light.

Even the term "conquest" is a sore point. Most Québécois refer to "la conquête," but many federalists argue that it was not really a conquest because the French won their religious and political rights fifteen years after the battle. Many English historians, and even Laurier LaPierre in his book *1759: The Battle for Canada*, see the event as an imperial European battle between two foreign expeditionary armies that just happened to take place in our back yard, and therefore it was not a defeat of the Canadiens. Even the highly respected Quebec nationalist filmmaker Jacques Godbout embraces this analysis in his tongue-in-cheek film *Le Sort de l'Amérique* (The Fate of America), which had just been released the year we were planning the series.

So the best way to settle the issue has been to ignore it. The battlefield of the Plains of Abraham is a national park along the Grande Allée outside Quebec City, but it's marked with a minimum of monuments, and a visitor would have to be diligent to find out that anything major ever happened here. The anniversary of the battle, September 13, is emphatically ignored by all levels of government. Such is the Canadian genius for resolving conflict.

But Godbout was right when he named his film *Le Sort de l'Amérique*, because on this abandoned farmer's field in 1759 not only was the fate of Canada decided, but the emergence of the United States was made possible.

Over a hundred years ago, the American scholar Francis Parkman, author of *Montcalm and Wolfe* and one of the greatest narrative historians of the nineteenth century, wrote this about the conquest of Canada: "More than one clear eye saw, at the middle of the last century, that the subjection of Canada would lead to a revolt of the British colonies. So long as an active and enterprising enemy threatened their borders, they could not break with the mother country, because they needed her help. . . . If [France] . . . had preserved but the half, even less than the half of her American possessions, then a barrier would have been set to the spread of the English-speaking races; there would have been no Revolutionary War; and for a long time, at least, no independence."

The Battle of the Plains of Abraham lasted less than fifteen minutes. Yet those fifteen minutes were pivotal to the fate of an entire continent, to the French-Canadian people, to the Indian nations, to the fate of the French and British empires, and would set off a chain of events that would bring about the American Revolution, the Loyalist flight, and the migrations of millions of Europeans to the Canadian frontier.

The fighting itself may have lasted fifteen minutes, but the buildup to that fateful quarter-hour and the events which followed it on the night after the battle, strain the imagination. It was all so capricious, such a roll of the dice. The fate of a continent would be determined by pure chance.

After two months, with a quarter of the British navy at his disposal and twenty-eight thousand sailors and soldiers, James Wolfe had nothing to show but devastation. He had reduced much of Quebec to rubble. He had burned the South Shore. His great invasion of the Beauport line at the Battle of Montmorency was a complete disaster that lost him seven hundred men. His generals had open contempt for him. In a modern equivalent, to make a Second World War parallel, he had been in command of the Normandy invasion, with the most powerful naval force in the world, and failed to take the beaches.

Now he spent days sick in his bed, stewed in a cocktail of medicines, racked by indecision and despair. He had just learned that his father had died, and he faced a humiliating return to Britain as a symbol of failure. Finally, the admiral of the fleet told him that time had run out. It was late summer; the water level in the St. Lawrence was dropping. Within two weeks the big warships and transports, whose hulls drew the deepest draft, would have to leave.

The tone of his last letter to the British cabinet is almost pathetic, given that this is the general of Britain's largest expeditionary force writing not in a private diary, not to an intimate friend, but to his political masters: "I found myself so ill," he wrote, "and am still so weak that I begged the general officers . . . to draw the enemy from their present situation, and bring them to an action. I have acquiesced in their proposal, and we are preparing to put it into execution." He wasn't taking command; he was giving up in despair – and admitting it to London.

His generals came up with the most rational plan: invade the opposite shore about fifty kilometres upriver from Beauport, and move on Quebec City. It was the plan they had proposed before, but Wolfe had decided instead on the disastrous amphibian landing right in front of the enemy trenches at Montmorency. On September 9, his generals had everything ready. Upriver, between Pointe-aux-Trembles and Saint-Augustin, a force of five thousand men, packed into massive transport ships with cannon, gunpowder, and provisions, was ready to clamber into dozens of landing craft and storm the thinly defended North Shore, in an action almost guaranteed to get the British army across. But it started to rain heavily, and continued for three days. With five thousand men cooped up in cramped transport ships, with full battle gear, for three days, Wolfe was still whimpering about himself. In his last letter to England, addressed to Lord Holdernesse, Wolfe was still despairing. "The weather has been extremely unfavourable for a day or two, so we have been inactive. I am so far recovered as to do business, but my constitution is entirely ruined, without the consolation of having done any considerable service to the State, or without any prospect of it." In this melancholic state, in the drizzling rain, the commander of the British forces wandered off back in the direction of Quebec City and studied the cliffs above the town through his telescope. And he focused on an abandoned farmer's field on the outskirts of the city. James Wolfe decided to gamble – again.

The image of Wolfe at this moment drew me deeper. Here was a despairing and desperate man, who knew he was dying of tuberculosis anyway, facing complete humiliation back in London. Five thousand men were cramped on a flotilla of ships upriver waiting to execute a fairly intricately planned landing. Suddenly Wolfe decided to change all that. It was a decision that enraged his commanders and endangered the invasion by changing its landing area, which his commanders had not had the time to assess. In fact, the proposed landing area was militarily reckless at the best of times and downright suicidal right now, with no reconnaissance. It was *a cliff*, over sixty metres tall, overgrown with trees and shrubs, with French sentries along the top, and a massive gun battery a few hundred metres away, guarding the river.

First the landing craft had to drift fifty kilometres downriver in a strong current, and with luck they would not be detected along this long trip. Then they had to find the thin strip of beach at the base of the cliff, and not overshoot it. They had to kill any guards along the beach, then disembark, which would take hours, undetected by anyone on shore or looking down on the river from above. Then thousands of men had to find goat paths up the cliff, and carry artillery up it. Then they had to somehow overpower 150 guards on the top of the cliff before they sounded a warning. And if this improbable series of contingencies worked, they would find themselves on a field no British officer had walked on or surveyed, and could expect to fight a battle within one or two hours of detection.

"It was worse than that," the researcher, Richard Fortin, added. "When they got to the top of the cliff, they had two fundamental military problems. One, Wolfe was actually placing himself between *two* French armies. The first was whatever forces Montcalm had sent from Quebec City. But remember there were two thousand French soldiers under the command of Bougainville who were scattered along the North Shore for fifty kilometres upriver to prevent the British from landing. Bougainville could muster them into a single army in two or three hours. Wolfe was walking into a guaranteed pincer action."

The second problem was just as basic as the first. "He had no avenue of retreat once he was on top of the cliff. If things went badly, he couldn't take five thousand men scrambling down a cliff back to their ships. You should never place yourself where you have no avenue of retreat."

At the next script conference with Richard, whose hand had healed enough for him to return, Sally and I kept coming back to this moment and the seemingly insane move. Richard quipped: "I guess you could develop an argument that Wolfe was intentionally committing suicide, and taking almost five thousand men with him."

Sally was also fascinated by this moment as a Wagnerian leap into the abyss. "It was a reckless grab for glory, for redemption – at any cost – by a man who just could not afford to return to England alive and face humiliation."

Why didn't Wolfe let the invasion take place upriver, where the generals had planned? After all, it would have been only lightly resisted, and he could have marched to Quebec within three days. One answer was that there was no element of surprise by taking three days to march to Quebec, the ground was soaked after days of rain, and the French would have destroyed all the bridges on the way. The less charitable answer is that there was no great glory in this plan. He had already told London he had "begged the general officers to consult together" and he had "acquiesced" in their plan. This last-minute move, however, was clearly Wolfe's plan, and no one else's.

The historical consultant on this episode was a thirty-eight-year-old dynamo with a goatee and a shaved head, whom we'd heard about from several people, including Ramsay Cook. The very mention of the Seven Years War made his face brighten and his eyes glisten. He would go into breathless flights of oratory on whatever point was in question, flights that were brilliant in their detail but never landed. The flight had to be shot down because the only way to stop Jay and move on to another point was to interrupt him. He always took such mid-air interceptions with good grace, aware that not everyone had his boundless capacity to absorb detail about the French army in North America in the mid-eighteenth century. After a few months, this was how I'd introduce him to others: "This is Professor Jay Cassel. His idea of a good time on a Saturday night is studying personnel files of marine regiments in the Seven Years War." He never took umbrage, because it was largely true. He was a historical heavyweight, completing his third book, *The Life and Death of an Army*, for Oxford University Press, and to research it he had literally gone through the surviving regimental records of France's army in North America. He knew every diary, every eyewitness account of every engagement in the war. He could literally name scores of soldiers on the Plains of Abraham and tell where they came from.

On the first day Gene Allen brought him in to meet the Episode 4 team, we went downstairs to the Mövenpick for lunch. Sally Reardon was there, along with Mike Sweeney, the cameraman, Murray Green, who would edit the documentary, and our senior visual researcher, Ron Krant. We had been worrying about recreating the bombardment of Quebec, a siege lasting nine weeks which had dropped twenty thousand cannonballs. Were there enough accounts by citizens describing the devastating siege? Could we reconstruct, minute by minute, the first night? I can only imagine what the lunchtime crowd around us thought as our table grew louder and louder, with Jay Cassel making wide arcs with his arms to show the trajectory of the signal rocket, or imitating the explosion of a shell.

"There is a description by Father Recher of women and children huddled against a wall, wailing and praying in distress," Jay said, and we reacted with delight. Diners around us began to cast glances. I remember being excited to learn that the British used more than cannonballs, which they would heat to glowing red in artillery furnaces so they would set roofs on fire when they landed; they had exploding shells as well, iron baskets full of combustibles and explosives which could set an entire block on fire. My excitement grew as I saw in my mind, for the first time, how we could film glowing balls of iron in satanic furnaces, seeing comets of light streak across the sky and hearing the rumbling of exploding shells. "This is fantastic," I said too loudly. "Listening to you, I feel like I'm in the London Blitz!" Sally had to caution me: "People are staring."

This was in April, soon after the video had been played to the board. Summer would be on us soon, and we had to devise a plan for reconstructing the Battle of the Plains of Abraham. And that brought us into contact with the curious world of the re-enactors. We all knew that there was a large community of groups in the United States that regularly staged Civil War re-enactments; less known were the groups that liked to recreate battles of the War of 1812, the Revolutionary War, and the Seven Years War. Sally Reardon plunged into that world, trying to find a major re-enactment being staged somewhere in eastern Canada or the United States that we could piggyback onto. It was inconceivable to us that we could stage our own event; we didn't have the uniforms, the muskets, or the money to bring a couple hundred men to a location.

The biggest such gathering was planned at Fort Ticonderoga in New York in late June. We hoped to shoot the battle there, even though the time of year was wrong – the Plains of Abraham was in September. But the plan fell apart when we realized the shoot would cost us $50,000, and that the fort wanted ownership of the copyright on everything we shot on their grounds. Ticonderoga was out. Sally convinced me we had to hold the battle ourselves, and that we needed only a hundred re-enactors. I said we'd need at least five hundred. Why? Well, I said, "Because there are at least that many in the *Barry Lyndon* wide shot," referring to the battle scene we had been studying for weeks in Stanley Kubrick's classic film.

"There aren't more than a hundred in that shot, I bet," Sally said.

Exasperated, I rummaged through the shelf, found the video, cued up the wide shot of the French army ranged across the crest of a hill, a breathtaking panoramic shot that actually looked like a thousand men, and froze it. "That's five hundred," I said. "That's one hundred," she said. We called Murray Green, the senior editor who'd be editing the episode. "About one hundred," he said. To settle the argument, we counted every little figure one by one: one hundred men.

Defeated, I finally said: "So one day we'd shoot them all in French uniforms. . . ."

And Sally finished the thought: "And the next day we shoot them in British uniforms. Just like Watkins did in *Culloden*."

I looked at Murray: "Can you edit that into a battle?"

"You bet."

We then asked Gilles Saindon from the CBC graphics department, who had composed the shot of the British fleet off Quebec that had so impressed everyone in the video, to come up. The frozen French line from *Barry Lyndon* was still on the screen.

"There's a hundred soldiers on this screen, even though it looks like a thousand," I told him, as Sally rolled her eyes to the ceiling. "Could you add different battalions, and artillery firing on the flanks, if we gave you the elements shot separately?"

Gilles stared at the shot closely, measured the length of the line, and nodded more and more as he conferred with Murray, finally pronouncing his diagnosis. "If you give me an element to disguise the stitch, for example a flag carrier at the end of each regimental line, I can stick a whole other battalion on, and then you can recostume them into artillery, and I can place the same men on the side as artillery. I'll need the better part of an afternoon with full control of the battlefield to do it, but we can give you two armies of four thousand men each."

"You guys can do that?" I asked, "That's *Titanic*-level stuff."

"If you can persuade the CBC to get us the new special effects software," Gilles said confidently, "we've got the skills downstairs to do it."

"Downstairs" was an improbable collection of young graphic artists with green or red hair, some with rings through their nostrils, who lived on the floor just below us. They usually had to grind out news graphics, and I knew they would kill to get their hands on a challenge like the history series. And I knew they were very, very good.

Now we needed two hundred eighteenth-century uniforms and cannon.

The next weekend I was at our family's farm in Cavan, where my old friend George Flak, a movie producer, had unilaterally taken over one of the smaller barns. He had even built a crude outhouse in the cornfield, for all passing traffic to see. He had been involved with the other Plains of Abraham movie which had kept me up nights a year ago, but which was now shelved. I asked him how one went about mustering two eighteenth-century armies in three months. "I don't know where you get the men, but I know where you get the uniforms: one company in London owns all the uniforms from *Barry Lyndon*, and another, in Los Angeles, owns the ones from *Last of the Mohicans*." That night, over the barbecue, he gave me a crash course in movie special effects, which persuaded me more than ever that we were totally out of our depth. "Get yourself a good assistant director, and a good explosives man," he counselled. (I had a fleeting thought of the first thing I would like an explosives man to blow up, and that was standing out in the cornfield.) He continued: "And get yourself the top military re-enactor you can find, the perfect general, to stage the battle for you."

The perfect general appeared in our office that spring in the person of Peter Twist, who had just finished working with Brian McKenna on his series about the War of 1812. Every military curator at every museum and fort had suggested Twist's name for staging battle re-enactments. Forty-eight years old, with neat brown hair and distinguished bearing, Twist was a specialist in military uniforms and artifacts who made models and dioramas for institutions like the National Museum of Science and Technology in Ottawa and designed full-scale re-enactments of famous battles. Twist could design and make anything needed for a battle – short of a cannon, and he could get a deal on that.

A group of us met with him for two hours in my office, and after a few minutes it seemed we had entered through a time portal, into a council of megalomaniacs. Laine Drewery, who had the most pressing needs because he was staging the War of 1812, held up his left hand and went through his shopping needs one finger at a time. "I need to capture Fort Detroit, I have to see Tecumseh dying at the Battle of the Thames, I need to burn the Mohawk Valley, and I need to fight the Battle of Lundy's Lane and the Battle of Queenston Heights." Switching hands for more fingers, he continued: "And I need carts, horses, and a mass of Loyalist refugees. I need a Loyalist family being expelled from their homes – and oh yeah, I need to invade Quebec City, but that'll be in winter."

Twist and Drewery went back and forth rattling off specific battalions, place names, and commanders I never heard of until, after fifteen minutes, they both settled back comfortably. Drewery had obviously been impressed with Twist's knowledge of history, and vice-versa. Twist was particularly keen about Drewery's plans for the American Revolution: "Finally, we're going to see it through the eyes of our people, the Loyalists. We're showing the civil war that was part of the revolution, and we're going to be telling our stories." One of those stories was the diary of an eleven-year-old girl, Hannah Ingraham, whose father had joined the redcoats and whose family was driven out by the neighbours. Laine wanted to use her poignant diary entries as the central narrative in the Loyalist flight to Nova Scotia. Twist would have to cast an entire column of refugees with ox carts, and a patrol of American Continental soldiers.

While the Loyalists are seen almost exclusively as helpless refugees in our textbooks, hundreds were far from that. They fought back, and hard, with daring raids against American units and settlements. The most famous of these Loyalist guerrilla bands was Butler's Rangers, who would winter in the Niagara Peninsula, then descend into the Mohawk Valley in upper New York State, where they owned land before it was seized by their neighbours. They fought Indian-style, often alongside Joseph Brant's Mohawk Volunteers, wreaking havoc against the revolutionaries. Drewery and Twist had so warmed to each other that Twist was already listing where he could find Ranger uniforms and the perfect re-enactors, and Drewery was listing which settlements they could burn. Anyone walking into this CBC office by accident would think they had blundered into a cell of arsonists.

When the conversation turned to the conquest of Canada and the Battle of the Plains of Abraham, Twist confirmed it was a bad idea to use Ticonderoga. "Half the people who participate in a re-enactment may be dedicated military buffs," he said, "but they look all wrong; many are portly, or have moustaches or goatees, whereas no one in the British army had any facial hair in that period, and with their diet, no one would be portly. Your uniforms will often be wrong, the age of the soldiers will be wrong, and you'll rarely get a clear shot without people in the background. If you want a period-correct battle, you're going to have to stage it yourself."

"Can you mount the Battle of the Plains of Abraham in three months?" I asked. "Yes," he said, "I can."

In fact, over the next five months, Peter Twist would have to stage more battles and invasions than Eisenhower did in a year of the Second World War.

Now I needed to find a director for the episode, a French director, or at least a fluently bilingual one. For months we interviewed people and spent countless hours sorting through names or staring blankly at one another. The people whose names came up were either unilingual or "auteurs" who were unlikely to be willing to work with a team and would want to turn the episode into a personal film.

By late spring, the situation was critical. We were beginning to spend money on costumes and props, and we were approaching the season of Wolfe's arrival in 1759, so we would have to shoot to match the climate and the leaves on the trees. We went back over the list of names and paused on a name that had come up earlier. We were reluctant to take a chance on someone we'd never worked with before on an episode as critical as this one. He might prove to be a difficult personality, someone who didn't run a team well, or someone who couldn't deliver on time. His name was Serge Turbide, a producer and director who had done some work for *Adrienne Clarkson Presents*. "He's never directed anything over an hour," I protested.

"What he has produced are arts portraits and a sweet little film on sand castles – and he has no journalistic experience." I hated interviewing people who had no hope of getting the job, because it just humiliated them and made us look dismissive and arrogant. Hubert, Gordon, and Sally pressed me to at least have a coffee with him, and I finally arranged to meet him, as much to get everyone off my back as anything.

You never know who is going to come into your life and change it. Serge Turbide came into mine in the outdoor seating area of Ooh-la-la, the coffee bar on the ground floor of the CBC in Toronto. Tall, reddish-brown hair, forty-two or so, with a scarf loosely tossed around his shoulder, Serge could have stepped out of a Krieghoff picture, his face was so classically French Canadian. He had a very gentle deep voice, with a strong accent I couldn't quite place till he told me he came from the Îles de la Madeleine.

"Look," he said, "I know you have a very important project, and it must be worrying you very much. If there is any way I can help you, I would like to." I can spot contrived empathy, but there was nothing contrived or calculating about Serge. He was completely disarming as he recounted his experience in theatre and in documentary, his achievements and his shortcomings. He was eager to help in any way he could because, he said, "I think this series might become the most important thing any of us ever do." Many candidates for director are jealous of their privileges and try to lay down strict conditions for independence and control. Instead, Serge was willing to chip in and become part of a team. I was so relieved, within minutes I was telling him all my fears of the series splitting along language lines, my doubts about writing an episode that reconciled two adversarial views of the Conquest.

I took him upstairs to my office to show him *Culloden* and some episodes of *The Civil War*, to show him the style I was after. He sat hunched forward, elbows on his knees, visibly excited by what he was seeing. "That's my vision of the documentary," I said. "Tell me about yours." He opened his satchel and pulled out a videocassette. "Have you ever heard of a French film called *Colonel Chabert*?" he asked. I shook my head. He inserted the cassette into the VCR and said, "This is just a couple of minutes where we see what is left after a large battle," he said. "This is my vision of what we should do."

A wide landscape of torn earth and human devastation appeared on the screen, with Napoleonic soldiers picking through scattered bodies in the foreground, women searching in the middle distance, and a line of carts in the background. It looked like the Russian version of *War and Peace*, except that it didn't have the feel of a costume drama; instead it was bleak, stark, a perfectly composed panorama of war. The camera moved hauntingly through the images like a cold witness at the gates of hell. *Colonel Chabert* had the indefinable quality of a documentary, not a drama. You believed what you were seeing.

He looked at me. "I would like to do that."

I extended my hand and said, "I think this is the beginning of a long friendship."

Over the next few days, the Toronto office went from the quiet ambience of a reading room to the kind of bedlam I was more familiar and comfortable with. The head costumer, Bill Fortais, and his seamstresses kept arriving with tricorne hats and sketches of eighteenth-century uniforms. Tim McElcheran from the special effects department brought muskets down to Laine Drewery, severed hands for Andy Gregg, and plastic bladders of fake blood for someone – I dared not ask who. Tim and Mike Sweeney and Casey Kollontay were all fired up about a new pyrotechnic technique for burning models, which they thought might work for the Quebec scene. They had to try it out, but all they achieved was to stink up one studio horribly.

Laine and Peter Twist were planning the surrender of Fort Detroit, to take advantage of a re-enactment in June, while Andy Gregg and his team were shooting migrations of the Porcupine caribou herd to illustrate the progress of Canada's aboriginal ancestors across the Bering Strait for Episode 1. Meanwhile Sally was ordering more explosives – and even pineapples – for an upcoming shoot in Louisbourg. (Apparently, the British commander had sent the French governor of Louisbourg two pineapples as a courtesy gift before opening his guns up on the fortress in 1758.) People in the office were starting to walk around in British and French uniforms, and Anne Emin had acquired an ornate and lethal-looking officer's sword from one of the shoots, which she used to emphasize the importance of respecting budgets. Things were looking up.

10
Battle for a Continent

Writing a historical script is a long, miserable, fickle business. Writing "Battle for a Continent" isolated me from my family and from my friends in the late evenings, as I smoked incessantly in my den, surrounded by files and books. I spent long hours poring over diaries that Julia Bennett, Richard Fortin, and Sally Reardon had sent me, and I'd often be on the phone to Jay Cassel until two in the morning. I was having a hard time finding the "voices" of people, other than generals and politicians. For such voices, we had to go to microfilms of original letters and diaries. We even hired a forensic handwriting analyst to decipher twenty letters written by one Quebec merchant. I couldn't believe we had not one single quote from any ordinary soldier who fought on the Plains of Abraham, only the laconic accounts of officers. There had been nine thousand men on that field!

The Seven Years War, to me, was one of those confusing memories from college, right up there with the War of the Austrian Succession and the War of the Spanish Succession, which I never got straight. "How do we even make anyone care?" I asked Jay. "It's just another European war."

"Tell them," he said, "it is considered by some to be the real first world war, because it was fought on several continents, on every ocean on earth, with the five greatest navies that ever set sail, and the largest armies in the history of mankind – bigger than those of Rome and Carthage. Tell them it was literally a life-and-death struggle between global empires, and it changed the destiny of nations."

"This is good," I said, typing, with the phone cradled on my shoulder.

I had never realized how savage and bloody and racial the struggle for this continent had been. It was true that the Seven Years War was a European war, between France and England. But I learned that the war had overlaid an already existing North American struggle among the American colonists, the Canadians, and their Indian allies. It wasn't simply an imperial war, fought between two distant powers in our backyard. It had also been a contest for America between North Americans.

"This is going to be one of the first histories seen through the eyes of North Americans," Jay observed at one point. "A history that recognizes we are all Americans. That's going to be quite radical."

The first thing that surprised me was the venomous hatred that drenched the peoples of this continent. The American colonies had attained a population of one million people by the 1750s, versus about sixty thousand French in New France. Yet to the Protestant American colonists, Catholic New France – Canada – was the evil empire of the time, the source of all terror, and the obstacle to their continental dream.

The other great fear of the American colonists was the Indian nations. The Indians were engaged in a war of attrition against the encroaching settlers and burned their settlements, slaughtered their pioneers, and took the women and children into captivity. Fevered stories spread of cannibalism and torture and unspeakable acts.

Most Indian nations of the interior had allied themselves with the French traders and soldiers, because they were united in a profitable fur trade, and because the French were not attempting to take any of their land. With this alliance of "savages" and "idolaters," Canada was, to the American colonial mind, the fusion of its two greatest night-mares. A number of battles – in the Ohio Valley, at Fort Duquesne, and at Fort Necessity – plus hundreds of incidents and massacres on all sides had taken place before the Seven Years War was even declared. Whatever imperial quarrels were brewing in Europe, there was already a continental war between neighbours in North America.

Another surprise for me was the character of Benjamin Franklin, whom I had been accustomed to see as the benign intellectual behind emerging democratic ideas and an accomplished scientist. He was both intellectual and inventor, but "benign" does not leap from the text of his papers and pamphlets while he was publisher of the *Pennsylvania Gazette*. His writings fan hatred for the French and call for their eradication: "The safety and security of all the English colonies in North America, their very Being as English Colonies, make such a measure absolutely necessary, and that without any Loss of Time." Franklin emerges as the Lenin of the American Revolution, the man who envisions a greater England spanning the continent, greater than the motherland itself, growing out of the million inhab-itants of the American colonies.

The first victims were not even in Canada but the Acadians, whose colony, strategically located at the mouth of the St. Lawrence, was now inside the American colonies. The Acadians had sworn to remain neutral, but anti-Catholic, anti-French lynch-mob hysteria swept the New England colonies anyway. In the summer of 1755, before any war was declared, hundreds of Boston civilians and mili-tiamen – blacksmiths, wigmakers, butchers, and clerks – answered the call for volunteers and boarded merchant ships and warships in what amounted to a massive posse of American colonists eager to deport an entire population of people. Together with British soldiers stationed in Boston, they burned the Acadians' homes, barns, and fields and shipped thousands into exile. Massachusetts governor William Shirley considered it just the first blow against Canada. "It is happy for us that we have now a fair opportunity offered of ridding the Province of its dangerous neighbours. . . . It would be wounding the Serpent in the head."

Now I knew what Roméo LeBlanc had meant when he said, "Don't look for your answers in London, look for your answers in the Boston board of trade." It was questionable whether London even knew about what was happening that summer. The Acadian Deportation was a North American affair. I had never been taught – and I doubt many Quebec students have ever been taught – that the lynch mob consisted of their American colonial neighbours, and the motive was the destruction of New France and control of the rich Ohio Valley. Nor is it taught that on both sides of this very American war, appalling atrocities were routine. French, Canadien, and Indian raiding parties deliberately planned and carried out the slaughter of civilian "American" communities, as in German Flats. This was, for over a decade, as bloody and ruthless a landscape of racial and religious hatred and economic greed as we had been seeing in the Balkans on our television screens.

This American war was overtaken by the larger French-English imperial war that erupted in Europe in 1756, and after a number of battles over the next three years, the focus of the Seven Years War fell on the St. Lawrence River. General James Wolfe was leading an armada so huge it stretched for a hundred kilometres, heading for Champlain's great citadel on the hill, which was now the bristling fortress of Quebec, commanded by Montcalm.

Claude Berrardelli had been right when he described almost inhabiting Champlain's soul by reading so much of his writings. I would feel the same, late at night, reading the letters of Montcalm, Vaudreuil, and Wolfe as they headed for their Armageddon. These midnight meditations were quickly burst by the realities of the office, such as the search for Wolfe's personal copy of Thomas Gray's *Elegy Written in a Country Church-Yard*. The famous *Elegy* was published just five years before his invasion of Canada and a copy was given to him, along with a picture locket, by his fiancée, Katherine Lowther. Wolfe had made several notations in it that we wanted to shoot. Perhaps with some portent of his fate, he had underlined these phrases: "The Paths of Glory lead but to the Grave" and "On some fond Breast the parting Soul relies." Next to the lines "Chill Penury repress'd their noble Rage / And froze the genial Current of the Soul," Wolfe wrote: "How ineffectual are oft our own unaided Exertions especially in early Life. How many shining Lights owe to Patronage and Affluence what their Talents would never procure Them."

The notation makes sense when you remember that Wolfe was a middle-class soldier who rose through the ranks and was held in contempt by some of his blueblood generals. Also, there was a widespread opinion that what drove him was his hunger for glory at any price.

Timothy Reibetanz was a very serious young intern whom we gave the task of finding Wolfe's copy. He found Katherine Lowther's locket at Raby Castle, home of Lowther's descendants, without too much difficulty. The copy of the *Elegy* proved more elusive. I offer the following detective story, as reported by Tim Reibetanz, partly so the reader will understand what we do for a living and partly as a vivid story about fate and chance. Reibetanz writes:

I found an article by Beckles Willson, Wolfe's biographer, from 1913. Willson writes that the copy returned to England where it was given to Lowther's servant, a Mrs. Ewing, who passed it to her daughter, a Mrs. Day. It then became the property of a bookseller in Le Havre, and from there it fell into the hands of a Mr. W.R. Colling, but that is as far as Willson traced the copy. I contacted museums across Canada and the U.K, including the Canadian War Museum, the Imperial War Museum, the McCord Museum, the New Brunswick Museum, the British Library, the Royal Commission on Historical Manuscripts (U.K.), Quebec House in Kent (where Wolfe grew up), Raby Castle, the National Archives of Canada, the National Library of Canada, and the interpretive centre at the Plains of Abraham. No luck. I was astonished that nobody knew where this important document was, or even if it still existed.

The National Archives had a microfilm of portions of Willson's manuscripts, and our archivist there, Monica MacDonald, told me that they were copied from the collection of a Mr. A. Willson of Twickenham, England. I found the number through U.K. directory assistance, and one morning in June 1998, Mr. Anthony Willson got a surprise phone call from me. He turned out to be Beckles Willson's grandson.

Anthony turned out to be very helpful. It turned out his grandfather's diaries had been dispersed throughout France, where he retired, and had only recently been returned to Anthony. The diaries confirmed that his grandfather had had the *Elegy* valued by Frank T. Sabin, an antiquarian bookseller. Unfortunately, when Anthony called the Sabin bookstore, he was told their records had been destroyed in WWII. He then called another antiquarian bookseller, Maggs Brothers, and someone there happened to remember that the *Elegy* had been sold to a bookseller in Philadelphia, from whom it had recently been purchased by Richard Landon, who had heard about the copy in Philadelphia from an antiquarian bookseller. Richard Landon was the director of the Thomas Fisher Rare Book Library at none other than the University of Toronto!

What followed was, without doubt, the most exciting trip I have ever made to a library. Within half an hour I was finally holding Wolfe's copy of the *Elegy* in my gloved hands. I imagined Wolfe pondering over the verse in his ship's cabin while he thought of Lowther at home. I imagined how Katherine Lowther received it, along with the news of her fiancé's death, and what she must have felt when she read his notes. I imagined the countless number of hands through which it had since passed.

While we were scouring the planet to look for documents that were six blocks away, Wilma Alexander and Bill Fortais were unpacking two hundred British and French uniforms no one had worn in twenty years that had just arrived from California. There was great consternation because they came without the white leather crossbelts and ammunition pouches, and of course, all the regimental lapels were the wrong colours. Some people in the series were prepared to take this in stride, but Peter Twist said we would be savaged by the historical community if we mixed the Forty-Seventh Regiment of Foot with the Light Infantry. Furthermore, there were no grenadier hats, whose purpose was to make their wearers look taller and thereby frighten the enemy. Bill Fortais set an army of seamstresses and tailors to Velcro on the correct lapel colours, while a purchase order for two hundred ammunition pouches and crossbelts went out to a local shoemaker, on the understanding that we'd sell them to the re-enactors after the battle. I drew the line at spending $2,000 on plastic replicas of the correct square belt buckles, and the reader might as well know that the oval belt buckles in the episode are incorrect. Peter Twist, disgusted by the CBC's penury, pressed his wife and children into service in his basement-cum-sweatshop, where they made for us eighteen grenadier hats out of felt and Velcro. They were delivered with the warning that they wouldn't survive the first rainfall.

In another basement, this one at the Broadcast Centre, carpenters were urgently lathing a period-perfect cannon barrel out of wood, light enough that the re-enactors could haul it up the cliff. These craftsmen were doing yeoman work, even though the CBC had handed many of them their notice.

The actual firing of cannons would be done not during the shoot of the battle but in a special weekend in November, at a conservation area outside Toronto, where every cannon anyone needed in any episode would be fired under the supervision of the Metro Toronto Police Tactical Squad in an apocalypse of destruction. But we would have to wait until the provincial wildlife authorities verified that every bird had left, which seemed reasonable.

Cannon can be fired near a city, but not with cannonballs, as they could land three kilometres away, in some subdivision. So only gunpowder is used, no projectiles. The effect is just as dramatic, no one gets killed, but neither does the cannon recoil. In movies the edit usually comes right after the mouth of the cannon spits fire. That's because there is no recoil, and the shot would look fake if it lasted longer. But sometimes we had to show recoil with field cannon on

gun carriages, so Tim McElcheran rigged up ropes, tied to the
wheels, out of sight of the camera. There are a lot of ways of working
for Her Majesty, even part-time. Being a rope recoil man for the
Canadian History Project was one. This involved ten or twelve men
lined up like tug-of-war players, hauling with all their might on the
gun carriage wheels when the cannon fires. All done within sight of
a twenty-storey condo tower. The carriage and barrel lathed for the
1759 battle were replaced, and bingo, we were in the War of 1812, and
twenty minutes later, in the Riel Rebellion. On top of all this, one
cannon would have to be fired at the Plains, in order to be in the wide
shot with the line of troops. This required many permits, the presence of a fire engine, police, a paramedic ambulance, oxygen tanks,
fire extinguishers, and a highway transportation permit complex
enough to move an atomic weapon.

"The Plains." We had to find some, and what grief that brought
us. We couldn't stage the battle on the actual Plains of Abraham, for
many reasons. First, they were bulldozed flat around the turn of the
century and now look like a golf course. Second, they are surrounded
by power lines, condos, phone booths, and passing traffic. Third,
crowd control would have been impossible. So where?

Peter Twist and his colleague Robert Henderson (no relation to
the senior producer Gordon Henderson) scoured what seemed like
every concession line between Quebec City and Ottawa in search of
the right landscape. We needed a hill – the Buttes-à-Neveu where
Montcalm's army arrived – bald on top but with cedars on either
side. This hill had to overlook a large overgrown field that had been
abandoned for about three years. Behind that field there had to be a
forest. To the left of that field, there had to be an old cornfield, with
most stalks withered, but some new. As if those requirements weren't
enough, it also had to be one-third scale so that our diminished
troops would be in proportion to the landscape. Lastly, the axis of the
sun had to be right, rising over the hill in the east and setting over the
forest behind the field below. Of course, no power lines; no flight
paths to airports which would leave airplane vapour trails. Motels
within twenty-five kilometres, but no hospitals or old-age homes in

case of sirens. "I drove every back road in the Ottawa Valley and Western Quebec," grumbled Robert Henderson. I can't imagine how many innocent farmers – or marijuana growers – still wonder why strangers were scouring their land with binoculars, taking notes and photographs with suspicious telephoto lenses.

The winner, or loser, was a Neil Perry, with the back forty of his dairy farm near North Gower, outside of Ottawa: "Drive three kilometres north of North Gower, turn right at the cheese factory sign." Perry, a youngish man, was surprised to find himself at the centre of Canadian history, since the nearest sign of political activity was a "Reform Party Information Here" sign attached to a nearby farmer's mailbox. The *Ottawa Citizen* was on to Perry instantly: "I was surprised when they told me my land would work as the Plains of Abraham. I honestly don't think it does. There's no hill here, just a four-foot rise," he said, unaware that the camera angle would exaggerate the rise to a hill. "They're renting it from me though, and I'm getting paid to haul away the garbage. Maybe we can have the North Gower Fair here next year." The *Citizen* chose to read political motives into our choice of site: "Could filming so far away be a conscious decision," the paper wrote, "something done to ensure Quebec nationalists are not offended, do not have to be reminded, on the anniversary no less, that they once had a country? And lost it."

Although the site was selected, the battle was weeks away. In the meantime, I was at my farm in Cavan with my family, trying to finish the script. Jay Cassel came up for a few days, and in the blistering heat we sat in the gazebo with files and books and a laptop, squashing mosquitoes on the computer screen, while my wife, Anne, mercifully fed us. We stayed up nights arguing and perspiring in the parlour, between two huge fans that blew script pages all over the room. Deciphering the battle had been one of the most intricate detective jobs either of us had been involved in.

Some weeks before, in a boardroom, everyone involved in the episode – Serge, Sally, Richard, Julia, and I – had a summit conference with Twist and Henderson, the heads of re-enactment, and Jay Cassel. We reconstructed the battle step by step, and in so doing, discovered some history ourselves. Jay ended up rewriting a large part of his book on the Seven Years War on the basis of that meeting. The first problem was that no historians knew exactly when the battle started. Even the diaries of officers gave contradictory times, either nine in the morning or ten.

"Historians haven't nailed this down," Jay said. "It's not important, really. You're going to have to fudge it."

"Fudge it!" I said. "The moment we turn on those cameras, the angle of the light and the shadows will say what time of morning it is. You just have to figure it out." We would have to go back to the original dispatches and calculate the time it would take Montcalm's troops to march a given distance, to resolve a 240-year-old question. That required figuring out the marching formations, deployment time, and the beginning of the French attack down the hill. The accounts said they marched quickly, at about sixty paces a minute.

"What is a pace?" I asked, and Twist and Henderson marched around the office to illustrate the loading drill, firing drill, then quick march, to the considerable wonderment of everyone at their desks, while we clocked them with stopwatches. "Bear in mind," Twist added, "that this is an abandoned, rutted field, full of tall weeds and some bush, and that it has been raining for days. The march will be sloppy, and it would be difficult to maintain ranks."

Jay grew uncharacteristically quiet, drifted off to my desk, and started scribbling furiously, then returned as Twist and Henderson acted out the British bayonet charge drill, the Highlander broadsword attack drill, and the Canadien militiamen's method of reloading: "The Canadiens would fire, then drop to the ground, roll on their backs, and load their muskets lying prone, so as not to present a target; then they'd scramble to their feet and resume marching." Jay popped up like a jack-in-the-box and resumed his furious scribbling in the adjoining office.

At the end of the evening, he paid Twist and Henderson the highest compliment a historian can give: "I have learned more today about the mechanics of the battle than in a month in the archives," he said. "You've resolved a lot of nagging questions for me. First, the question of why the French line was so ragged as it descended the hill – because of the ruts and bush and wetness – and the issue of why the Canadiens disrupted the French line. The French soldier beside a Canadien militiaman would keep marching, and probably thought the man was hit; by the time that militiaman got up after firing and reloading, he had lost his place in the formation. Montcalm had never properly trained the militia to fight as part of a regular formation!"

Jay, who had been skeptical of re-enactors up till now, became inseparable from Twist and Henderson, and during the actual shoot, he paced off positions in total rapture. After researching dispatches, incidentally, we established that the battle began at nine in the morning.

Back at the farm in Cavan, Jay and I had finally worked the script down to a modest fifty-two pages, which would take an hour to re-enact.

"Are you insane?" Sally Reardon phoned back after reading the draft. "I never should have left the two of you alone – little boys with guns." I protested that this was only an assembly draft, we'd cut it drastically. But no matter how often I typed "Draft," a ripple of panic went through the unit, and there was an outright explosion in Montreal.

"The goddamn battle lasted only fifteen minutes," Hubert stormed. "It took me an hour just to read this!" Wilma Alexander, Anne Emin, and Gordon Henderson met to figure out how to contain my enthusiasms, and I began to feel like Captain Queeg in *The Caine Mutiny*, when all the officers realized he was insane. Serge Turbide, the calm diplomat, assured everyone this was only a draft for comment, then took me aside to suggest I not be so liberal in distributing drafts until I had it down to twenty minutes.

Once we'd hacked it back to twenty-two minutes (still seven minutes longer than the battle), the script went to the wardrobe, makeup, special effects, graphics, and casting teams, the assistant directors, and the business unit, to be parsed into numbers of wigs, bayonets, boots, pounds of gunpowder, litres of water, and servings of hot meals. I was particularly worried about the food. As a former newspaperman, I knew that one of the cheapest tricks a hostile journalist can pull is a sentence like: "After bayoneting three French-men through the gut, Malcolm Fraser dined on a delicate *saumon en croûte*, with a side of fiddlehead greens and *risotto milanese*, cour-tesy of the CBC, which laid off another fifty people last week." I asked for a meeting with Wilma and Anne to review the on-site catering plans. Wilma had negotiated a great deal with a company that catered to the film business. They submitted the lowest bid by far and would be bringing their brand new catering truck. We reviewed the menus, and all my fears were realized. It looked delicious, and politically fatal: California gazpacho, chilled apple and pear soup, spinach and ricotta canneloni, ravioli with pesto, and California rice and five-bean medley. "This is suicide," I said. "Can't we give them chili and hamburgers?"

"They're travelling hundreds of miles at their own expense," Wilma protested, "and they deserve a good meal. Besides, this is actually cheaper than chili and hamburgers." She showed me the other bids, and they were all higher. "But it doesn't look cheaper," I protested. Finally, the caterers were persuaded to bring their two old catering vans instead of the shiny new one, and Wilma changed the names of the dishes to "rice and beans" and "cold vegetable soup."

We hoped the re-enactors were travelling toward North Gower, but we couldn't be certain till the day of the battle itself. Peter Twist had distributed flyers at various re-enactment events; he had called all his contacts and cashed in every favour. It hadn't been easy to find enough people. The soldiers had to be young and have no facial hair, because of the age of the soldiers on the Plains and the fact that beards and moustaches were not the fashion at the time. Plus we weren't paying their room and board, and they had to foot the expense of getting to Ottawa. If a hundred men didn't show up, we'd have a lot of ravioli left over.

11

The Hinge of Fate

On one Saturday morning in September 1998, my daughter Madeleine and I drove to Neil Perry's farm. As we crested the last hill, I nearly had a stroke. Below me was the largest tent I had ever seen outside the circus, with three tall peaks, each flying a long streaming flag that suggested a medieval tournament. There were two more large tents, about five Winnebagos, an eighteen-wheeler, a generator truck, an ambulance, the North Gower Fire Department truck, a field with at least a hundred cars, two large equestrian trailers with horses grazing nearby, two catering trucks emitting smoke and steam, two cannon on gun carriages being fussed over by special effects men, regimental flags streaming in the wind, dozens of men in red and grey uniforms wandering around with muskets and swords, and a party of Indian warriors in brilliant war paint smoking near the long row of blue portable toilets.

I could barely make it down the long hill, because of the cars full of onlookers parked along the side. Half of North Gower was there to watch the fun. I parked the car somewhere, and Madeleine and I picked our way through the visitors and past the barrier. Farther on were the two makeup trucks, the wardrobe tent with two hundred costumes arranged by regiment and size, the humming generator truck, and a truck marked "DANGER: EXPLOSIVES." It was a small city, joined by snaking black electrical cables.

The first person to greet me was Analisa Amoroso, our enthusiastic series assistant. She and other members of the unit were giving guided tours through the battlefield for the public. To my immense relief, half the people on the site were local people and the families of cast and crew. We had decided that since we were likely to draw a crowd and didn't want to turn people away, we'd make this an open set for visitors. But I'd never imagined so many. It was a frightening leap, going from squashing mosquitoes on the computer screen in Cavan a few weeks ago to this.

The writer is just an irritation on a production set, quite superfluous, even more than the executive producer, so I was shunted off to be a part-time tour guide and unofficial photographer. Madeleine, on the other hand, was seen as an asset and was given a job as a water girl, with the task of running across the battlefield to revive any parched combatants.

There were re-enactors from everywhere, pitching their tents in a neat military encampment in an adjoining field. The Milice de Chambly was here in force from Montreal, Butler's Rangers from Toronto and Hamilton, many with their wives and children in costume, Quebec militia units, aboriginal warriors with traditional tattoos and dress, and two re-enactors from the United States. The last to arrive were the Fraser Highlanders on a bus from Montreal. We had a total of ninety-eight re-enactors and two horses. Twist and Henderson, dressed as British officers, took command and started drilling the men into standard British firing sequence for the period. Jay Cassel inspected the troops like Napoleon.

The *Ottawa Citizen* did arrive and did its best to find some misuse of federal money, but was chagrined to find the catering reasonable, the re-enactors paying their own way, and the public not only welcome but given guided tours. Finally, the reporter, Ron Corbett, noticed something amiss, which he wrote about in the next day's *Citizen*:

I noticed Beryl Boyd, standing beside a CBC truck, shaking her head when she saw the Highlanders finally take the field. . . .

"The bagpipes are all wrong," she told me.

"What do you mean?"

"They have three drones. At the time of the Battle of the Plains of Abraham they would have had only two drones."

"Ma'am, what in the world is a drone?"

And she told me. A drone is one of those pipes sticking out from a bagpipe. . . .

I caught up with Starowicz a few minutes later and asked him about the Highlander's bagpipes. He called over Robert Henderson. Asked him if the pipes were "period accurate."

"No," said Henderson, "they have one too many drones."

Starowicz glared at that bagpipe for the next ten minutes. I got the impression he wanted to rip it out of the shot.

The next day everyone would be in a French uniform, but right now everyone was in a British uniform, including all the Quebec re-enactors. "If my great-great-grandfather could see me now," said a member of the Milice de Chambly, as he slipped on red pants, "he'd send a bolt of lightning to kill me." Half the soldiers were franco-phone, wearing Grenadier and Forty-Fifth Regiment uniforms, snapping group photographs of one another. All the various groups came with their own commanders, so Peter Twist had a general staff of about six officers, French and English, who deployed everyone into the required formations with crackling efficiency. First we'd shoot the British arriving on the field, then we'd show them forming into columns, then the British being hit by Indian and Canadien snipers in the bush. Serge was in overall command, with a megaphone. He'd consult with Twist, then point in turn to individuals: "You're dead. You're shot in the knee. You're grazed in the head. You catch your buddy to the left falling." Twist then shouted, "Battalion will come to attention." Serge called "Action," and without any shot being fired, the men enacted their fates. "Cut," Serge called, and makeup artists dashed in and rapidly painted wound marks as Gail Boyd walked down the line of the standing and the fallen, reading from her clipboard: "Grazed in the head," "Shot in the knee," "Dead with unseen wound." Gail was followed by a continuity assistant who shot Polaroids to record the precise position of each man. Then we readied everyone for the next shot. All the British action in the battle had been parsed into dozens of separate shots, each one taking about twenty minutes, with three or four scenes being shot simultaneously. Sally was in the adjacent cornfield with the second unit, shooting Canadien militiamen and Indians stalking through the withered corn and firing at the British. I wandered over and was startled by four very mean-looking militiamen in tricorne hats and three Indian warriors screaming out of the corn past me. Then I heard Sally on a bullhorn saying, "Stay out of the shot please, Mark."

On the main field, they were testing the cannon. The test explosion was startling, like a bolt of lightning bursting right beside you, and it actually hurt the eardrums. But at Serge's position there was a shaking of heads, followed by the bullhorn command: "Smoke. We need smoke on the field." Tim, the special effects man, got on the walkie-talkies and gave orders. "We need smoke. Bring out the condom."

The "condom" is about sixty metres of flexible white plastic tubing about half a metre in diameter, with five-centimetre-wide holes every ten or so centimetres. It is attached to a machine the size of a steamer trunk which, in just one minute, can blanket the entire field in fog made out of atomized lanolin. Depending on how the condom is placed and the direction of the wind, the effect is startling. "Too much smoke," Serge called over the bullhorn, since we could barely see one another now, and that was followed by Tim's voice ordering, "Shorten the condom." The deafening artillery sequences were then shot in quick succession, along with the reaction shots of soldiers in the line engulfed in smoke.

Finally, around four in the afternoon, all ninety-eight men in British uniforms were aligned, this time facing the setting sun (which would appear on TV as the rising sun, to match the morning's shooting). The big shot of the day was being prepared: the one of the single volley, more than a kilometre wide, that decimated the advancing French troops. And it was here that the computer software we had to almost extort from the CBC three months before came into play. On a platform made of scaffolding, Mike Sweeney had a stationary camera and a monitor. Below him, Serge, Gail, and Gilles Saindon from the graphics unit watched the same shot on another monitor, which had transparent acetate overlays taped to its screen, with grease-pen lines radiating on the acetate, like Mercator lines on a globe.

Using bullhorns and walkie-talkies to talk to Peter Twist and Robert Henderson, the graphics people repositioned each regiment until it fit one of the lines on the screen. There was always a regimental flag carrier at the end of the line. They were all real-life pieces being fitted into a moving jigsaw puzzle. The camera rolled, then action was stopped, uniforms altered, grenadier hats put on, regimental banners changed, and the new group was positioned farther down the imaginary front line. Each time they were shot standing and waiting, then shouldering their arms, then getting into position to fire, then firing, and so on, for over ninety minutes.

Between shots, the makeup artists leaped out from hiding again to splatter the dead, and Madeleine ran back and forth with armloads of bottled water, then with a garbage bag to reclaim every last bottle.

Finally, the squibs were brought out, bladders of red stage blood attached to a weak explosive charge and a wire threaded under the clothing to a small switch controlled by a special effects technician. On command, he pressed the switch and exploded the bladder, blowing a hole in the re-enactor's shirt and jacket, and spurting the blood out. It is remarkably effective, but as it also ruins the uniform, we could afford to use only five or six on uniforms we had had made, since we couldn't deface the rented ones.

That night Maurice Chabot, the Prince of Darkness, worked late with Wayne Chong to shoot night sequences for the next episode in the series, the War of 1812. Some of the re-enactors were bundled into 1812 uniforms to stand guard in front of General Brock's tent. Finally, at around eleven, we brought in a few cases of beer and a bottle of Scotch, and Serge Turbide, Mike Sweeney, Maurice Chabot, and

Derek Kennedy relaxed for the first time since they had got up at four that morning. We would all be back eight hours later, which was the Day of the French.

On Sunday morning, Madeleine and I woke to behold our worst nightmare come true: rain. It hadn't rained during the Battle of the Plains of Abraham 239 years ago, and no amount of computer graphics could erase rain if we shot today. All the re-enactors had to leave by four o'clock, and even if we could reconvene them sometime, it wouldn't be till next spring, and we couldn't afford it. I picked up the *Ottawa Citizen* to find a snarky full-page spread on yesterday's shoot and said to Madeleine, "Well, they'll have a real laugh in tomorrow's paper if everything crumbles this morning." We drove to North Gower and met a sombre production crew, including the assistant director, Ian Campbell, who was on two cellphones, trying to get radar readings. By this time, the rain had eased to a drizzle. "There are patches of rain all over the radar screen," he reported. "It could be sunny three kilometres away, and then change back to rain. We'll have to chance it and avoid shots with too much sky in them because of the low clouds."

There was on-again, off-again drizzle for the next two hours but no raindrops, which would have appeared as stains on the light grey French uniforms. "As it is, it's going to be a hell of a colour-balancing job back in Toronto," Mike Sweeney muttered, "with the sun on the British and no sun on the French." With nervous eyes to the sky, we started shooting on schedule. Twist and Henderson cut handsome figures in their French officers' uniforms, and all the anglophone soldiers had just been trained by the Milice de Chambly in French firing drill. The morning went at an even more furious pace than the previous day's, and it was more complex, since there were Canadien militiamen in civilian dress within the French ranks and parties of Indian snipers on the flanks. Then two splendid horses were brought onto the field with the saddle blankets and bridles of a French general.

Peter Twist, a practised horseman now dressed as Montcalm, mounted the first horse, which reared and nearly threw him. The second horse also spooked and trotted sideways into the thickets, not responding to any command. Only the owner, a woman, could control them. With time running out, Serge called a huddled war council, and within five minutes, the slender, long-haired woman, who was half Peter's weight, was dressed as Montcalm, with the aid of padding and safety pins, and her hair tucked under the tricorne hat. Since we had never intended to show Montcalm's face, just a ghostly presence in silhouette, it worked perfectly.

All day, drizzle came and went, and the winds kept shifting and blowing the smoke from the condom in the wrong direction, but Serge steadily made almost every shot on the production schedule. Now it was time for the grand shot of the whole series: the entire French army massing on top of the hill, artillery firing, then launching the offensive. Like yesterday's Thin Red Line, the image would be shot in stages and then assembled. Even before it was stitched a week later, the sight on top of the rise was awesome. First came the Canadien and Indian snipers, the regiments with all their colours streaming, the artillery being pulled by teams of men pulling block and tackle, and then – if you didn't know any better – General Montcalm.

The dramatic centre of the script was a list of names which would be read while we showed the faces of marching men – the Canadiens who had come to the defence of New France. This was the sequence I had dreamt about, which I modelled on *Culloden*. It was our tribute to Peter Watkins.

After panning the faces on the British line and naming the Scottish Highlanders who were at the Plains of Abraham because their families had been driven from the Highlands, the sequence ended with "These men have nothing left to lose." Then the Canadien sequence begins:

> Marching in the ranks of Montcalm's regiments, however, are hundreds of men who have everything to lose – fathers and sons of the great Canadien families: d'Argenteuil, Courtemanche, Repentigny. Unlike the French soldiers, the Canadiens are defending their homes and their way of life.

"François Clément Boucher de la Perrière. At fifty-one, he feels his age. "I can no longer see clearly now," he says, "though I have glasses on my nose."

Not far from him, the next generation of his family: René Amable Boucher de Boucherville. The Bouchers are defending almost 150 years of family and history.

"Charles Deschamps de Boishébert spent two years protecting fleeing Acadians from the British. He leads the Acadian militia this morning.

Under him, Joseph Trahan, eighteen, an Acadian who escaped the Deportation. This morning he's a refugee and a soldier-at-arms.

It had taken months to track down the biographies of these few ordinary men, to place them on the field of battle that day, and to give face and voice to the Canadiens on the Plains of Abraham. Tim Reibetanz had tracked Joseph Trahan through archives in Scotland and Normandy and descendants in Acadia, finally finding an interview with him in the records of the Fraser Highlanders. When he was an old man, his account of the battle had been recorded because he had been right in the line of the Highland charge.

The most challenging scene was now upon us: the French line firing on the British line, while standing no more than twelve metres away. Most of the re-enactors were in French uniforms and were preparing to fire, while a handful were in British uniforms so we could see who was being shot at. Even knowing that what was unfolding before us was staged, it was terrifying to watch. The French commander shouted "Feu!" and the field exploded with flaming muzzles and a concussion that we could feel. Everything was choked in smoke.

I finally understood how that battlefield was the mass of confusion that I had read about in contemporary accounts. In the smoke, the soldier could see only immediately around him. For a moment he didn't know if he himself had been hit somewhere, or if his sergeant or commander had been hit. He had no idea if his side was devastated. The wide line would be a confusion of shouted orders, and the enemy line might even have started a bayonet advance that would come at him in the smoke. His side might have sounded a retreat that he hadn't heard. For what must have seemed like an eternity, he was lost in hell.

Now came the final scene: the French line being hit by the British volley, then breaking and retreating. This was the moment I was most worried about, as it is a lot to ask men to re-enact the fall of their own ancestors, in the battle where they lost their country. It's also a complicated scene that requires the men to act, and these men were not actors. With the sky looking as though it would rain any minute, and the clock approaching three, Serge and Peter urgently choreographed the line in about ten minutes: "You fall on the ground, and you pick him up like this," Serge instructed. "You, hold your ground and fire off one wild shot before you run. And you, you look dazed and confused." I ran up to the top of the hill, where Mike Sweeney had set up his camera for the master shot. Chabot and Kennedy were below to shoot the close-ups of the French line breaking, but the drama would culminate with the soldiers rushing toward Sweeney's camera. From the top of the hill, I could see Serge in the distance, moving down the line in a series of pantomimes, reeling onto his back, kneeling and firing, or grabbing someone and running – in short, looking like a man possessed. Madeleine was running through the line passing out water bottles, while the makeup people inflicted appalling wounds and the props crew fussed over the giant regimental flag in the hands of the colour-bearer.

Finally the wind was right, the condom emitted billows of smoke along a thirty-metre line, all cameras were rolling, and the signal shots were fired. The activity below was frantic. While Chabot and Kennedy picked close-ups through the line, some men were falling, others firing, others breaking into a run. They scrambled, limped, or crawled up the hill toward the camera, flitting past us as if we weren't there, engulfing Montcalm, who was behind us on a rearing and panicked horse. After two minutes of watching an army disintegrate,

Serge called "Cut!" and the scene was over. I thought it was great, particularly since Chabot and Kennedy had not shot prearranged scenes; they had behaved just as documentary cameramen would, catching what action they could on the fly. But after a few moments, I could see something was wrong. There were clusters of re-enactors huddling below. Richard Fortin, who had been beside me at Sweeney's camera position, went down to talk to some of the soldiers.

"I saw a group of French soldiers who were very upset," he says. "When I asked them why, one answered, 'We just filmed a scene in which we abandon the regimental flag to the enemy – that's unacceptable.' They explained that you never abandon the flag, because that is the honour of the regiment, and the French and Canadien soldiers on the Plains of Abraham had never abandoned their colours."

This is what I was afraid of, a mid-battle debate, and I went down to see what was happening and found myself surrounded by English re-enactors, in French uniforms, who couldn't understand what the French were saying, but who repeated their complaint: "The French would never abandon their colours," one insisted. "This makes this whole scene unreal." I told them we had run out of time and promised we'd edit around it, but this didn't please anyone. Finally Serge came down with Richard and Gail, and huddled briefly with Twist and the cameramen. "If you're willing to stay a bit longer," he called out, "we'll redo the shot." There were cheers and applause from the ranks.

On top of the hill again, Richard and I and Sally were watching on a monitor as all the "Stand by" and "Rolling" sequences were called, and the condom started spewing smoke again. But the wind had shifted and the smoke was not only covering the field, it was creeping up the hill toward us. In a minute we could see nothing, neither on the monitor nor in reality. Soon soldiers were running at us out of the white wall of smoke, and I was almost trampled by the retreating flag-bearer. When Serge called "Cut," Mike was shaking his head. "Did you see anything on the monitor?" he asked me. "Not much," I said gloomily. "We oversmoked it. What a rotten ending to a shoot." We started packing up. Once the smoke cleared, we saw everyone below us congratulating one another, unaware that the shot was ruined.

The tapes from each cameraman were immediately taken by a runner down to the main tent, where Murray Green had a screening station set up to check all tapes and monitor picture quality. Slowly, Serge and Gail and Madeleine and I wandered down there, passing the cannon crew hauling the gun carriage off the field. "Boy, I really felt sorry for that guy," Madeleine said, pointing to one of the men in the gun crew. "Why?" I asked, since he seemed no worse for wear. "I was next to him most of the time this weekend," she said, "and he had to repaint the whole gun three times." I didn't know this. "Yes," she said, "every time you guys switched armies, he had to repaint everything." We strolled slowly, picking up trash.

We were practically the last to reach the screening tent. "Have you seen the last shot of the retreat?" Murray asked. I told him I had seen it live on Mike's monitor, and it had been smoked out. "Watch this!" he said. The wide field came into view, with ghostly figures moving in the smoke, then slowly, the army disintegrated and clusters of men started running up the hill in the fog – completely visible! In the background, we could see four Canadien militiamen in habitant dress form a line and fire at the English, then out of the smoke appeared the figure of the French colour-bearer, running directly at the camera, his regimental flag filling the screen. It was magnificent! It could not have been more perfectly framed if Sweeney had been able to see the action, which he hadn't.

Over the next hour, Murray was made to play the tape over and over for all the re-enactors and production crew. "It's the series poster shot," he declared. Hubert was beaming: "The French colours defended by four Canadien militiamen," he said. "You couldn't pray for a greater shot." Richard, who had reason to take considerable credit for persuading everyone to retake the shot, said with quiet satisfaction, "What's good about this is that 239 years after the battle, the re-enactors themselves are animated by the same passion as their ancestors." What was more remarkable to me was that half the re-enactors who were applauding were descendants of the English side.

The day ended with great relief and satisfaction. This had been a baptism of fire for a documentary unit thrown into drama-scale production, and after months of hand-wringing over narrative and visual style, we had crossed from theoretical debate to reality. We knew it would work. And we had set the benchmark for the series.

12

Mission to Caraquet

While Jay Cassel and I were writing the Plains of Abraham episode that summer, battling mosquitoes and chasing windblown pages, Laine Drewery was shooting the American Revolution and the War of 1812, the next episode.

In Toronto, Laine, who managed to have a permanent five-day growth of beard, could usually be found smoking in front of the building, pacing worriedly, looking more like a racetrack tout with a bad ticket than one of the best documentary producers in Canada. When he wasn't outside, smoking, he could be found in his office, glaring at his computer monitor. People learned not to ask him how his script was going because they'd get a half-hour answer. "He's crazy," Alan Mendelsohn would allow. "But he's good. He's intense." Laine described Mendelsohn in roughly the same terms, adding, "Granted, he's a bit colourful."

The three of us sparked a lot of ideas in one another, which was difficult since we all spoke at once. Going out for a drink with them in the late afternoon meant writing off the rest of the day and at least half of the next, and the business department shuddered at the thought of the grand schemes we'd dream up. Laine had a theatrical speaking style that involved a lot of gestures, and at the bar he would perform scenes from the American Revolution, the flight of the Loyalists, and the War of 1812 – all in vivid and voluble detail and punctuated with modern observations like "You know, Brock was really a bit of a shit" and "The governor's daughter was a real babe." Like the rest of us, he was learning much of the story for the first time. "I didn't know any of this going in," he said. "I had never been taught that the American Revolution was a civil war between Loyalists and rebels. It made me realize just how much the Americans have succeeded in mythologizing their history and burying the Loyalist side. This wasn't just a war of liberation against a colonial power, it was a long and bloody struggle of Americans versus Americans."

The Loyalists have been portrayed as effete British fellow-travellers in American mythology, and as displaced victims in the Canadian story. In fact, most Loyalists – or Tories, as the rebels called them – were ordinary farmers and shopkeepers, just as the rebels were. They were anything but passive victims, and some of their guerrilla units were brilliant and ruthlessly effective commandos. "Why didn't we know anything about them in school?" Laine asked. "They were ten times more swashbuckling than Davy Crockett and Daniel Boone."

I asked him if researching and directing his episode had changed him. "It was a complete revelation to me," he said. "For the first time I realized that these Loyalists were my people. That we were born of the revolution, just as the United States was. I understand why we feel so deeply connected to the Americans, but also why we are so different."

Laine had a difficult task. In a single episode, he had to cover from 1774, where we had left off my episode after the Quebec Act, to the end of the War of 1812. Unlike my task in "Battle for a Continent," Laine's brief involved shooting in many locations in period dress uniforms that changed over forty years.

The weekend before the Plains of Abraham shoot in September, he had taken over Upper Canada Village, west of Cornwall, Ontario, and staged an impressive number of reconstructions: American rebels expelling a Loyalist family, the flight of the Loyalists, the surrender of Fort Saint-Jean, the Battle of Châteauguay, and the raids by Butler's Rangers into the Mohawk Valley. The latter involved setting a barn on fire. "We found this log building without a roof," he reported, "and persuaded the park to let us use it. They said OK, providing we didn't burn it down, or there'd be real trouble." A special effects technician, Gus White, rigged propane pipes along the upper walls, then donned firefighting equipment and entered the structure. "He said he could give us twenty seconds of flames," Laine said, "and then he'd have to douse them. He was actually inside the place while it burned." The blaze went perfectly, without a scorch mark, but Mike Sweeney's tripod had been jostled by a few pigs. "These were huge, black things," Laine recounted, "easily 800 pounds each, the size of a hippopotamus." Gus White had to restage the fire while kicking giant pigs out of the way. "The final shot looked terrific. Good man, Gus."

While Laine was fending off giant pigs in Upper Canada Village, he was also getting nervous about the Plains of Abraham shoot scheduled for the next weekend. The battle was having an inflationary effect on all the other battle scenes planned in the series. "I had to do the Battle of Lundy's Lane in the War of 1812 three weeks after the Plains shoot, and I was feeling that my battle was going to look pretty scruffy. And yet this was one of the defining moments of Canadian history." He knew he couldn't go over budget, so he rescheduled other small shoots to the weekend he was staging Lundy's Lane, raising the number of soldiers on site from twenty-two to eighty.

Laine was new to large-scale dramatic reconstruction. Pim van der Toorn, his unit manager, remembers how Laine slowly realized what he had gotten himself into. "A production meeting is standard in the drama world," he recalls, "but a bit intimidating when you haven't been to one. This is where directors tell the different departments what is expected of them during each scene. Well, as the room filled up with one or two people each from hair, makeup, wardrobe, props, special effects, carpentry and paint, lighting, staging, camera, and so on, I could see Laine's face drawing tighter and paler. After a while, I leaned over and whispered, 'Laine, do you want me to start the meeting for you?' and he said, 'Yeah. Good idea. In fact, why don't you run the whole thing?'"

In one weekend at Fort George, outside Niagara-on-the-Lake, Laine had scheduled a virtual Armageddon: the outbreak of the War of 1812, the Battle of Châteauguay, Brock leading the charge up Queenston Heights, Brock being shot, and of course the Battle of Lundy's Lane. The only bloodless scene was a recreation of the governor's ball. In that one weekend, Peter Twist had to go through enough costume changes to get a skin rash. He was an American officer, then a British officer, then a *voltigeur* at Châteauguay, then another British commander, then one of Brock's infantry, then an effete British toff at the governor's ball. It was a masterwork of planning and logistics by Drewery and Pim van der Toorn, but it was a killer schedule. "I slept six hours in three days," Laine said, "and all I could do was pray for it to be over and promise that I'd never, ever do anything as complicated as this again." Then I arrived and nearly destroyed his shoot.

I had driven down from Toronto just to watch and learn and take stills for the publicity department. I arrived to find batteries of lights, cannon, and an entire graveyard erected in a field opposite Fort George. The nighttime Battle of Lundy's Lane, fought in a cemetery, was Canada's last desperate defence against American invasion and also the bloodiest of the war. Six thousand British, Canadian, and American soldiers had ended up bayoneting and clubbing one another in hand-to-hand combat. Sergeant James Cummins described the aftermath: "The morning light ushered to our view a shocking spectacle. Americans and English laid upon each other . . . Nearly 2,000 was [sic] left on the field." An American soldier had described the scene Laine was trying to reconstruct: "The opposing lines were so near each other that at the flash of the enemy's guns [we could] see the faces and even mark the countenance of their adversaries. . . . The darkness and the smoke combined with the fitful light made the faces of those in the opposition ranks wear a blue sulphurous hue, and the men at each flash had the appearance of laughing."

I watched as the twilight faded and the battery of lights simulating moonlight were switched on. The scene became eerily real. The outlines of soldiers marching through the graveyard, the flashes of the cannon, and the gleam of bayonets conveyed the grim hellishness of this terrible battle. The re-enactors were sombre too, respectful of the horror that the soldiers had gone through. Laine had given a couple of soldiers small camcorders to supplement the three big cameras that were shooting the action, and the disarrayed shots he got that way captured the chaos of the battle.

Laine was racing the clock. The permit the municipality had given us to fire muskets and cannon expired at 11:30, after which there could be no noise. At 10:30 he made a controversial decision: he wanted to stage the hand-to-hand combat. Pim objected strongly: "We don't have stuntmen, we don't have rubber bayonets, we aren't insured for this. It's crazy!" Peter Twist agreed with Pim, but the re-enactors took Laine's side. They proposed to do it safely by first pairing off and choreographing movements one man to another, so there would be no improvisation during the actual shoot. Pim and Peter relented, and the re-enactors rehearsed their movements. When they were ready, the field was hushed, and I moved over to the monitor at the main camera position. Field sound was essential for the shoot, and the boom mike was beside me. The action was unleashed, everyone watched tensely, and then: *breeep, breeeep, breeep*. I had committed the cardinal sin of leaving my cellphone on during a shoot, and it was beeping into the mike. Everyone, including soldiers in mid-combat, turned to glower at me. I reddened and flipped open the phone. It was my wife. "I can't talk now," I said, "I'm in the middle of a battle." Later that was voted the single most ridiculous sentence uttered in the series. A household emergency required me to rush back to Toronto, which was just as well, since I was too embarrassed to hang around the shoot. With me out of the way, the retake went brilliantly and no one was injured, just my pride.

The success of the Plains of Abraham and Lundy's Lane shoots worked wonders for the morale of the unit in Toronto, but Gordon, Hubert, and I were anxious about the 1837 Rebellion shoot, which was to take place next. Peter Ingles, the director, and his producer, Frédéric Vanasse, were diligent, organized, but taciturn, so we had no idea if they were shooting in the same style as the rest. The three of us went to Carillon in Quebec, to play observer while they filmed the Battle of Saint-Denis. I drove from Montreal and was surprised when I arrived to find painted plywood panels erected here and there. One was a two-metre house, painted on a two-by-three-metre sheet of plywood. Another was a tree; another a shack. All of them had a distorted perspective that made them look cartoonish. I drove down the main street and up the hill to the shooting location, past people dressed in top hats and frock coats, in habitant dress carrying muskets, and in British army uniforms with tall hats. I looked at the top of the hill and saw a large farmhouse rocking in the wind. It was unsettling until I realized it wasn't really a farmhouse, just a twelve-by-six-metre painting of a farmhouse on a flat.

I found Hubert in the field on his cellphone. "What's going on with all the flats all over town?" I asked. "I feel like I'm in Toontown." The flats were masking fire hydrants, newspaper boxes, and modern buildings, Hubert explained. "They look like cartoon buildings in real life, but that's because of the camera angle and correcting for parallax view." I went to a camera and looked through the lens, and the difference was incredible. The village was now pure 1830s. Nothing looked fake.

"You know the skirmishes we've been having with the Montreal plant?" Hubert said when I'd satisfied myself that the town looked the part. He was alluding to the foot-dragging and lack of co-operation we had been getting from those in charge of technical services, staging, and production. For months we had been told that all facilities and services had been booked months, even years ahead and that they had nothing for us. They were treating us like an outside production, a private company with no direct access to Radio-Canada services, unless we paid full market rates. "Well, they've gone too far this time," Hubert said in barely controlled fury. We were short of stagehands at Carillon, and on Friday the team had called for more. The technical producer at the Montreal plant had not returned the call. Another was on sick leave. In desperation, the unit called the technical assignment department and asked directly for stagehands. We had a huge, expensive shoot, and we should have had a technical producer there to help us.

"Now," Hubert went on, "listen to this message which I just got from the deputy plant head. I saved it." It was almost like a call from a Mafia hit man. The voice said we were creating unacceptable pressures and tensions and that a directive had gone to all their people, forbidding them to speak with the Canadian History Project people. This can't go on, the voice said, adding, "It's going to get ugly." Hubert and I had both thought the foot-dragging from the Montreal plant was just bureaucracy. Now it was clear we were facing open hostility at the upper administrative level.

As the shoot started and muskets began firing, Hubert and I walked grimly off to the side and digested the realization that we had a major war to fight of our own. We had been virtually threatened with sabotage. "The period was for me the most difficult and nastiest part of the whole project," Hubert says. "From the start we had been hemorrhaging money because the plant was treating us as an outside production, and we could never get a proper accounting." Hubert was bearing on his shoulders all the weight of properly representing French-Canadian history, only to find his enemies were not in Toronto but in Montreal. "At one point," he says, "the costume department told us they would rent Radio-Canada costumes at the commercial rate they charged outside productions. This despite the fact that our unit had *bought* more than $10,000 worth of costumes from the series *Big Bear* which were now *their* property. When I pointed that out, they were prepared to let us use the costumes we had bought at no charge, but we would still have to pay for all the others. This was presented as 'a policy' from higher up."

Their intransigence made Hubert recall something he hadn't paid much attention to before. "One of our production assistants once told me that one of the location directors had told him over a beer that his job was to make sure we failed – 'qu'ils se cassent la gueule' [let them bash their faces in]. I told the PA this was nonsense, that it must have been a joke. Now I believe him."

If there was someone in Montreal plant management, or higher, who was trying to screw us, it wasn't evident from what happened at Carillon that weekend. Radio-Canada drama production units are the best in the country, and the precision and skill they brought to reconstructing the 1837 Rebellion was impressive. The Battle of Saint-Denis had been a victory for Patriote rebels fighting for democratic rights against a draconian British regime. Civilians had erected barricades at the edge of the village and forced the retreat of a major column of troops under the command of Colonel Charles Gore. Later, in retaliation, the village had been burned.

Peter Ingles and Frédéric Vanasse were shooting an epic story, every bit as powerful as the Plains and Lundy's Lane episodes. Once again I felt the terrifying reality of a column of men with fixed bayonets coming at the barricades. René Chartrand, our historical adviser, was there to pronounce on the authenticity of every garment, every artifact. Even for him, the national expert on the rebellions, the event was frightening. "I am a military historian," he wrote to me later, commenting on this shoot and the subsequent Battle of Saint-Eustache, "but like most people, thank goodness, I have never experienced battle, and certainly not the linear tactics in use previous to the twentieth century, with troops in battle lines, volley fire, and bayonet charges. After this experience, I would much rather continue being an 'armchair general.' Another thing that struck me was seeing troops accurately uniformed and equipped for once, skirting along the walls of street houses, occasionally and methodically breaking into some of them. Would you like to see this on your own street . . . ? It must have been horrid for the ordinary, innocent people."

In the days after the Battle of Saint-Eustache, the British soldiers and volunteers spread terror throughout the county of Deux-Montagnes, looting and burning scores of homes and entire villages. A year later, one thousand Glengarry Highlanders and militiamen from Upper Canada burned the whole Beauharnois region, leaving a ten-kilometre-wide trail of destruction, which even the fiercely pro-English Montreal *Gazette* described as horrific: "All the country back of Laprairie represented the frightful spectacle of a vast expanse of livid flame."

The Patriotes and their counterparts in Upper Canada, led by William Lyon Mackenzie, were fighting for basic democracy and elementary liberty, but hardly any English Canadian has ever heard of Saint-Denis, Saint-Charles, and Saint-Eustache. Had this happened in the United States, the Americans would have made a national holiday to commemorate the French and English insurrections.

Walking down the street in Carillon, I was greeted here and there by a group of Patriotes or by British soldiers returning from the food tent. I recognized faces but couldn't place them, since they were in such different clothing. Many were veterans of the Plains and Lundy's Lane shoots and had made the long journey to participate in Saint-Denis. I was heartened to see people so devoted to the honest portrayal of history that they were prepared to recreate a crime like the burning of a church committed by their own ancestors. René Chartrand was also impressed and later told me, "Perhaps a fine ray of hope for me was that all those involved were from diverse backgrounds but mostly from the two 'founding nations,' as we used to say, and all worked in harmony and made fun and jokes between shooting scenes for Saint-Denis and Saint-Eustache, no matter what their personal politics were."

I spent the evening in a chicken and ribs tavern with the Radio-Canada crew and was moved to see about thirty people rise at the end and raise their glasses in a raucous toast to Radio-Canada. They were proud to be involved in telling their own history and proud that it would be seen by the whole country. Whatever the bad faith in Montreal, this team was making sure everything was done impeccably, because it was their story.

While churches were being bombarded for the episode on the 1837 Rebellions, Jim Williamson was browsing through the archives of the Grey Nuns in Montreal. The order ministered to the sick and the abandoned and kept meticulous accounts of their work. Their

vaults contain "one of the greatest treasuries of Canadian history,"
Jim says.

Jim was writing and directing the complex, three-hour episode
on Confederation, and the records of the Grey Nuns were indispensable for an accurate social portrait of the 1860s. When they were first
approached, the nuns had been cordial but cautious. "Finally," Jim
says, "one of the senior nuns came out with it. She asked my colleague Johanne Ménard if this history was a sovereignist project or a
federalist project. Neither, replied Johanne, it's as objective and accurate as we can make it. The sister visibly relaxed, and soon we had
access to everything. It was a reminder of how politics in Quebec
permeates everything."

Jim had been a member of *The Journal*'s senior editorial staff and
had worked with Hubert Gendron in Montreal. He is fluently bilingual, and his knowledge of Quebec history and his relationship with
Hubert made him ideal for this episode. He knew that to make the
complex constitutional negotiations interesting, he had to tell the
story through its characters, not its committee meetings. One such
character was Jane Slocum, the English mother superior of the Grey
Nuns, whose diaries gave a picture of how hard and desperate the
lives of Irish immigrants were in Montreal. The order had cared for
hundreds of babies deposited at their door by mothers unable to
look after them. On the political side, the words of the Irish revolutionary turned Canadian nationalist Thomas D'Arcy McGee and the
bombastic, anti-French George Brown brought the passion of the
times to life.

Jim covered the closed-door Quebec Conference as a news
camera would cover it today – from the outside, with no access to the
committee rooms. "Half the drama occurred during the social events
at night," he said. "It was more dramatic to describe the great negotiations through the gossipy diaries and spicy letters of the delegates
and their wives." He shot the exteriors in Quebec City, reproducing
the endless rainy days of the negotiations with the aid of the local fire
department, which pointed its hoses into the air. Then to stage the
night of the great ball, he took over the St. Lawrence Hall in Toronto,

brought in dancers from the National Ballet, actors, and extras, and caught on video every facet of that glittering night.

"Usually, a film set is only partially dressed to cover only what the camera will be pointing at," Jim says. "But here, we were shooting the entire ballroom, as the camera swept across the floor during the waltzes, so we dressed the entire room. It wasn't a set, it was a time machine. After a while, people weren't acting, they had become the characters in a Victorian ball."

We were very busy that fall, with many simultaneous shoots, among them the Acadian Deportation, which was being staged in Caraquet, New Brunswick, under the direction of Claude Lortie. He brought back superb footage that rivalled anything we had shot. The series was starting to feel truly epic, and the documentary directors had all risen and met the dramatic challenge. But while the unit's morale was high, Hubert, Gordon, Gene, Anne, and I knew we were caught in a trap. Our fortunes would take us back to Caraquet very soon, on a very different mission.

It had been six months since I had written the memo saying the series would cost $25 million. Although everyone in Toronto from Jim Byrd down took this to be the operating estimate, we still had no clearance to spend at that level. So I had kept deferring critical decisions and episode divisions in the expectation that I would soon receive word. Furthermore, fourteen months from air date, we still didn't know if the series would have a full commercial load or not. If the series was to be thirty hours, full commercialization meant it would have to be six hours shorter than if it carried no advertising at all. No one was giving us an answer on commercialization, or even the ultimate budget, because they were hoping we'd raise $8 million in corporate sponsorship. And that hadn't happened. In fact, for five months, no one had even tried to get sponsorship because the president and the chair seemed unable to communicate.

Was the series spending $20 million or $25 million? Was it thirty hours of content, twenty-four, or twenty? The variables were so wild that it was impossible to plan. I was now telling directors to plan their episodes to be either 120 minutes long or 96 minutes long, and that I didn't know if they would be broadcast in two-hour blocks or one-hour blocks. This is like trying to bake a cake and delaying the decision if it's chocolate or vanilla till it's in the oven. My instructions to them were absolutely absurd, and I'm surprised and grateful they even tolerated such wildly oscillating parameters. I didn't tell them the whole story behind these vague instructions, because the worst thing that could have happened was a leak to the papers that made it look like the project was on the road to disaster. In the senior group, we were still loyal to the CBC chain of command, even if it made us look like idiots before our own troops.

But the human toll this was taking was becoming intolerable. Directors were frustrated, the business unit in despair, historians in disbelief, while Hubert, Gene, Gord, and I swung between depression and pure fury. There were weeks of anxious, sleepless nights for all of us, and much family grief as a consequence. It seemed impossible that the CBC would leave us swinging in the wind like this simply out of departmental and divisional gridlock, and head office paralysis. Yet it was happening. It was almost comic: a head office where no one had ever produced a program was like having military chiefs of staff who had never fought a battle. It was something out of *Yes, Minister*. A giant fundraising plan where no one was allowed to make a phone call to raise money was absurd, surreal. But it's just not so funny when it's backfiring on people who have only one asset: their reputations. Yet Gene, Gord, Hubert, Sally, and Anne would all be seen as the people who screwed up the history of Canada.

"We can be complicit in an evolving disaster and tell the true facts later, when no one will believe us anyway," I wrote in my journal. "Or we can force the facts out now, with the result that we're fired, or the problems are solved. Anything to end this senseless limbo." Hubert and I had been talking for hours late into the night for days, trying to wrestle with all this, when he finally said: "Mark, I'd rather be unemployed at fifty-five than live one more day of this horror."

Perrin Beatty had dropped in to see me in late August, and I had outlined our dilemma, how nothing had been done about corporate sponsorship. "It's a personality thing, I guess," he said. "I just can't seem to get the chair's agreement." I asked him what I was supposed to do. "Mark, if anyone can find an answer," he said, "it will be you." I was irritated, because he was just throwing the problem back into my lap. So finally I came up with the answer, though I don't think it was one Perrin had contemplated. We would go over the heads of the chair and the president, something that's never done in a corporation, nor should it be necessary to do, because it violates every rule of corporate governance. But it had come down to a choice between two disgraces: either botch making the history of Canada or end-run management. The choice was easy.

We knew, from the team that was working on the Acadian Deportation, that one member of the board surpassed the others in his support of this project. Clarence LeBreton is a community leader in Caraquet, a tall man with a moustache and an effusive personality who speaks his mind. At the board meeting of March 1997, he had said, "If you ever need my help, call me." Now I proposed to take him up on his offer.

I unveiled the proposal in a late-night conference call with Louis Martin and Hubert Gendron. Of the three of us, Louis Martin seemed to be our best envoy. His reputation as one of the great statesmen of journalism, especially French-Canadian journalism, was unexcelled. Was he prepared to fly to New Brunswick and meet privately with LeBreton to describe the paralysis we were caught in? The unspoken stakes were these: If this collaboration between the French and English CBC turned into a disaster, then there wouldn't be another attempt for at least a generation. It would play into the hands of anyone who believed there was no point in collaborating, and there were plenty of people in both language groups who would enjoy the failure. This was something neither Louis Martin nor Clarence LeBreton wanted. It was certainly anathema to everything LeBreton, as an Acadian, believed.

The idea was for Louis to call LeBreton and ask for an off-the-record meeting on a matter of great importance to the Canadian History Project. We had a crew shooting in the vicinity, so there was a justification for Louis to check on their progress. He would fly out the next day to Moncton, drive to Caraquet, and reveal everything to LeBreton. The question was whether LeBreton would be willing to place an item about the history project on the agenda of the November board meeting, which would force decisions on budget, commercials, and length of the series.

Louis agreed immediately to undertake the mission. This was a dramatic move for someone who had been in management at Radio-Canada in his last job. It felt like mutiny, but, as Louis said, "We are turning to the legal board of directors of the CBC, which is hardly terrorism."

Louis arrived in Caraquet and told LeBreton the sorry story, which scandalized him. "It didn't take a lot of explaining," Louis reported. "For LeBreton, this French-English unit was everything he had been fighting for. He said to leave it with him. I stressed that this meeting had never occurred. He understood." Clearly Louis's mission had succeeded, for, as he reported, "We had a bottle or two of rather good wine. He is a very good host."

We waited. None of us in the senior group was at all comfortable with this kind of end run. In my thirty years at the CBC, I had never once considered resorting to this. Furthermore, we really didn't have an adversary – just entropy. Hurling the white ball at the cluster of coloured balls on the billiard table, which we had just done, is not exactly playing tactical pool, since you don't know where any ball will go.

LeBreton called Louis Martin back to inform him that he had phoned Guylaine Saucier, and the issue was now an item for the November meeting. No more detail than that. To marshal all our facts and arguments in anticipation, I sat down to write my second "Status of the Canadian History Project" report in six months. At this stage, there was no point mincing words. "The combined French-English unit has worked. But its environment has been, frankly, hell," I wrote. "The solitudes of CBC/SRC [Société Radio-Canada] have complex immune systems to reject such collaboration." I recalled that we were promised "full mobilization" and that the president had declared the project to be the top priority of the corporation. "Instead, we have paid for every nail, every piece of construction, every incremental infrastructure need, every field camera case, every cost of going against the gravitational laws of the system." Other programs operate within departmental infrastructures that have production managers, unit managers, and cameramen that are provided to them – departments like news, drama, or sports. We weren't part of any department, because there was no such thing as a French-English department, so we had to build our own infrastructure. We estimated that it had cost us $2.5 million just to function as an isolated unit between the CBC and Radio-Canada universes and we did not want to be billed for that out of a budget that was meant strictly for shooting a series. "*We should not have to pay out of the production budget,*" I wrote in italics, "*for the structural flaws of the system.*"

The problem was systemic. "Every step we take," I wrote, "we seem to have to first perform a marriage between two graphic departments, two sound post-production departments, two industrial relations departments. This has been mind-numbingly time-consuming."

I thought it was important to put the cost of *Canada: A People's History* in some international context. Far from being lavish, our series was a bargain. *The West*, by Stephen Ives, cost the equivalent of $13 million Canadian to produce thirteen hours – a series less than half our length, in only one language, and it was five years in production. *Liberty! The American Revolution* cost $7 million for six hours in one language – that's one-fifth of our series length – and it took five years to produce. *The Great War*, a PBS-BBC series, was five years in production and a quarter of the scale of our series, with no recreations because it was all in the photographic era, and it cost $8 million. "Factor in language," I wrote, "and *Canada: A People's History* is strikingly cheaper than all models above. Time from assembly of unit to first airdate: *less than two years.*"

I concluded: "There is going to be a day – not far off, 15 months – when this series is no longer a debate about how things should be done or not be done. It will be on our launch pads, carrying every controversy of our history and our peoples, from the Northwest Rebellion to the Manitoba Schools Question, and carrying the very definition of this Corporation's raison d'être. It will be watched by children, every historian, every parliamentarian; it will be scrutinized for every shade of bias, for every exclusion, for every portrayal. There will be acres of media attention. We have, for better or worse, invested our corporate image as two language networks in one great enterprise.

"It's going to feel really tense and scary. That will *not* be the time to ask: 'Maybe we should have paid a little more attention to what the team was trying to tell us.'"

I sent the memo to Bob Culbert and Claude Saint-Laurent, to arm them for the board meeting. Soon afterwards – too soon for the memo to have reached Ottawa – Rachel Brown got a call from Guylaine Saucier's office, saying the chair would like to meet with me the next time she was in Toronto. I saw this as evidence that our mission to Caraquet had set wheels in motion. Rachel arranged for Saucier to visit the office, meet the team, and screen some footage.

The meeting had been scheduled for four o'clock. Everyone was on high alert not to go out between four and six in case we came by with the chair. All day, desks were being cleared, old piles of newspapers and coffee cups were thrown out, half-dead ivy in hanging baskets was pruned and watered. Two floors up, in the screening theatre, Casey Kollontay drove the maintenance people crazy testing speakers and tweaking the notoriously fickle video projector. Rachel had worked out the route of the tour and a system to alert each post when the royal visit was about to turn the corner.

At 4:00 P.M. I walked into the office Saucier kept in Toronto. "Everyone's eager to show you what we're doing, Madame," I said as I entered.

"Sit down, Mark," she said sternly. "I'm not going anywhere."

I sat down across the desk from her, and she rocked back and forth in her swivel chair and looked at me like a school principal addressing an errant student. She was clearly furious as she spoke.

"This whole history project has become a scandal," she said. "I have just come out of the PMO, and it is making us look very, very bad."

For the life of me, I had no idea what she was talking about. What could the PMO possibly know about the history project that I didn't? For a few moments I expected to hear some revelation of malfeasance by one of our units, or some appalling action by someone that would be in tomorrow's papers.

"I live in the same condominium in Montreal as Red Wilson," she continued. Red Wilson was the chairman of the CIBC bank and of Historica, which was trying to raise millions to set up a fund to support Canadian history studies and projects. "And I saw Red in the parking garage, and do you know what he told me? He said he would never dream of supporting the 'People's History of Canada' because of the irresponsible spending of your project. This is making the CBC look bad, look very very bad in the PMO, and do you realize what a critical point this is for the CBC with the government?"

I interjected after a few minutes to ask: "Madame, what precisely is the financial scandal?"

"You have spent all the money – millions," she replied. "You have already gone over your budget."

"What is your source for that, Madame?" I asked.

"I've been hearing reports everywhere. It was even in *Frank* recently."

There isn't a word in English that describes the mixed sensation of relief at discovering your fear is unfounded and horror at discovering another, even greater fear, dawning. I couldn't believe that anyone would get their political and financial intelligence from a magazine that no one takes seriously. It was staggering.

"As I recall, that was just a couple of paragraphs buried somewhere in the magazine," I said, and laughed in disbelief.

"This is not a humorous matter," she snapped. "You have changed your original financial projection until it is three times what we were told it would cost us; first it was $12 million, then $20 million, and now you have run out of that too. Do you deny that you have spent your budget already?"

There was no way this meeting was going to end well, I thought. The project looked like it was up the flue, so there was no point being delicate any more.

"You've had your say, Madame," I began. "Now you will be gracious enough to let me have mine. First, I am still sitting here in disbelief that you are quoting *Frank* to me or getting your information from a parking lot conversation. Second, not a single statement you have made is accurate. We are not over budget by any stretch. We only began shooting six months ago, and it would be physically impossible to go over budget. To date we have spent approximately $5 million, which is about a fifth of the projected budget.

"There never was a budget that said the series would cost $12 million. That figure is the CBC's portion of a $20.5-million estimate from when we were in partnership with the National Film Board. Last July, in a properly documented meeting, the president and several vice-presidents signed off on the full amount. In fact, we warned them at that meeting that the series would more properly cost upwards of $25 million.

"There was only one budget revision, and that came in a memorandum written by me prior to the board meeting of last March, which discussed the project and which you did not attend. In fact, I don't believe you have seen anything of this project to date. We submitted revised budget estimates that showed the higher figure of $25 million was the realistic figure and requested permission to operate at that level. Submitting a revised estimate based on preliminary operations, two years before broadcast, before spending the funds, and giving the management other options, is perfectly responsible business procedure. Not to present revised projections would be the irresponsible act. Monthly costing reports of every aspect of this project have been routinely sent up the chain."

I went into detail about the various budget estimates and reporting procedures. While I spoke, Saucier's face was impassive. She swivelled slowly left and right in her chair, but she was listening without interrupting. I was convinced the project had died in this office, this afternoon, and I was almost relieved. I wanted no further part of this lunacy.

So I told her, "There are, however, scandals surrounding this project, you're right. And since you have been frank, Madame, you will perhaps not be offended if I am equally frank.

"For the first time in CBC/Radio-Canada history, a team of French and English journalists, historians, technicians, and artists have attempted to bridge the cultural divide which you have eloquently addressed yourself as the greatest tragedy in the CBC. The first scandal, then, is that Head Office has thrown up every conceivable bureaucratic obstacle." I described the long delays about getting cameras and edit suites, the proposition that we should buy our own cameras, and the chaos all this created. "We have not only two language solitudes, but two technical solitudes which don't even use the same equipment, two accounting universes, two totally different universes of labour unions so that it's impossible to sign rational contracts with actors, even impossible to call one person a journalist in both jurisdictions, two different pay levels, computer graphics departments which don't even use the same computer programs and therefore cannot send files back and forth. The French network was treating our own French team as if it were an outside production company, and billing us for tens of thousands of dollars of costs.

"The senior management's job was to protect us and support this expedition into the no man's land between CBC and Radio-Canada. That was promised by the president in the July meeting: full corporate support. We got nothing. Instead we have been abandoned by Ottawa. That's the first scandal.

"The second is that we have spent months trying to bring all the disparate parts of the CBC and Radio-Canada together to go out and look for corporate sponsorship. Bear in mind that that's not even our job as journalists, and we could face criticism for crossing the line between production and fundraising. But never mind – we went to banks, we went to John Rae and Power Corporation, we even had the active support of the governor general. Finally, John Lewis managed to get everyone in one room and sign off on a fundraising plan." I described the meeting and Perrin Beatty's final comment: "I think I should fly this past the chair."

"Since last May – and this is November – I have heard absolutely nothing. The CBC hasn't gone out and tried to raise one penny. Total gridlock. I'm too embarrassed even to talk to the governor general. Now, I'm prepared to take responsibility for a lot of things, and I miscalculated a lot. But the biggest thing I miscalculated is the competence and even the goodwill of Head Office. And I'll be damned if the people waiting downstairs are going to take the rap for the worst management mess I've seen in my life. We should not have been put in this spot. We are not taking the rap for a dysfunctional corporation. Thank you for listening to me. I realize you have to go. I'd better get down to the unit and tell them the visit is off."

I rose, she rose, we shook hands awkwardly, and I walked to the history project office, on the other side of the building, trying to think what I would tell everyone.

"So what's happening?" Rachel asked eagerly. "Where's Madame Saucier?"

"She's not coming," I said. "Tell everyone to stand down in the edit suites and shut down the theatre. Tell them she had a conflicting appointment." In the conference room, all the senior editors from Toronto and Montreal had started into the sandwich tray Rachel had ordered. They looked up eagerly.

"It was a disaster," I said. "It was the worst single meeting I've ever been to in my life. I was reamed out, and I felt like a student being scolded by a Mother Superior. I'm still reeling from it." I recounted the conversation in detail. They could scarcely believe what I was saying. We talked for two hours, trying to absorb what she had said. At the end, we agreed not to tell the staff, yet, for fear of panicking them. Besides, I needed to brief Jim Byrd, Slawko Klymkiw, Bob Culbert, and the rest of the network management, as well as Claude Saint-Laurent in Montreal. We stuck to the story that Saucier had a schedule conflict, and apologized to everyone for the misunderstanding. Then we went downstairs to the Mövenpick bar and commiserated into the evening, after which I went home and wrote down a complete account of the conversation, which was still ringing in my ears. I didn't do any work on the project that weekend, except to rehearse how to announce the cancellation of the project and what to do for the people who would be out of work.

It was true that we weren't that popular in the rest of the CBC and Radio-Canada. The Canadian History Project was the subject of considerable difference of opinion within staff ranks. Many were cheered by the bold move of launching such a large in-house production, because it gave a signal that, despite the mass downsizing, we were not closing shop. For others the project, and its cost, seemed like a vast indulgence. Hundreds of people were losing their jobs, entire service departments were disappearing, every employee of a regional station feared his local station would be closed, and yet the CBC turns around and gives an elite group in Toronto and Montreal millions of dollars for what would probably be a tedious view of an obviously boring subject. I could hardly blame those who felt that way, given the sorrow and the injustice of what I could see happening to my friends and colleagues. It didn't help that no one could see the fruit of our work. This wasn't a weekly or monthly program, this was a series that would not appear for two years, and no one could see what we were doing. The *Globe and Mail* called us "the raccoons in the attic of the CBC," unseen but causing strange bumps in the night.

By the following Monday we had briefed the Toronto and Montreal managers, who calmed us by reiterating their support and saying they would make sure it was clear we had spent only 20 per cent of the budget. Two days later, I got a message to call Guylaine Saucier urgently in her room at the King Edward Hotel in Toronto. I called, not knowing what to expect.

"Mark," she said, "I am very sorry for last week, and I feel bad because you are the people who have been working so hard to achieve everything I have been fighting for in the CBC, and I should have been more understanding. When you talked about how the CBC and SRC are structured to almost prevent collaboration, you are right, and I have always believed it. But when you talked about different computer platforms, different accounting systems, different sound equipment, and what your people are going through, I have to say even I had no idea how bad it was.

"You are right. Your team in Toronto and Montreal are doing something that has never been done before, you are a pioneering team, and I understand it will be difficult and costly. But I will support you."

This was a totally different Guylaine Saucier from last week. This morning, on the phone, she sounded anguished and vulnerable. "You have no idea the problems we have with the government and with the opposition," she said. "We are fighting for our lives. Literally fighting for our lives."

It was a heartfelt and generous call, made all the more memorable by her spending many minutes talking about her dreams of breaking down the Berlin Wall between French and English CBC. We talked about what we needed. I warned her that we had to go with the higher budget estimate, if only because the costs of doing business in French and English exceeded everyone's expectations. We needed to have the paralysis about fundraising, whatever was causing it, cured, and we needed a decision on whether there would be commercials during the series.

"We'll do everything we can to support you, Mark," she ended warmly.

I reported the conversation to the senior group, and the relief was a measure of how despondent we had all become in the last few days. Everyone broke into broad smiles and cheered.

"So we have a father and a mother now?" Gord Henderson asked.

"Mom and Dad don't get along," someone else quipped, "but they've accepted joint custody of the children."

On November 7, because of Clarence LeBreton's intervention, the CBC board of directors approved the revised appropriation and seventeen episodes for the Canadian History Project, including $2.5 million for infrastructure costs. A few days later, the good news was confirmed, and authority to go out and raise corporate sponsorship was transferred from Ottawa to Slawko Klymkiw. The board had saved the project, and we were free and clear.

A footnote to the financial wars: A few months later, in May 1999, Hubert Gendron called me at home in a state of great agitation and said, "Mark, I have let you down badly. The end-of-fiscal-year figures show us massively over in our expenditures, and we're virtually broke. I accept responsibility, and I offer my resignation."

I was flabbergasted. All of our tracking had shown us on budget. But the Montreal unit manager, Michel Legault, found that tens of thousands of dollars of charges had been dumped onto our budget at the very end of the fiscal year. I rang Claude Saint-Laurent, and he was livid at the news. The next morning he brought in a trusted former production manager and executive producer and ordered an item-by-item audit of every single charge.

"We discovered things like extensive double-billing," Hubert recalls. "For example, stagehands, already paid by the corporation, would take a few minutes to move accessories like canoes in the props area and charge a half-day of their time to the project. For unexplained reasons, some drivers at the garage charged their time to the project on days that we weren't shooting and went nowhere. Because we weren't 'dans le plan,' many of the plant employees were on 'overtime' when they started a shift with us, because their 'regular' hours had already been used up by 'normal' programs which were 'dans le plan.'

"One day, during a meeting, where Michel Legault and I were told for the nth time that we were 'comme une production extéri-eure,' I exploded. 'Est-ce-que j'ai l'air chinois? Est-ce que vous pensez que je suis de Radio-Pékin?' [Do I look Chinese to you? Do you think I'm from Radio Peking?] This is the biggest internal production in the CBC/Radio-Canada, and you treat us like strangers!"

Saint-Laurent's audit uncovered the fact that, while no money had been stolen, we had been overcharged by at least $120,000 because we were billed for services as an outside company. We also learned that many people within the support departments of SRC were disgusted by how the Canadian History Project had been used as an ashtray for unattributed costs. Eventually, some senior plant people were replaced, and for the rest of the production we were no longer treated like strangers in our own house.

But the most satisfying moment for me that December came when we viewed rough assemblies of the autumn's shoots. I'd asked each director to select six to seven minutes of his or her episode and put actors' voices in them and temporary music, to see if we were all using the same grammar. It was stirring beyond description. I felt like I was in an IMAX movie, as the screen showed Champlain's vast canoe convoy and the magnificent faces of Huron warriors. Louis-Joseph Papineau addressed the Assembly of the Six Counties and it seemed there were a thousand people waving banners of liberty. Magnificent vistas of the Arctic filled the screen, with muskoxen and herds of caribou. The team of documentary producers had tackled the impossible and pulled it off.

One rough cut had a particularly strong effect on me: Laine Drewery's, which chronicled the flight of the Loyalists from the American Revolution. The story is based on the diary of Hannah Ingraham, who was eleven at the time. We first see her in a column of refugees marching along a dirt road with all their possessions on carts and donkeys. They are fleeing to New York, where the harbour is teeming with tens of thousands trying to board ships bound for Jamaica or London or Halifax. We follow Hannah onto a ship that takes her family to Nova Scotia. Later, the narrator says: "The flood of refugee Loyalists that lands on the shores of Nova Scotia nearly triples the population overnight. Twenty thousand refugees flood into the coastal towns of Yarmouth and Annapolis Royal. Whole communities spring up where nothing existed before. The Caldwells and the Dodds, the McKays, the Moodys, the Thompsons. Surveyors frantically lay out townsites and homesteads. The wave of new settlers spreads up the Saint John River, creating the towns of Saint John, Queenston, Gagetown, and Fredericton. It is here that Hannah Ingraham's family settles. They spend their first winter in tents but by spring Hannah's father has built their first rough home." And the actor reads from Hannah's diary: "There was no floor laid, no windows . . . no door but we had a roof at least. A good fire was blazing and mother . . . boiled a kettle of water. We . . . all sat at our breakfast that morning and mother said: "Thank God we are no longer in danger of having shots fired through our house. This is the sweetest meal I ever tasted."

The lights went up slowly, and I looked down so no one would see the tears in my eyes. Wayne Chong, the producer, was in the room; so were Hubert Gendron and another producer, Grazyna Krupa. Not a Loyalist descendant in the bunch, yet I saw everyone else was teary-eyed just like me. Why did this one affect us so much? After a few minutes, I realized why. Because, in some way, it was my family's story too. For Wayne, Grazyna, and Hubert, it had also struck the same distant memory of refuge. It was then, I think, that we first glimpsed the unifying idea of our series.

13

No Memory and
No Money

As soon as the board's decision had been put in place and administration of the series given to Slawko Klymkiw, the English network's program director, he became Saint Paul on the road to Damascus, transformed from skeptic to zealot.

"Thank God we've got that zoo off our backs," he said. Within days he was calling scheduling and publicity meetings and telling everyone that *Canada: A People's History* was going to be the centrepiece of the 2000 and 2001 schedules. "I'm talking movie theatre trailers, bus posters, and covering the country with promos," he said.

Slawko, a tall man with curly long hair and a shaggy moustache, has an effervescent personality subject to great enthusiasms and despondency. He and I have known each other a long time and talk to each other with mock rudeness. In good times we could be found together in a bar in the evening, indulging our fondness for Cuban cigars; in bad times we'd be storming into each other's offices accusing the other of some dramatic transgression. We are both, after all, eastern Europeans, and the reason anglophones always think that Poles, Ukrainians, and Russians sound like they're shouting at each other when they talk Polish, Ukrainian, or Russian is that they usually are shouting at each other.

Eva Czigler, his deputy program director, is the most fashionable woman at the CBC. Eva, a Hungarian refugee from 1956, considered working for Slawko and with me – "impulsive eastern Europeans" – one of the crosses she had to bear. She is married to Peter Herrndorf, and the two of them were the social centre of our circle, which means they were the only people with matching placemats and capable of entertaining guests with more than takeout pizza.

Sometimes Slawko's office smelled like a deli, because he had brought in some Ukrainian sausage, and Eva had brought in Hungarian garlic sausage, and they had exchanged jars of homemade dill pickles. And on one such afternoon in November 1998, with the scent of garlic seeping into the hallway, Slawko landed her with the task of raising the corporate sponsorship money for the series.

My idea of getting a citizens' committee together for the job was clearly dead now, and we didn't have the time to set up an internal team. Eva thought it was best to hire an outside fundraising company. This is how Nina Kaiden Wright came into our lives. Short, bright blond, Nina has a strong New York accent and the bluntness that goes with it. Her personality fills a room the moment she enters it, and any remaining space is occupied by her elegant assistants. She is the chairman of Arts and Communications Consultants, a fundraising company specializing in high-end arts projects. She watched the video with her assistants, then shot up in her seat and declared, "Love it, love it, love it! I am reduced to tears. I don't usually do this kind of thing, but this is an honour, this is so exciting!" I decided I liked her.

Within two days Nina had us all working for her, writing summaries, finding images for portfolios, creating charts of corporate logo visibility and lists of sponsorship opportunities. I started worrying when she talked about making historians available for corporate picnics, but I decided I'd cross that bridge when we came to it. One of the first people to agree to help us was the former premier of Ontario, Bill Davis, who strongly supported the project. In the ensuing weeks,

Nina and her associates drew up an exhaustive list of potential sponsors, complete with their recent donation history and their corporate image goals. Every couple of weeks she would breeze in with her assistants to report to Eva on who in the corporate stratosphere had spoken to whom on our behalf.

Meanwhile, in our own corporate stratosphere, everything blew up. On December 14, 1998, barely a month after our budget was steered through the board, two memos appeared, one announcing the departure of Jim Byrd from the CBC, another appointing the head of English Radio, Harold Redekopp, as his replacement at the helm of English Television. Jim Byrd had been dethroned, pulled down by Guylaine Saucier, the finance heads in Ottawa who had been closing in on the English network, and the executive vice-president, James McCoubrey. I feared the history project was a factor in his demise, but I learned it wasn't. The constant attacks on English Television from Head Office finance, from Radio-Canada, and from the board had culminated in a demand that Byrd get rid of some of his senior lieutenants – all of whom were thought to be resisting the new order of things. Jim Byrd refused, and his lifelong career with the CBC was over. The man who had taken the bold chance almost three years ago of announcing the Canadian History Project, and who was our biggest ally and protector, was unceremoniously ousted. The Beatty-Saucier civil war was clearly over, and Saucier had won.

Finding out that some of the project's biggest supporters had been in disfavour was awful. Jim Byrd was so widely liked and respected in television that, if it was possible for morale to sink lower, it was now funereal. His farewell dinner at the inappropriately named Club Lucky bar and restaurant seemed to close an era. All the most famous producers and stars of the last twenty years came to pay homage to him, and Jim was so moved, he had to stop his remarks for a full minute, trying to keep his lips from trembling.

Three weeks after the announcement of these radical changes, on the night of January 4, 1999, Jim McCoubrey was driving home in a snow squall from a restaurant on the outskirts of Ottawa. His Jeep Cherokee skidded on the ice, flipped against a hydro pole, and plunged into a snowbank, leaving him upside down and buried headfirst in the snow. He suffered a massive concussion and would spend the next three months in intensive care and rehabilitation. The general feeling was that he would probably not return.

Nobody had any clear idea who was running the CBC any more. Saucier had won her battle with Perrin Beatty, but the job of chair of the CBC was only a part-time position (about two days a week), and Saucier sat on many other corporate boards. McCoubrey was in hospital, and Perrin Beatty's authority had been mortally damaged by the chair. What little power he had left was being rapidly eroded. He was now a lame-duck president whose term expired in just three months. If the Prime Minister's Office intended to renew him for another term – which he indicated he wanted – they would have announced it by now. Leaving Perrin Beatty to swing in the wind through the winter of 1999 was not only shabby toward him personally but an indication of the PMO's indifference to the CBC. At the last possible moment, Beatty's term was extended, but for six months only – a further insult to him and a slap in the face to the CBC.

It was hard to imagine things could get worse, but they did. A month after McCoubrey's accident, on February 16, three thousand technicians walked off the job, reducing English Television and English Radio to repeats and a skeletal news bulletin. The technicians' union had little appetite for striking, but the massive budget cuts had forced the CBC into such draconian economies that the technicians had to fight back. Their wrath was aimed at the government as much as the CBC.

In the history project, the cameramen, the video editors, and of course the studio technicians were all members of the striking union. Even before the strike, shoots were being cancelled in case crews were stranded somewhere. Laine Drewery had painstakingly planned a major shoot in Quebec, with re-enactors and special effects and snow-blowing machines staging the American invasion of Quebec by Benedict Arnold in 1776. We pulled it down because of the looming strike, and it's good that we did, or thousands would have been spent in vain. By the third week in February, the Toronto end of the history project was dead in the water, edit suites abandoned, studios dark, cameras locked away. Sweeney, Kennedy, Chabot, McElcheran, all the special effects and production teams we had worked with were out on the picket line in a bitter and windy winter.

Oil drums burning scrap firewood billowed black smoke out front of the CBC, as hundreds of strikers, muffled like characters out of a Siberian film, tried to keep warm. The once gleaming entry to Broadcast Centre now looked like a military roadblock in Sarajevo. The strikers marched slowly back and forth in a grim circle, with their signs, for weeks. Though their production colleagues were obliged to cross the line, most of us would march with them for up to an hour before entering. Wilma Alexander, Anne Emin, and Casey Kollontay were in management, so they were taken out of the history project and assigned to operate broadcast equipment to keep the stripped-down schedule that the CBC was barely maintaining. There was no point phoning anyone inside the CBC, they had all been reassigned to emergency services. There was no mail or courier delivery to the CBC, so hundreds of archival black and white prints from museums and colour transparencies of ships and portraits ordered from museums around the world by Ron Krant for various episodes were stuck in a mountain of mail somewhere.

Because the French technicians in Montreal belonged to a completely different union, the Montreal history unit at first kept working at full tilt, which made up for their late start from the ice storm the previous year. But the Toronto shutdown eventually affected Montreal staff, who were unable to get archives, sequences from Toronto graphics suites, or any shots that Toronto producers were supposed to be getting for them.

The previous winter, we hadn't had enough cameras to shoot winter scenes nor edit suites to assemble them, so we were counting on this, the last winter before broadcast. Instead, our work was paralyzed by the strike. Nevertheless, our costs continued to accumulate because we were still paying for researchers, producers, cost clerks, and the truncated infrastructure. If we laid them off, we'd never get them back again. As for CBC Television's audiences, they were evaporating since original programming had disappeared. We were doing bare-bones national newscasts but all local newscasts, *Air Farce*, *22 Minutes*, *Midday*, and most Newsworld programs hadn't been on for weeks. By the end of March, the strike was still on, winter was almost gone, and all hope of *Canada: A People's History* being ready for January 2000 had vanished.

At our house, it had been a grim fall and winter too. For months, my wife, Anne Wright-Howard, had been suffering from excruciating back and leg pain that virtually immobilized her. She had to go to painful rehabilitation, suffer through misdiagnoses, wait for weeks to see specialists and even longer to get an MRI. It was as if we were living the collapse of the provincial health system. On top of this, the future of her program, *Undercurrents*, was in doubt – yet again – even though it was one of the freshest programs on television, attracting a young demographic and seeming to meet every stated objective of the CBC. At March break, I pulled out my credit card and practically forced the family to Puerto Vallarta, Mexico, for a week. It was a godsend for everyone. Madeleine made a close friend, Caitlin danced the macarena till the wee hours every night, Anne rested, and I sat on the beach, reading about the British conquest of Canada and thinking I could always open a bookstore in Puerto Vallarta if worse came to worst. The strike was still not over when we returned. I alternated between finishing the script for "Battle for a Continent" and working with Eva, Slawko, and Nina Kaiden Wright, trying to raise sponsorship.

BCE Inc. had shown interest in the digital and Internet opportunities, and for weeks, complex negotiations had gone on with various vice-presidents and development executives. More weeks were spent assessing Internet opportunities and designing digital plans that would suit BCE's objectives. One of the BCE people said she would need us to persuade all the divisions in the conglomerate to come on board, since they would have to be sold on it one by one. "Doesn't Jean Monty just make the decision?" I asked, referring to the legendary CEO. "Eventually, yes," she said, "but we have to sell the divisions themselves. Bell Mobility, for example, might not see it as a

useful vehicle for selling cellphones." I allowed as how this was probably true. I was impressed that BCE was an even more complex
bureaucracy than the CBC. I thought we had cornered the market on
divisional intricacy.

We decided that Slawko and I would be used only to talk to
likely clients in general terms about the project. I didn't want to
field specific content questions like "Are you doing the founding of
Molson's?" or "Do you have a chapter on Alexander Graham Bell?"
Nina and the CBC were scrupulous in protecting me from that. But
the presentations and the preparation of various documents about
Web site plans for BCE and other interested parties consumed a lot of
time. At one point, Slawko and I made a presentation to the CEO and
marketing heads of Canadian Tire. Clearly the CEO was intrigued but,
equally clearly, his marketing heads were not. I was getting the idea
that CEOs have a lot less power than I had imagined, and our problems would come from the marketing divisions. In the cab on the
way back to the CBC, Slawko and I slumped in the back seat and I
said: "If anyone had told me this is what I would be doing to produce
a history of Canada, I'd have called them crazy." Slawko added, "If
anyone had told me this is what being the program director would
mean, I would have stayed in Newsworld."

John Rae called me from Power Corporation, months after indi-
cating they would probably be very interested, to tell me that they
had decided that a series like this should be funded by the CBC itself.
"At the cost of how many cancelled programs?" I asked with irritation, and he replied: "I understand, I'm sorry."

Throughout the year-long hunt for sponsors, there were many
close calls – Canada Post, Via Rail, Canadian Pacific, the Bank of Nova
Scotia – but nothing came to fruition. Slawko and I made presentations to institutions that were focused on Canadian history, such as
the Historica Foundation and the Bronfman Foundation, but without success. I was shocked. It had never occurred to me that major
Canadian corporations wouldn't see the series as an opportunity for
corporate positioning or, at the very least, that they could afford to be
seen as indifferent to Canadian history.

The Historica Foundation had already gathered several million dollars in corporate donations for the support of Canadian history; Jack Granatstein's book *Who Killed Canadian History?* was a national best-seller. The *National Post* had an article or editorial at least once a month calling for the reform of Canadian history education. Furthermore, we were within a year of the millennium, and this millennium project promised to be the most visible of all. But no one was touching us.

"I don't understand it." Nina would throw up her hands. "We are getting real interest from the CEOs of companies, but then the project is turned over to their advertising departments for 'evaluation.' And they seem to be confused about the difference between advertising and the subtle benefits of arts sponsorship. In the U.S., there would be a bidding war between Microsoft and General Electric and a dozen other companies within minutes."

The search for corporate sponsors continued, but we reduced the money we were asking for. We approached every major Canadian corporation in every major sector: the financial, airlines, railways, communications, high-tech, petrochemical, and service industries. Well-connected members of the CBC board opened corporate doors for us, Guylaine Saucier and Slawko Klymkiw met with Jean Monty of BCE in Montreal, and many prominent citizens aided the sponsorship hunt.

But it was to no avail. It slowly dawned on us that a lot of companies were afraid of the series because it would be dealing with combustible incidents in Canadian history, from the Acadian Deportation to the exploitation of Chinese workers in the construction of the railways. But the biggest fear seemed to be Quebec, and how we would deal with the history of French-English relations. This was a double-edged sword, because if we were too sympathetic to the French, it would anger English viewers, and if we were too federalist, it would anger Quebec viewers. We never heard this directly from the companies, but it would come up discreetly from advertising agencies who would speculate that "this would be a problem for Hydro-Québec" or "BCE is heavily dependent on its Quebec base."

Not only was corporate Canada skittish about Canadian history, it appeared, so were parts of the federal government. Some friends in the Ottawa press gallery told me ministerial assistants or press aides occasionally asked them, "Do you know if this series has any bombshells?" or "Do you think it's something that we're going to have to prepare for politically?" The French press in Montreal and Quebec City seemed to have decided that we were a federal government propaganda effort secretly funded by Sheila Copps. *Le Devoir's* first story about the series was not that Radio-Canada was broadcasting thirty hours of Canadian history, not that we were restaging some of the great moments of the history of New France, but that "Radio-Canada denies that the project is subsidized by special federal money." While in Montreal, many saw us as a federalist plot, in Toronto many assumed we'd be soft on separatists.

Those companies and agencies that did not see the series as a hazardous substance saw it as a guaranteed audience repellant. Vice-presidents of marketing expressed great skepticism that Canadians would watch Canadian history. "You have to admit, it can be a bit boring at times," some said, quickly adding, "Not that it's not important."

In January, I was invited to give the banquet speech to a huge history conference at McGill University, organized by the celebrated military historian Desmond Morton. The title of the conference was "Giving the Past a Future," and hundreds of historians and history teachers attended from across Canada. I was nervous, given that I was no historian and hadn't been to a history class since 1968. I sought Gene Allen's wisdom and borrowed all his ideas, and he edited the speech carefully, finally letting me out in public with the admonition, "Don't stray from the text," which I didn't. The title of the speech was "A Nation Without Memory," and it suggested that Canadian history was fascinating, but that we were afraid of it and therefore barely taught it in schools. The consequence was, I argued, "that Canada seems to have suffered a stroke which has wiped out any national memory, condemning us to live every linguistic and regional crisis without any historical context, buffeted by any random sound bite or stampeded by a phone-in show." Canadian history was as vivid as any other country's, and we were hiding it from our children not because it was boring "but because it is alive – too alive for authorities afraid to discuss language and race." The *Globe and Mail* published it afterwards, and I soon found that suggesting our history was vibrant was drawing some unexpected fire.

Sitting on yet another morning flight to Montreal weeks later, I opened *En Route* magazine to find my friend Gwynne Dyer firing a broadside at my remarks, arguing that we are blessed to have a tepid history, and where it had been controversial, we should let sleeping dogs lie.

Months later, I opened the Saturday *Globe and Mail* to find another salvo against my January speech, under the headline "Napoleonesque It Isn't – Is It Possible to Be Too Patriotic About Canadian History?" by Robert Fulford. This time, I was lumped with Jack Granatstein, and we were denounced as cheerleaders who were merely "justifying personal career choices and appealing for financial support." He warned, "They run the danger of making themselves, and the study of Canadian history, ridiculous." He did, I had to admit, call me to account on some of my more overwrought phrases. But he concluded, "Granatstein and Starowicz, by overkill, will have joined the assassins of Canadian history."

I was finding not only that Canadian history was controversial, but that even the very assertion that it's interesting or exciting is controversial. One Quebec commentator went so far as to suggest we were "hijacking" Quebec history and paving it under the asphalt of Canadian history.

On the fundraising front, none of this sniping was helping us land sponsors. It was difficult to sell something that was too boring for some VPs of marketing and not boring enough for others.

In the meantime, things were at least settling down a bit in the management at the CBC, where beheading our leaders was routine and life was treacherous but never boring.

Harold Redekopp, the radio VP who had replaced Jim Byrd, was doing well, given that he had never worked in television production.

Harold and I have known each other since our earliest days in radio, nearly thirty years ago, when he was a producer for what was actually called the Serious Music Department. That department regarded us upstarts at *As It Happens* as a biker gang that had just roared into Massey Hall in the middle of the Goldberg Variations. But over the years we had lived through several adventures together, and our antagonism had mellowed into a mutual respect. At our first meeting in his new incarnation, in front of twenty people, he remembered that once, in our radio days, I had called the Serious Music Department "pastoral." He was right, I remembered this. But I wondered, in that winter of 1999, how such a benign word had the power to survive thirty years as an insult. They had been an odd bunch in Serious Music.

Harold is a Manitoba Mennonite with an M.B.A. and with the conviction that Jesus Christ travelled economy only because there wasn't third-class seating. This was refreshing after the years when executives travelled business-class to be "fresh" for meetings three hours' flying time away, while correspondents flew in steerage for fourteen hours to get to war zones. Harold knew nothing about television and had the good grace to admit it. His first question about the history series, when we were alone, betrayed his roots: "Who are your composers?" His face fell when he didn't recognize the names. But his next sentence surprised me more. "This is the project that could save the CBC, and more important, it's critical to this country. You've gone through a lot of crap. How can I help you?"

The meeting we'd been in before our private one was to brief him on corporate sponsorship. The CBC budget was in the toilet, a third of the corporation was on strike, and there was a lot of pressure to fully commercialize the series. The nightmare of not knowing how long the series was, because I didn't know if it would have six hours' worth of commercials, snuck up on me unexpectedly during this boardroom briefing. But it disappeared in ten wonderful seconds for which I will be eternally grateful to the Mennonite brotherhood. "We're not going to commercialize the history of Canada," Harold stated baldly. "It would be wrong." And that was that. Six hours of Canadian history that would never otherwise see air were suddenly on the screen. It had been years since I had heard a financial argument at the CBC settled with "It would be wrong." I would come to disagree with a number of Harold's decisions in other areas in the coming years, but I've never had any quarrel with his moral compass and the depth of his feeling for Canada, and for public broadcasting.

The strike ended in mid-April. But with the winter completely gone and dozens of winter scenes still to shoot, the launch of *Canada: A People's History* was put back nine months, to October 2000. This not only bought us breathing time but actually made a lot more sense, since October was the start of the fall television schedule. The strike had crippled a lot of other production for fall 2000, so the history series would fill the breach.

A month later, around the end of May, Hubert Gendron, Louis Martin, and I were having lunch together when I felt a hand squeeze my shoulder. I turned, and there stood Jim McCoubrey, with a warm smile. I stood up, stunned to see him, and he clasped me by the shoulders and said, "It's good to see you."

"I thought you were still in rehab," I said.

"I'm not supposed to be back," he said, "but I was so bored that I'm coming in half-time. What are you doing these days?"

"The history project still," I said. "Come up one day and I'll show you some of our rushes." He said he'd like that a lot, we shook hands, and he walked away. He seemed a transformed man, warm and somewhat wistful. The next day he called to take me up on the offer. The theatre was free, so I told him to come up in an hour.

I planned to show him four six-minute excerpts, but to show the progress since last year, I played the original thirteen-minute video first. We sat beside each other, and when it ended, he turned to me and said: "That's terrific. Have I seen this before?" I hesitated, confused, and slowly said, "Yes. Fourteen months ago during the board screening, right in this theatre." He sighed, and with the theatre still dark, recounted his remarkable story. Most of McCoubrey's recent life had been completely erased from his long-term memory by the accident.

"I have no recollection of the accident, of the Christmas before that, nor anything since the accident till a few weeks ago," he said, shaking his head. "I can't remember anything that happened in the past five years if it has any sad or tragic association. Even a fishing trip with my son, where I guess we had an argument or something, is completely erased from my mind. Anything bad, anything negative, for five years, is totally lost." His short-term memory only started returning a month before. He asked his wife how his mother was. She had the painful task of telling him she had died two years ago.

He talked, with sadness and sometimes an ironic smile, for over an hour. Murray Green, who was at the control console at the back of the theatre, could hear him, and sat quietly, moved by what McCoubrey was saying. McCoubrey described how a small group of loyal friends had saved him by coming regularly and talking with him, which helped restore his spirits and his context. There were dozens of people, some close friends, whom he didn't remember, and entire stretches of time which no longer existed in his mind.

"Not being able to remember unhappy moments," I said finally, "could be a blessing in the CBC." He smiled.

"I'm surprised I don't remember this film, though," he continued. "It's so powerful, how could I forget it? Maybe something sad was associated with it."

We showed him excerpts for the next forty minutes, and when he left, he seemed tremendously grateful. I sensed this afternoon was important to him. It was for me, because whatever our differences before and since, it was a reminder that there is always a humanity in an adversary. And on another plane, life was too short to be living through the grief we had been going through in this series, and this corporation.

May turned to June, and still no one was appointed as the new president. Articles and editorials began appearing in the papers, criticizing the prime minister for leaving the CBC swinging in the wind and for appearing to be indifferent to public broadcasting. In July, Perrin Beatty left the CBC and named Jim McCoubrey, who couldn't remember much of his past years in the CBC, acting president of it.

Also that month, Bob Culbert, the executive director of news and current affairs who had backed the project from its inception, was told his time in his job was ending. Harold Redekopp wanted big changes in Newsworld and in news and current affairs. Bob, however, had made it clear he was opposed to some of the proposed changes, and Harold decided he wanted someone else in the job.

It was the summer and autumn of farewells. I visited Roméo LeBlanc in Rideau Hall, and we spent an entire afternoon in rambling conversation. He had learned that he had diabetes, and he had decided to end his term early. I told him about our problems, including the times I had been too ashamed to talk to him. He smiled, patted me on the arm, and said: "You're talking to an old warhorse, Mark – I understand."

He saw me out, we shook hands warmly, and he said: "It's going to be terrific, Mark. It's going to work. Good luck." In October, LeBlanc left Ottawa and moved home to New Brunswick.

After the unfilled vacancy at the CBC provoked outrage from the arts community, the PMO finally announced the appointment of Robert Rabinovitch to the post, effective November 15. The appointment was well received. Rabinovitch had been a respected civil servant and a strong believer in public broadcasting.

In December, I attended yet another mournful farewell, this one for Bob Culbert. We had been together for the launch of *The Journal*, the death of Barbara Frum, and the inception of the Canadian History Project. Hundreds came to pay their respects. About the only bright spot was the deteriorating weather and the bitter cold. We could finally resume shooting winter scenes. Laine Drewery again fired up all the elaborate preparations for staging the American invasion of Quebec on December 31, 1775.

On December 30, 1999, all the technicians in Radio-Canada went on strike, shutting down all shooting and editing of the series in Quebec, including the American invasion. And at about the same time, BCE informed us that, after due consideration, they would not be sponsors of *Canada: A People's History*.

By now, I didn't care about any of this, because I had barely slept for days. Two weeks earlier – in mid-December – my wife of nearly twenty years had told me she wanted a divorce.

On December 31, Anne, our friends and family, and I went down to the CBC to the control room to watch the millennium broadcast going from time zone to time zone around the world. Then, toward midnight, we walked over to the base of the CN Tower to watch the shower of fireworks that would greet the new century – and the year *Canada: A People's History* would be launched. The sky erupted in spectacular columns and fountains of light, and I never felt emptier in my whole life.

14
Countdown and Meltdown

These weeks immediately before and after the turn of the millennium were the make-or-break point of the project. They were also pivotal in the lives of many of us working on it. We were reaching our limit.

The breakdown of my marriage sent me into a tailspin. I still loved Anne and couldn't conceive of breaking up the family unit. Our separation has no place in this book, except insofar as it forms the background for the rest of this story. Nobody else was involved and no incident provoked it; but, as Anne put it finally, "People change, Mark." At work, I told only Gene Allen, Anne Emin, and Sally Reardon.

Poor Anne Emin found herself propping up two people going through the same thing. That winter Sally Reardon's long-time relationship dissolved, and she had to sell her beloved farm in Nova Scotia. The two of us were a sorry sight. On weekends we'd meet to finish the script for "Battle for a Continent," and Sally would start us off by saying, "The meeting of the Losers' Club will now come to order."

The news from Montreal was also grim. Louis Martin had been diagnosed with a serious degenerative ailment. It would be impossible for him to continue the gruelling travel between Montreal and Toronto, vetting scripts and rough cuts, and supervising all the content for Radio-Canada. He took medical leave, and Hubert found himself virtually alone with the weight of the French series on his back. To compound the Montreal crisis, we were having serious problems with the three hours on New France. Scripts were not coming together, and many characters and scenes we thought were essential had not been shot. Finally, with Louis gone and the New France material in deep trouble, I went to see Claude Saint-Laurent and told him we had to reorganize Montreal – and put all of our cards on our best writer and clearest thinker there, Hubert Gendron. We'd have to hire a hard-nosed senior producer to take the management load off his back, and give total control of what appeared on the air to Hubert. "He's pretty stressed out already," Claude cautioned. "Can he do it?" I said he could, but if he so much as caught the flu in the next six months, we'd be dead. Then I did the one thing I hoped I wouldn't have to do in this series, and let a director go.

If New France was the weak link in this series, we'd lose our audience in the second episode. I couldn't let that happen. At this late stage there was no time to bring in a new writer/director, so the only answer was for Hubert himself to write it. Then, to direct and re-edit these New France hours, I turned to Serge Turbide. That meant Serge would be directing three hours of New France, as well as two hours of "Battle for a Continent," which was a huge responsibility. Sally and I could take up the slack for Serge on the "Battle for a Continent" episode, though where we'd find the time I didn't know. Toronto was also having difficulties with a major episode – on the fur trade, which was foundering on delays and disagreements. As in the case of New France, there were no margins left, so I asked Gordon Henderson to move into the edit suite and take over authority for it.

We were stretching the top people in both cities dangerously thin. Gene Allen was at the centre of a maelstrom of paper and e-mails:

all the historians' comments were flooding in at once, all the final script revisions poured in and had to be vetted with him, and he was also supervising the two companion books we were publishing. The books were massive undertakings that involved two writers. Don Gillmor had been working for two years, writing two-thirds of each book, and was a dream to work with. Pierre Turgeon in Montreal had been hired to write one-third of the first volume, based on the episodes produced in Montreal. Everything was late, because the scripts were late, and then hundreds of illustrations had to be cleared, sidebars and captions written, quotes checked against the original documents, and translations rewritten into fluid prose.

Dedicated Web sites, one in French and one in English, had been promised from the beginning and formed an essential part of the concept. But they got caught by the same bureaucratic tar baby that had got us, and nothing had been done in the past two years. Then we discovered that the sites – and the money allotted for them – had been cancelled. When they were finally restored, it was almost too late to do them. Only a superhuman effort could recruit a bilingual staff and put twenty thousand years of Canadian history into two major sites in just six months.

Then there were the home video and DVD sets, which needed to be designed, with liner notes and additional supportive material. Beyond that – and most important of all – were the educational guides. From the beginning, I had promised that the series would be made available to schools, with curriculum guides adapted for every province and grade level. At the end of 1999, however, hardly anything had been done.

We also had yet to design the promotional campaign and press strategy, and although there was a CBC department to handle that, it would need our help and our material. Finally, the hunt for sponsors had to be revived. Nina Kaiden Wright's contract with the CBC had expired, and English Television was going to try one last massive push with its own staff. The sales people who had resisted the project two years earlier were gone, and the new team were not only eager but determined to pull a rabbit out of the hat.

There was no way to coordinate all of this while completing the first wave and starting the second. "This unit is a television production operation," I told Slawko Klymkiw and Eva Czigler. "It has the infrastructure of a 7-Eleven store, not a multinational. We need someone to coordinate sales, publicity, educational, and press strategies. We needed someone a year ago." Their hands had also been tied until recently by the paralysis in Ottawa, but Eva Czigler was able to start looking for someone to take on the job. It would be May, five months before air time, when a communications manager came on board.

On the editorial front, however, blessed reinforcements arrived. In Montreal, where Hubert was drowning, Claude Saint-Laurent had come up with a replacement for Louis Martin. I knew Mario Cardinal was an eminence in Quebec journalism and the former ombudsman for Radio-Canada, but that was all. And I wasn't at all sure a former ombudsman was what we wanted. We needed a results-oriented and tough-minded managing editor to back up Hubert and I feared Cardinal might be a bit pedantic and academic. I approached the lunch Claude had set up in mid-January with some skepticism. "We don't need a French political commissar," I told Claude, and we had gotten somewhat bristly with each other.

It took me about fifteen minutes to form a deep liking for the snowy-haired, trim man with the infectious laugh. Cardinal also had an impish sense of humour and a lust for adventure that had taken him to Africa to teach journalism after his retirement. "I hadn't planned to take on any work," Mario said. "I promised my wife we'd go to Spain this winter." But as we described the scale of what we were doing, I could see his interest grow. The more obstacles we described, the more he behaved like a retired gunfighter thinking of strapping the holster on one last time. By the end of the lunch, we were embracing each other.

"I didn't hesitate to get on board a train that was already moving," Cardinal says. "I saw it as a chance to plunge once more into a history that had been a part of me through my childhood and which was everywhere during my career as a journalist for Le Devoir, which had been founded by Henri Bourassa, and which remained profoundly nationalist. To be a journalist in Quebec is by definition to walk hand in hand with history. I saw my participation in the project as being part of an unprecedented production in Canadian television history, but also as a responsibility to work toward seeing that Quebec's distinctive character would be present within it." His focus on Quebec, however, did not blinker him against the wider story, and as the winter progressed we saw that he was enchanted and fascinated by all of Canadian history, and profoundly moved by the aboriginal story.

At the same time, Claude had found the man to take the production load off Hubert's back in the person of Denis Boucher, a producer in the private sector with the reputation of a sergeant major. Denis was affable, but also blunt and impatient with delay. When the strike ended in Montreal, we'd be burning rubber with Denis in charge.

In Toronto salvation came in the person of Kelly Crichton, and I couldn't believe my luck. She had led the television news department, had been executive producer of *the fifth estate*, and had headed the London bureau. She was an experienced documentary producer, and I had worked with her as far back as *As It Happens*. Because of yet another reorganization, the CBC wasn't sure what to do with her, and Kelly was thinking of retiring. Within minutes of hearing this, I told Slawko we had to have her, and I made her life miserable until she joined.

"Gordon, Hubert, and Gene are stretched to the limit and I'm in a rough patch personally," I told her. "We're neglecting all the second wave producers, we don't have anyone editorial to recruit the narrator or to supervise narration and post-production, the Internet is shaping up to be a disaster, and there's a hundred loose pieces cropping up every day. I want you to worry about all of that while the rest of us get the first wave on. You'll be senior producer in charge of everything that's broken."

"In other words," she said, "you're looking for fresh meat."

"That's about it," I conceded.

"OK," she agreed, "I was hoping to polish my French anyway."

All this – the books, the Web site, the teaching guides, the hunt for a sponsor – started to take off in January of 2000, just as the team was expanding to start production of the second wave of eight episodes, which would take us from Confederation to 1990. The senior team members were barely keeping their heads above water, and the production load was doubling. New directors and researchers were being recruited, as well as historians who were specialists in the twentieth century. There was a tumult of activity and a lot of new faces in January 2000. I would find myself asking Rachel, "Who's that?" as a young researcher brushed by. She'd say "That's So-and-So. She's on your payroll."

All the edit suites had been working double shifts for months; the graphics departments laid on extra staff to produce not only the intricate special effects compositions but also hundreds of maps and chapter title cards in both languages. We became, overnight, the largest single employer of actors in Canada. We had to record two hundred actors who appeared on camera and four hundred actors for voice-over only, and all this just for the first nine episodes. For every actor we selected, we had auditioned four in each language, which meant more than two thousand people came in to read for the parts. Gail Carr ran the casting in English, and Céline Halle conducted it in Montreal, in an operation that was the equivalent of casting two years' worth of Stratford seasons in one autumn.

Some of Canada's most distinguished actors appear in the series. Robert Joy plays James Wolfe and Guy Nadon plays Montcalm. August Schellenberg plays Pontiac, David Hemblen plays Captain Cook (and would do the voices of Adolf Hitler and J. Edgar Hoover in the second wave), Graham Greene plays Kondiaronk. Louise Marleau plays Thérèse Baby and Ghislain Tremblay plays Champlain in both languages. Also featured are Tantoo Cardinal, Zachary Richard, Nigel Bennett, Lorne Cardinal, and Domini Blythe.

Two hundred on-camera actors meant two hundred costumes and wigs and makeup sessions as well as two hundred backgrounds, so by late 1999, we were running almost full-time studios in both cities. We were asking actors to do something most had never done before: be in a documentary. That meant they had to avoid any trace of theatricality. "I had a 10 per cent strategy," Gordon Henderson says. "When the directors had finished with the actors on camera and were satisfied, I would say, 'One more time, just 10 per cent less.' I was terrified of overacting. TV is a small medium so play it small, not too big. A director's natural instinct is to ask for more, to make it bigger. I kept saying make it sound real, not like theatre."

The backgrounds behind all the actors turned out to be one of the stickiest debates in the unit, and it took us longer to solve than it took the Vatican to pick the last two popes. Building sets was out of the question; it would have bankrupted us. But when we told the directors they had one close-up face and an out-of-focus background, and that was all, they nearly revolted. Mike Sweeney and I wanted to use nine or ten standard background flats like stone walls, brick walls, parlour panelling, and outdoor woods. Hubert wanted to have the actors perform with a green screen behind them and have the backgrounds inserted electronically. Mike and I were adamant that we had rarely seen this done well.

Finally, Mike and I were defeated by sheer cost, and our defeat was the best thing that could have happened, because it forced us to solve the mystery of chroma-key, as the green-screen technique is called. Mike experimented for two weeks and determined that the reason the technique looks fake is that the lighting is different for the background than it is for the foreground figure. Mike had a set of real backgrounds shot and wrote accompanying lighting instructions for the studio. That way, the lighting on the actor could be matched to the background shot showing on a separate monitor. It saved us a couple of hundred thousand dollars and gave us total flexibility to use the same background in either city with no props or set-up crews.

There are three main stages in making a documentary: shooting, editing, and post-production. The closer it gets to the third stage, the more the enterprise resembles an entire army on the move. Every part depends on every other.

When a team returns from a shoot, they arrive in the edit suite with dozens of twenty-minute tapes, each with several takes and retakes of the shots. To winnow everything down, the video editor enters all the best takes into the hard drive of an Avid, which is a very powerful computer that stores moving images. He or she will then do a rough "assembly" of the shots in logical sequence and begin to work on reducing them to a workable rough cut of a sequence and, eventually, of the whole episode. It is usually at least 30 per cent too long, with a lot of shots missing, and paintings and stills yet to be found, which are represented by "Painting of Madame de Pompadour to go here" or "Graphic of Beauport trenches to come." The "scratch narration" is usually just the director's own voice. The on-camera and voice-over actors have not been recorded yet, and are usually represented by the voices of other members of the team. It is very rough, but it's what you show your senior producer to get an idea of the story flow – where it sags, what is confusing, and what is just plain boring. This is the first thing the historians see too.

The full senior group from Montreal and Toronto would then screen and comment on this very rough assembly, something that often took most of a day. On the basis of all these comments, the next version of the script would be written – still far from the final one – and the rough cut rearranged, shortened here, expanded there, screened again, altered again, until we had a "fine cut."

When the fine cut has been screened and passed by everyone again, and any final adjustments made, and the documentary fits its time slot perfectly, then it is "picture-locked." Picture-lock doesn't mean the documentary is finished, but the visual skeleton of the documentary is now totally set. The documentary will open with the ship blowing up, and precisely seven seconds later it will dissolve to a shot of the actor's face, and he will speak for thirty-seven seconds. No image can be made longer or shorter.

With this picture-locked blueprint, a dozen production departments are now activated. The visual researchers know what images have made the final cut and will order high-resolution transparencies from the appropriate museum or gallery. The business unit then buys international broadcast, book, educational, and Internet rights to these images. Casting departments in both Montreal and Toronto know how many actors they have to audition for the voice-over roles, and the production crew know they have to book and schedule studios. The graphics team know which composite wide shots they have to create, and they prepare a montage. The sound effects studio can prepare soundscapes for, say, London streets, inserting the correct bell sounds, or they can build a soundtrack that covers Versailles and exterior sounds of Quebec streets in ruins. The foley technicians know what close-up sounds they have to manufacture, such as all the loading and firing sounds for a firing squad. The composers of the original musical track are now able to begin their work as well. Until now, they have known the broad outline but had no idea how many bars to write for each part of the sequence. When they have composed the music, it will reveal how many flutes, French horns, cellos, or harps are needed, which will allow the production and business and music-mixing people to book the recording facilities and hire the appropriate musicians.

Picture-lock thus unlocks everything, and a virtual army of craftspeople goes to work. It is called the post-production stage of the process. Now the business unit can precisely cost every single minute of the documentary and track whether it is running over budget.

The woman in charge of this post-production army was the opposite of what you'd expect. Far from being a martinet, Pat Goodland was quiet and soft-spoken, and sat at her post wrapped in a shawl, an island of calm in an electronic storm. By all rights, she should have told us to go to hell. "I was to start in January 2000 as the post-production supervisor," she says, "on a series that was airing that fall. Basically we had to do the equivalent of sixteen movies in two years."

Pat's first challenge was dealing with a human catastrophe: "On the first day of the foley sessions in February 2000, the CBC laid off a large number of technicians. One by one, the sound effects technicians were called out of our sessions and given their layoff notices. In the end, the entire TV sound effects department was laid off, effective the end of June. I spent most of that day trying to help people deal with the shock. Most of them had been with the CBC for over twenty years. No one knew it was coming." I am absolutely convinced that, had it not been for Pat's skill and the loyalty the technicians felt for her, the series would never have made it to air.

The pace and range of activity now resembled an invasion. It was all run by the weekly conferences of the senior producers and business and production managers, which were like meetings of a war cabinet. With boardrooms in Toronto and Montreal linked by conference lines, Anne Emin would go down the list and we would update the status, episode by episode. A hard-drive crash in Edit Suite 3, courier shipments with images delayed by the Montreal strike, an episode slipping its picture-lock date by yet another week because the director's father died, a museum refusing to sell Internet rights, a snowstorm delaying a shoot in New Brunswick, a map animation that put the coureur de bois route in the wrong place, more script delay in Episode 4: "I won't authorize your ticket to Ottawa until you finish that chapter," Anne would chide, skewering me with a withering look, and Hubert would chime in on the speakerphone, "If I delay my chapter, can I get out of going to Ottawa too?"

It was war footing in other ways too – all leaves cancelled. Everyone was working flat out, nights and all weekends. March break plans were in ruins, weddings missed, tax returns unfiled, credit card bills unpaid. Murray Green, a father of three, got one weekend off all winter. The Toronto office was a sea of pizza boxes, with whiteboards covered with cryptic scrawls like "Constantinople falls . . . ," "Trade turns west . . . ," "Monk says mass on whale's back. . . ."

Laine Drewery was pressed into service to help out in the second episode, which had to explain how the Spanish conquest of the Incas led to gold fever in Europe. I wandered upstairs on a smoke break, heard a shot coming out of a studio, and peered in to see a conquistador, several Incas in loincloths, a stone wall, some potted palms, and Laine Drewery tearing his hair out. I walked up to the conquistador and opened the face mask. "Peter Twist, is that you?" He grinned sheepishly. "A little out of your period, aren't you?" Things like this were happening all the time that I didn't know about.

Another bizarre encounter occurred while I was waiting for an elevator on the sixth floor. The doors opened, revealing an associate producer, Lynette Fortune, clutching what appeared to be a pillow. As we rode down, I could see it was actually a transparent plastic bag of white granules like soap powder. "What's that?" I asked. "Artificial snow," Lynette replied hurriedly. "I'm just rushing to Winnipeg for the Duck Lake shoot. They phoned to say there was no snow out there and to bring some. Apparently if you blow this stuff at the lens it looks like a blizzard." With that, she was out the door like a shot, and I had lived long enough to see someone taking snow to Winnipeg in winter.

I can't think of a more difficult thing to do than to join the Canadian History Project at the peak of its lunacy, but that was what Julie Dossett did when she became our communications manager, an addition to staff that I had been pleading for for over a year. Young, dark-haired, enthusiastic, and very businesslike, Julie had only ever worked in the private sector. It didn't take her long to realize she had landed on the dark side of the moon. I had warned her that she was walking into a mare's nest of interdepartmental jealousy in the CBC and two years of bureaucratic paralysis, but I think she discounted this as creative exaggeration. But not for long. Julie discovered that her title really meant "head of everything nobody has done anything about." "I was stunned," she says. "I should have been hired at least a year earlier. No press kits were ready, no posters ordered, no Internet, no movie trailers, no on-air promos, no public receptions, no coordination with the educational side. My head was spinning."

Her first job was to escort reporters and photographers from *Maclean's*, *Time*, and local media to the last major re-enactment in the series, the Battle of Batoche, which was being staged at Canadian Forces Base Shilo in Manitoba. It was her first television shoot. "I was perplexed," she says, "when after a half-hour of driving along a dusty road through an endless landscape of identical scrub and prairie grass, the convoy screeched to a halt and the director, Bill Cobban, determined we had arrived at 'the spot.' Nothing distinguished it from the previous twenty-five kilometres. The experience, which included standing around for hours on a tick-infested, sun- and wind-beaten prairie, quickly proved my suspicion that television is quite possibly the least glamorous business of all. Thirty volunteers from the local Métis community and an equal number of young men from the Royal Winnipeg Rifles out of the Princess Patricia Canadian Light Infantry donned the historical costumes brought for them. The hours – and the ticks – ticked by, and at one point I apologized to one of the soldiers who had to set up tents early in the morning, then sit and wait while Bill chased after shots of oxen and Gatling guns. The soldier sprawled on his kit and said, 'Ma'am, we're in the army. All we do is set up stuff, then hurry up and wait. It's what we do.'"

But the Métis who had gathered here this morning had a different purpose. Lynette Fortune, who worked with Bill Cobban, had tried several weeks earlier to find Métis extras to participate in the Batoche reconstruction. "I lucked into Steve Racine," she says, "a mover and shaker in the Métis community. He agreed to help us because he wanted the young Métis to take pride in being Métis; he didn't want them to feel like garbage. I remember him giving a rousing speech about this in the local restaurant. Everyone in the place was listening, and I almost signed up for it, I was so moved. He managed to put together Métis men from all over the province – some came from five hours away and our shoot started at seven in the morning! These men, many of them descendants of those who fought at Batoche, were big and strong with large necks like walruses. One of them held up his rifle and yelled at the young soldiers from Shilo, 'Today we rewrite history.' They actually looked afraid!"

"It could have been tense," Julie remembers. "Several Métis volunteers were playing out their own blood relatives' deaths at the hands of an army that could not have looked much different than the one that stood before them. For the Métis re-enactor Ken Lefort, a retired grain elevator worker from Turtle Mountain, this day had a special meaning. He was reconstructing a period photograph that showed his great-grandfather Daniel Ross lying dead after the battle. Phil Beaudoin was re-enacting a key scene in a thicket, which in real life was the place where his great-great-uncle Demasse Carrière died. "Christ, it's no wonder we lost," he told Brian Bethune from *Maclean's*, looking at the antique rifle he was holding. For Steve Racine, who had persuaded the Métis volunteers to come today, this day had special meaning. In 1885, English-Canadian society and the eastern press had treated these men like criminals and terrorists. Over a century later, the national broadcaster and the Canadian army regiment that fought them were reverently reconstructing the event as a legitimate fight for identity and liberty, and the men who had died on the Manitoba prairie would be portrayed as defenders of their people. Racine had waited a long time for that: "We can now show everyone what we're really like, what really happened."

Lynette Fortune, herself part Mohawk, and Bill Cobban later went to Poundmaker Reserve, two hours north of North Battleford, Saskatchewan, to film the signing of Treaty 6. "I was assigned the job of being the horse wrangler," she remembers. "I sat in the back of a pickup roaming the reserve, looking for horses. But what I saw were shanties not fit for habitation. An old woman pulled me into her home and showed me the leaking roof, and she talked about the bad water being pumped into the reserve that was making everybody sick. I saw a water truck deliver water to those who had money. I watched a wheat field catch on fire, billowing black clouds of smoke because someone had sold the fire truck. I listened to stories of poverty and corruption."

Lynette had researched the last great days of the Cree and the Blackfoot, who had been reduced to starvation in 1885 because of strict government ration policies. By 1879 the buffalo herds had stopped coming north, and the Cree and the Blackfoot had been reduced to begging. "I saw this legacy alive today in the rusted, rundown mobile homes, and the lack of hope in the people," she said.

Something remarkable was taking shape that winter and spring in Toronto and Montreal, as everyone involved in the first wave was returning from the last shoots and sharing stories. There was almost a collective consciousness forming as directors and researchers recounted experiences among the Cree, among the Inuit, on the

Acadian shores, and in the Saguenay. Like Lynette, they had been shaped by their work over the past two years, and I could see that they were not entirely the same people we had hired. Immersing themselves in other people's history, breathing in their stories, had affected them. There was less talk of technique and more recounting of experience. They were becoming storytellers for the people whose heritage they were recounting, and they were assuming the responsibility with gravity. I could sense it in the edit suites and see it in their scripts. The project had taken on the indefinable air of a shared mission, something larger than the sum of its parts, a regimental pride that they were working on the project of their lives. Now, if we could only beat the clock, I knew we would win.

During this time Knowlton Nash called me to say that I had won the Lifetime Achievement Award of the Canadian Journalism Foundation – just about the highest honour a Canadian journalist could expect. There was a gala dinner with six hundred people at the Metro Toronto Convention Centre, and even a ten-minute film about my career. Claude Saint-Laurent, Mario Cardinal, Jean Pelletier, and Hubert Gendron made a special trip from Montreal to be there. As I stood at the podium thanking everyone, including my wife for her considerable part in supporting my career, I looked at the table where my family was sitting and just felt dead.

In the ensuing days, I realized there was an unusual consequence of being the youngest to win the Lifetime Achievement Award. It took me a while to figure out why so many people were asking me if I was all right, or saying, "If there's anything I can do to help, you know you can call me." I knew almost no one knew about the impending divorce, so I assumed it was because I looked pretty tired and had bags under my eyes. Finally, I said to Gene, "You know, I think people think I've got cancer or something because of this award." "Well," he replied, "in my experience, lifetime achievement awards usually mean you're dying, or you're about to be fired." Given the hurricane we were flying into, the latter seemed more likely.

15
The Road to October

On May 26, 2000, the sales and communications departments pulled out all the stops. One of the giant studios had been converted into a virtual Canadian History Project theme park. Giant illuminated posters that Julie Dossett had ordered for the series hung from the lighting grids like banners at a political convention. A huge screen filled one end of the studio, with risers and a podium. Along the sides, uniformed chefs standing at steaming servers were preparing to dole out the power breakfast of all CBC power breakfasts.

The invited were bank vice-presidents and heads of marketing and communications for railways, airlines, auto manufacturers, and oil companies, as well as advertising and media buying agencies. President Robert Rabinovitch launched the pitch, calling it a landmark series. The wide screen filled with panoramic views and surging music, and I marvelled for a moment – gazing at the giant posters, the wide screen, the tables of guests – at how far we'd come. Half the post-production suites in the building were currently processing some part of the series.

And there was a new kind of pressure growing, which had me frightened. The press, having largely ignored us up to now, was starting to write major pieces on the series. Delivering the series on time was the apex of my ambition; a second coming for public broadcasting was raising the bar too high. The trick in publicity is to raise curiosity and interest but not unachievable expectations.

Just before the big sales breakfast at the end of May, Stephanie Nolen of the *Globe and Mail* had begun working on a major feature on us. She asked a great many skeptical questions, but she also spent considerable time observing the unit and viewing some rushes. The long piece she wrote appeared a week after the breakfast. She reported, "The infamous CBC rumour mill is abuzz about the show. There are reports that it is well over its original $25-million budget. . . . The other persistent rumour about the show is that it simply isn't very good." She quoted one current affairs producer grumbling, "People just disappeared up there . . . and nobody's seen a thing, no one knows what the hell they're doing."

But she also declared, "In truth, the show is good." She wrote, "It isn't what you might think when you hear 'Canadian history.' Its promotional tag is 'Canada, as you've never seen it before' and with good reason. . . . It is not dusty, it is as thrilling as it is earnest. . . . It's big, it's slick and for the CBC, it is a shot at redemption." She called it "gripping" and added, "The battles are dramatically re-enacted, the ships are satisfyingly ka-boomed, the scripts are compelling."

Since so many media people knew the *Globe* had been looking for a disaster story, Nolen's report stating the very opposite had great weight. It made us "hot" again and back in the redemption business. But Nolen had also done some digging in the advertising and marketing world and had called many of the people who had attended the sales breakfast. What she learned was that they were skeptical that anyone would watch the series. Though the sales presentation had distributed surveys showing that Canadians were interested in Canadian history, the *Globe* quoted one marketing executive saying, "But that doesn't mean they want to watch Canadian history on TV."

This same buyer, unidentified but reportedly one of the biggest agency names in Toronto, was then quoted further, and I almost spilled my morning coffee over my shirt as I read it. "It raised for him," the *Globe* said, "some of the most chronic criticisms of the CBC. 'You look at these people, at Rabinovitch and Redekopp and Starowicz, and they're a group of people living in a different mind space, a different century,' he said. 'I think it's an amazing exercise that the CBC would commission a 30-hour series of Canada, without knowing if anyone will watch it. As the parent of teenagers, I'm not sure anyone under 30 cares. Or that anyone west of Thunder Bay will be too interested in the Upper/Lower Canada axis on which the first half of the episodes inevitably spins. . . . They've made 30 episodes of this thing – but if no one's watching, are they going to run them all?' "

In my four years on this project, I encountered more mediocre thinkers and impenetrable jargon in the marketing world than anywhere else. That hundreds of them charge vast fees for dispensing the kind of ignorance quoted in the *Globe* article is mind-boggling; that corporations are deluded into believing these marketers actually know something is merely tragic.

But I did learn something valuable from the marketing world. Every Friday night during the previous winter I took Madeleine and her best friend, Zoe, to a movie. Before the feature, a commercial appeared on the screen for Molson's Canadian-brand beer, featuring "Joe," a Canadian Everyman. His rousing speech culminating in the proclamation "I . . . am . . . *Canadian!*" made the whole audience burst into enthusiastic applause. I'd never seen that before. By the time spring arrived, the ads had been on television and had become part of the popular culture. I took it as further proof of a latent nationalism across the country that perhaps augured well for us.

Our hopes rose and fell almost weekly. Canadian Pacific was interested, we were told, then Canadian National, then the Bank of Nova Scotia, then Canada Post seemed to be within reach but had been thwarted by some internal problem. BCE was out, Air Canada and Petro-Canada were never interested. All these names glittered like fireflies for a second and disappeared. I was even told by one of our sales people (I don't know on behalf of which client) that we were asked to offer assurances that we wouldn't dwell too much on the numbers of Chinese who died building the Canadian Pacific Railway. Gene and I stared at each other in disbelief. "You read about this in histories of radio in the 1930s," I said. "I really didn't think it still went on at such a crass level." On another occasion, a different customer expressed the hope that we wouldn't be concentrating excessively on the building of the CPR. I still have no idea if such concerns came directly from the railways or from some functionary in the media buying agency who was trying to anticipate a client's concerns. The new sales team rose even farther in my estimation when they made it clear to all potential clients that there was a brick wall between the sponsorship and the content of the series; that the integrity of the series was not an inconvenience but the core asset itself.

Betty Chiu, Gaye McDonald, and Sandra Hammond worked tirelessly to find sponsors; Gaye even postponed surgery for a painful shoulder by months until the campaign was over. "We're in the sales business," Betty Chiu said one day as we waited for an elevator, "but if no one buys in, to hell with them. I'm just so proud that the CBC is determined to put it on, no matter what the marketplace says." Karen Bower was another person whom I barely knew in a department called non-broadcast sales. She sat quietly at a coordinating meeting that Harold Redekopp had convened, until he asked people around the table if they saw any potential for their departments to get involved. "I have been waiting for a project like this for twenty-five years," Karen said with a flinty determination. "I'm going to put it into every bookstore and video store and make sure it's in every school in the country." In the weeks following, she was like a woman possessed, researching every provincial curriculum, hiring educational specialists to design lesson plans, putting out tenders for home video sets, attending teachers' conventions, and setting up the entire machinery for mass-producing home videos and DVDs.

That summer of 2000, I think most of the Broadcast Centre was working on one part or other of the series. We were playing the promo and excerpts in the eighth-floor theatre so many times each day for potential clients and reporters that we ran into a crisis in the adjoining foley studio, where they made all the live-action sounds like feet marching on dried grass or soldiers running on a battlement. "You're setting back the foley production so badly we're going to have to lay on weekend overtime shifts," complained Pat Goodland. "You mean they built this theatre so cheap that the sound comes through the wall?" I said. "This is supposed to be a soundproof studio." She shrugged.

Throughout the spring and summer of 2000, Gene Allen and I were going through every minute of the series, line by line, and polishing the scripts. Documentary writing is a reductionist process. Reduction isn't so much saying what you mean in the fewest possible words as distilling the essence of the thought, using metaphor and simile as your tools.

The producers and directors had already written the scripts, but their drafts needed to be smoothed into a series style. Gene and I played good cop, bad cop with each other, saying "I don't understand that" and "Why should I give a shit about this?" until we got the balance right. We were determined to make all the scripts comprehensible to anyone above the age of twelve. I would ask Gene to explain a chapter as he would to my daughters if they were there.

I have enjoyed writing with Gene ever since we worked on *Dawn of the Eye*. We were perfect foils for each other, pacing the room while trying to come up with a noun, homing in on it like some elusive moth: "Heritage..." "Inheritance..." "No..." "Legacy!" We took turns sitting at the laptop, playing secretary to each other's thoughts. Gene was irritated because I was always late, and I bristled when he slurped his tea loudly, but otherwise the weekends we worked together were the most pleasant moments in the series for me. Gene had the grasp and the knowledge of Canadian history, and I'd interview him to find the human drama underlying each story. Gene's marriage had also recently collapsed, and he was staying with friends and looking for a place to live, too. Sometimes, between Jacques Cartier and Captain Cook, our conversation would drift to kitchenware.

Like all really great journalists, Gene has a childlike capacity for wonder, which survived all the years he spent earning a doctorate in

Canadian history. "Think of it, Mark," he'd say when talking about the ancient burial site at L'Anse Amour in Labrador. "Before the pyramids in Egypt, before Athens, before the invention of the wheel in Mesopotamia, people buried a child here, people with their own gods, their own language and social organization." The "gee whiz" expression would animate his face and he would look at you, eyes wide and eager, like some kid who'd found a giant marble. The phrase "Baldwin-LaFontaine alliance" was enough to put anyone to sleep, until Gene explained it. First, he'd bring the people alive. "Robert Baldwin was a man so deeply in love with his wife," he said, "that he never forgot the pain of her having a baby by Caesarean. He left instructions in his will that on his death, a cut be made on his body to match the incision on his beloved wife." After the failure of the 1837 Rebellions, Britain united the two assemblies of Upper and Lower Canada into one assembly of United Canada, which effectively marginalized the French and the reform parties in each province. Baldwin then made the move that shaped the destiny of the country. He dispatched a letter to the reform leader Louis Hippolyte LaFontaine in Lower Canada, offering an alliance between the English and French reformers. Gene would stand up and read from the script by Peter Ingles, Frédéric Vanasse, and Andrew Burnstein, "He writes to LaFontaine, 'There is and there must be no question of races. It were madness on one side, and guilt, deep guilt on both to make such a question.' LaFontaine accepts the alliance, but he can't get elected in his own riding of Terrebonne because the governor general put the only polling station in an English village, and thugs block his supporters!" By now, Gene would have everyone transfixed. "Baldwin prevails on his father, William, to give up his nomination in the Toronto riding of North York and offer it to LaFontaine. Think about it! A French Canadian – a supporter of the 1837 Rebellion – runs in a Toronto riding, and he wins! It probably wouldn't happen today." The first time Gene related this story, everyone broke into applause. "That's not all," he continued. "Later on, when Baldwin is defeated in the riding of York, LaFontaine returns the favour, and Baldwin runs in the French riding of Rimouski, and wins! What do you want for a great yarn?"

Our biggest writing challenge was Episode 1, "When the World Began. . . ." It ranged over twenty thousand years, had little recorded history, and risked sounding like an anthropology lecture. It was the episode that worried me most, because it had the fewest quotes and few characters on whom to hang a narrative. Finally we decided the character would be Canada itself. Andy Gregg was determined to produce an episode that saw aboriginal history from *here* and not just through the eyes of explorers from *there*. "I want to show it in all its complexity," he said, "before the white man finds it." I had been skeptical until I came across a photocopy of a pre-contact map of North America, which showed the approximate "borders" of all the nations that existed before the arrival of Europeans. It was as complex as a map of Europe today. It was like seeing a picture of the other side of the moon for the first time.

It was hard to explain the complexity and diversity of North America, so finally we created one scene, early in the first episode, based simply on the map. For almost three minutes the camera just pans across the map while the narrator reads a list of the aboriginal nations. The beauty was in the names. It was one of the most powerful sequences in the series.

In the rough cut, when the camera pulled back to reveal the map and the music swelled, Julie Dossett shouted, "Yeaaahhh, team!" and people applauded. I took note that people with names like Dossett, Gendron, Burnstein, and Chong felt pride in a prehistory that had nothing to do with their ancestry. Why? I would think about that often in the weeks to come.

Sometimes, when I needed to get away from the beehive the unit had become, I would head to the relative peace of the eighth-floor narration studio. After two years of hearing only temporary "scratch narration," it was heartening to hear the "voice" of the series. It had taken us two months of auditions in Toronto and Montreal to decide on the English and French voices who would be the guides through the history of Canada. After much debate, Marie Tifo, an experi-enced television personality with a wide popular following, was hired to narrate the French version, and in Toronto, we chose an actor who had performed on stage for twenty years, Maggie Huculak.

Gene and I were now a frantic writing factory, creating or killing words on demand, not only doctoring scripts but writing the head-lines and introductions for each episode, network promos, and even a major trailer for the movie theatres. As soon as a page was "locked," it was whisked by Rachel to all the various departments, and to narration.

Meanwhile, in graphic compositing, Stephen Dutcheshen was commanding a platoon of artists in creating digital armadas and erasing modern intrusions that had snuck in. He remembers that somehow, "through all the screenings, everyone had missed a car speeding by in the background of a Lundy's Lane battle scene, and it had to be carefully removed." At other computer stations, artists were removing electrical lines from shots of steam trains chugging through the prairies, and three different compositors struggled for long days and nights to create a fleet of ships from a single shot of the *Endeavour* to recreate Wolfe's invasion of Canada. "The rocking water and shaking camera made it a nightmare of image tracking," complained Dutcheshen. "The computer has to take the movement of the ship, memorize it, and apply the same movements to new cloned ships. There was much aggravation and hair-pulling." This team was working on graphic compositions equal in complexity to those in *Titanic* and had become one of the leading digital graphics shops in North America. In Montreal, Alain Provost was single-handedly setting barns and fields on fire in the Acadian Deportation with electronic fire that was startlingly real, digitally subtracting cars and stop signs from video of the Place d'Armes, and designing the master animation for the entire series.

It seemed that, for all the apparent turbulence, the series was in good hands and in good shape. I appreciated the words of a six-teenth-century theatre producer in *Shakespeare in Love*, which came out that summer. In the midst of chaos, he shrugs and says, "It always comes together somehow. I don't know how. It's a miracle." But not everything was.

Hubert called on a Sunday in June to say that Serge wasn't feeling well and had gone to an emergency room, and that Gail Boyd would take over directing their shoot in the Saguenay. It was a tricky reconstruction of the Great Peace of 1701, when thirteen hundred native delegates of more than forty nations gathered in Montreal to sign a treaty to end the Indian attacks on New France. Since Hubert had written the scene, he went up with Gail.

I called the hospital late that night and miraculously reached Serge. They had found something, he said, and they were going to have to do some more detailed tests. I thought I was talking to him in his hospital room, but in the background it sounded more like a Metro station. "No," he said, "I've been in the corridor for the last ten hours, waiting. I sent Jacqueline and the kids home." I called him again on Monday. He was still in the corridor, in pain and waiting for a room.

By Monday night, they had finally found a bed for him, and by Wednesday he had been diagnosed with advanced colon cancer. Serge was forty-five years old, the father of an eight-year-old daughter and a newborn son. His contract with us was running out this summer. As a freelancer, he had no disability coverage, no survivor pension, and the future for him and his wife suddenly looked terrifying. Anne Emin and I talked, then I called Jacqueline to tell her not to worry about money; we would extend Serge's contract as needed and find work for him when he was well.

This was the fourth tragedy to hit our team. In Toronto the head of wardrobe, Vasile (Bill) Fortais, had died unexpectedly. The Montreal team had been struck by two serious illnesses: Mechthild Furlani, a gifted producer and mother of a young child, was on disability, battling cancer. Louis Martin was gravely ill. Now Serge.

When Serge came out of the hospital, he insisted on returning to the edit suite to work on his episodes. But his smiles grew scarcer, his body thinner, his face gaunt, and his eyes ringed in black. Hubert thought Serge was coming in out of a sense of obligation, and told him, "You know, your health and your family are more important. We can finish it for you." Serge said he wanted to finish his work. Then he added: "We all know we're going to die, it's just that some of us have a clearer idea when." Still, we all hoped he'd beat the cancer, and Serge talked about how he'd take me to the Îles de la Madeleine, as promised, maybe around Christmas. In the meantime, he asked me to look after the orchestral scoring of "Battle for a Continent."

Up to now we had been using temporary music in the edit suites, usually tracks taken from film scores to approximate the mood and effect we wanted. After picture-lock, however, the composers set about the mammoth task of scoring every minute of each episode. The composers were Eric Robertson, an imposing Scot who looked like Rasputin and was music director of his church, and his partner Claude Desjardins, a shorter, heavy-set Métis who wore his long greying hair tied in the back. They had started work a year ago on the master theme of the series at a meeting where I'd thrown out phrases like "epic but not pompous," and they talked about "attack," "resolution," and "undertow." It was like two blind men trying to describe an elephant to each other. The process can test the limits of the language. For the part where Wolfe has failed to take Quebec and all his officers are mocking him, we'd say, "We need a military theme over flags and tents, but an undercurrent of decay and desperation." They always nodded, though I suspect they were humouring us. They were scoring sixteen hours for the first wave, the equivalent of ten movies, so they were as sleep-deprived and harried as the rest of us, on top of which Claude was in agony from a kidney stone. He'd be greeted in the mixing studios with "Do you have the 'Continent of Nations' theme, and have you passed the stone?"

There are certain moments you live for in a series, but perhaps the greatest is the day the orchestra comes in to record. I rounded up people from the edit suites and the library and practically dragged them to the huge sixth-floor music recording studio. "It's better than sex," I said. "You have to experience it." The control room looks like the bridge of Captain Kirk's *Enterprise*. The mixing board has over a hundred tracks, some of the fader controls so far from the operator that they are run robotically. There are several couches against the glass panels that overlook the three glass rooms that separately house the brass, the percussion, and the strings. The scene for which the musicians are laying down the score is projected onto a huge screen, and the speakers inside the control room are so large and so sophisticated that they envelop you in the music – it is a physical experience.

Eric Robertson conducted twenty-two musicians – mostly from the Toronto Symphony Orchestra – scene by scene. A scene that to me meant freezing on a battlement in Louisbourg, then an ashtray full of cigarettes while writing the script, then images on a small screen became, finally, with music, the scene I had imagined two years before.

The next urgent task was to publicize the series. Of late, television has become as competitive as the movie industry, which is as much about promoting a film as producing it: you have to shout loud to have any hope of being heard in the din of the American and Canadian television launch season. Our air date was Sunday, October 22.

Slawko Klymkiw and the executive director of communications, Diane Kenyon, made our series the priority for all publicity and the keystone of the CBC fall launch. "We're going to carpet bomb the country with promos," Slawko said, and he was true to his word. Spots were going to appear on radio and television stations across Canada and on border stations in the United States. Six different posters were readied to be deployed in bus shelters around the country; full-page newspaper and magazine ads were going to accompany every weekly episode. It was a thrill for me to sit in a movie theatre with Madeleine and Zoe and during the trailers suddenly watch the battlefield of the Plains of Abraham appear. The orchestral music swelled and the screen exploded with a magnificent sixty-second trailer for "Canada – as you've never seen it before." I could hear gasps and murmurs ripple through the packed theatre. No one had seen anything like this about Canada before. This wasn't a Heritage Minute, this was a Canadian production being advertised with the same rocket fuel as an American film.

The CBC had decided to repeat the series during each week, as American specialty channels and PBS had been doing with their big-ticket series. Each episode would run at 8:00 P.M. Sunday, be repeated at 11:00 the same night, then again at 8:00 P.M. the following Thursday. In the thousand-channel universe, you have to pursue the viewer with multiple viewing opportunities.

French network publicity was downright tepid in comparison to the CBC's, about one-tenth the scale. The Radio-Canada publicity people informed us that their instructions were to treat the series as one of six or seven big events that fall, not the centrepiece of their schedule. The idea of running the series in unison on both networks had been reduced to airing them the same week. We would launch on the same night, but then go our own ways. The symmetry was lost. Radio-Canada had no intention of repeating each episode during the week, we were advised.

One day in midsummer, all the publicity and communications heads from both networks spoke in a lengthy conference call to coordinate plans to promote the series. It didn't take long for it to become clear that Radio-Canada was not even playing in the same league. The CBC people on the Toronto end of the conversation were shaking their heads in amazement and despair. Finally one of the most senior CBC publicity people – whom I don't feel free to name – leaned toward the speakerphone and said loudly, "The real scandal in this room is what Radio-Canada is *not* spending and *not* doing to promote this series." For Hubert and Mario and the Montreal team, who had been stretched beyond all human limits and who had fought so relentlessly to make sure the series reflected Quebec history, this was further confirmation that their own network was a lukewarm supporter at best.

Our frustration led us to break ranks temporarily with the Radio-Canada communications people in late summer. We told them we would contact the editors of the major Quebec newspapers ourselves and try to break the silence around the series in Quebec. Mario Cardinal had the stature as a Quebec nationalist and – more important – the respect as a journalist to call the editors of the

Montreal dailies personally and get them to a screening at the Château Champlain. They were briefed on the series and shown excerpts that established that the series was pulling no punches. To counter the assumption that this was some kind of Sheila Copps "Save Canada" initiative with special funding from Ottawa, Mario made a very effective speech, putting his integrity on the line and declaring that this was an honourable, objective journalistic effort. By now, we pointed out, every major publication and newspaper in English Canada was preparing lengthy features on the series. No French-language paper or publication had yet demonstrated any serious interest, however. "Analyze us, criticize us," Mario said with passion, "but it would be a crime to ignore an enterprise of this uniqueness, magnitude, and honesty."

In English Canada, *Maclean's, Saturday Night, Toronto Life*, and *Time Canada*, plus over a dozen major newspapers, were all committed to run features on the series in the first half of October. But the Montreal press continued to ignore us, despite Mario's personal intervention with the editors of the Montreal dailies. *Le Devoir* was the only paper to interview us. How the press could be indifferent to the large-scale portrayal of the iconic events in their own history, broadcast to their own readership, was incomprehensible to me.

Corporate Canada was also acting indifferent to the series. Gaye McDonald and the CBC sales team had extended the sponsorship deadline to the absolute last minute. The Royal Bank of Canada might come aboard, the sales people thought. Its chairman and CEO, John Cleghorn, was a big advocate of supporting Canadian history and had expressed interest in the series when it was first announced. Then, out of the blue, another sponsor appeared and became the first to commit itself to the series. Sun Life Financial is a venerable Canadian insurance company that had expanded into a full financial services institution and needed to enlarge its public profile. It was a daring move that locked out any other financial institution, because CBC was offering "sector exclusivity" – only one financial company, one transportation, one oil, etc. By jumping in when no one else had the nerve, Sun Life was rewarded with a great deal of free publicity in the business press.

What flabbergasted me was that the author of this tactical move was none other than my nemesis from the death of *The Journal*. Robert Pattillo was now the vice-president of public and corporate affairs for Sun Life Financial and had gone to the board of directors and urged the move. On the executive floor of the CBC, I was the butt of endless ribbing: "Are you going to be able to stand there in public and praise Pattillo?" In fact I did, many times and quite sincerely, allowing that, while he may not have redeemed himself completely, he had taken a major step in the direction of a holy life.

Sun Life Financial produced excellent spots for the series on just three weeks' notice, and its army of salespersons and representatives handed out flyers and schedules for the series at all their locations. Of the five available sponsorship slots, four were still unsold when the series went to air. Sun Life had the field to itself, a point even the business press repeated regularly in the months to follow, as it jeered other corporations for lacking courage.

Radio-Canada did finally stage a proper series launch on Tuesday, October 10, at the old fort on Île Sainte-Hélène just across the river from downtown Montreal. It was very colourful and well-organized, with the Milice de Chambly in full dress greeting invited guests from the press, museums, and historical and community groups. A dozen native warriors who had worked with the series came in magnificent war paint and dress. We screened "Battle for a Continent." Serge came for the occasion and sat at the back, looking very thin and his eyes set in dark rings. At the end of the episode the room burst into applause, and it gave me great satisfaction to ask Serge Turbide to rise in the back and accept the accolades. He smiled and bowed his head slightly in acknowledgement of the applause. I could see he was deeply moved.

Outside, some of the re-enactors in French and British uniform were smoking with the painted warriors, affording as incongruous a scene as anyone could imagine. "Hey," one of the guests shouted as he emerged from the screening, "weren't you guys bashing in each other's heads in there a second ago?" A large tent had been erected on the grounds, and some two hundred participants and guests, many in period costumes, toasted the launch of the series.

Gail Boyd, however, was nowhere to be seen. Hubert told me she was feeling sick and had a fever. He had persuaded her to go to hospital. Four days later, he called me in Toronto. "Gail Boyd has acute leukemia," he said. "It looks very, very bad." We were both silent for some time. Gail was a former dancer, ate healthily, and took very good care of herself. She had two young children and was only in her early forties. We hoped fervently that someone so young and strong would beat the disease. "What is it about this project?" I said, thinking of Louis, of Serge, of Mecky Furlani. "I've never seen so much tragedy strike a single group of people in my whole life."

By October, everyone was so emotionally drained and physically exhausted that a doctor who saw some of us at a dinner told me, "Everyone I've seen here has every symptom of combat fatigue." We just wanted this nightmare to be over; it had gone on too long in a permanent state of crisis. Vindication would be nice, but termination would do. Then magazine features and advance reviews began to appear on the newsstands. They ran the gamut from cruel ("An experience verging on narcolepsy," Alex Strachan in the *Vancouver Sun*) to enthusiastic ("Probably the most remarkable programming achievement in the history of the CBC," Tony Atherton of the *Ottawa Citizen*).

Time Canada, which had to bump us from the cover for the bombing of Yugoslavia, nevertheless devoted the most space – thirteen pages – and the most play of any publication, with a viewing guide to each episode. The article by Steven Frank proclaimed, "The epic that unfolds later this month is a masterwork of dramatic storytelling" and called the cinematography "extraordinary."

Maclean's bumped us for a cover not about Yugoslavia but about the importance of keeping fit, but still did a seven-page special report on the series. Brian Bethune concluded, "The television achievement is undeniable, and in terms of telling the stories – reliving the experience – of individual Canadians, unparalleled. . . . Now we can see ourselves as never before."

Toronto Life had come out with Robert Fulford's article earlier in the month. I waited till I got a large coffee, then closed the door and laid it out on my desk. Instead of the negative piece I had expected, Fulford had written a generous appreciation of the risk our team had taken, of the narrative and visual techniques we used, and paid tribute to the CBC for daring to back us. In the last paragraph of page 83, he tersely declared, to my surprise: "After seeing samples of the work-in-progress, my foolhardy guess is that . . . the latest work of Mark Starowicz will be among his triumphs."

Fulford's article was a turning point for the enterprise. The approval of Canada's leading cultural critic was crucial to the success of the series.

On Friday, October 20, Slawko called me. "Good luck, buddy. I don't care what the ratings are. We're doing the right thing." I predicted 400,000 viewers, which is the best an episode of *Witness* will get. "I'll declare success at 400,000," I said, "and I'll set the church bells ringing at 500,000." Slawko said he would too, though he dreamed of a million, and I told him he was crazy. I invited everyone to my home to watch it. Saturday I spent buying beer, wine, and cold cuts. Seventy-five people came over to watch the opening of the series. Someone showed up with a placard reading "Oppose Narrative Cleansing" as a joke. Caitlin and Madeleine played bartenders. I called Hubert to wish him luck on the Radio-Canada launch, then I called Serge to wish him the same, but I was afraid to disturb Gail.

A silence falls when a production team watches a broadcast, because any talk is an act of disrespect to the writer, the music mixer, the foley man. Then it comes on and rushes like water through your fingers, entire months and years pour through. As the credits rolled by, we applauded every contributor, but then suddenly it was 10:00 P.M., the big train moved on to the news, and all of those stories in Baker Lake, and the polar bears, the muskoxen, and Cartier and

Donnacona were gone. Friends called to say it was terrific. But in the end, everyone went home, and I was left facing a postpartum void. It would be Monday, late afternoon, before the Nielsen ratings came in. The morning was shapeless, filled with nervous small talk, as we wondered if we had collectively won or laid an egg. More than that, did anyone give a damn about Canadian history?

Antonia Zerbisias in the *Toronto Star* that weekend found the series "breathtaking in its breadth and fascinating in its details." But she also wondered, "Will Canadians watch ... ? How I would love to say ... yes. But years of monitoring our TV habits have taught me that most of us seek entertainment and not enlightenment from our screens. You can lead Canadians to their high-minded history – and CBC was right to do so – but you can't tear them away from *The X-Files*."

16

Something's Happening Out There

About thirty-two hundred homes in Canada are rigged by the A.C. Nielsen company with devices that log what channel is being watched by whom. On the basis of this sample, the next day computers spit out the data detailing how many viewers watched every television program in Canada, minute by minute, by age, gender, income, education, and region. These data spell life or death for entire series and determine the rate card for millions of dollars in advertising. I was so nervous I even read my horoscope in the *Globe* that weekend, and I was surprised to find this: "Something miraculously wonderful will happen to you tomorrow, which will vindicate everything you have been working towards."

The ratings wouldn't come out till late afternoon, but all morning in the Broadcast Centre, everyone in the project was being warmly congratulated and thanked wherever they went. Producers and researchers were approached in the cafeteria and on the elevators by people they didn't know and told that the series made them proud to be part of the CBC. Of course, I found a reason to worry about this too, fearing that people were getting their hopes raised only to have them dashed when the ratings came out.

At four o'clock, Slawko called and my heart sank – if it was good news, I knew he would have come storming through the door in person. "Are you sitting down?" he asked gravely. "One million, seven hundred thousand viewers for the main broadcast. Two hundred twenty-one thousand on the 11:00 P.M. repeat. Five hundred and fifty-eight thousand on the French network. Congratulations, buddy. That's two and a half million people, and we still have the Thursday repeat to add to that."

The *Ottawa Citizen's* Tony Atherton was the first to report the stunning results and understand their significance. In a page three story headlined "CBC Special Knocks Out Millionaire" he wrote: "Canadian history outdrew American trivia Sunday night as the audience for CTV's top-rated *Who Wants to Be a Millionaire?* plummeted in the face of withering competition from CBC's *Canada: A People's History.*" It was the largest audience for any CBC program since the season began, and "its viewership rivaled some of the peak moments of the network's Sydney Olympic coverage.... The ratings for the opener of *Canada: A People's History* are on par with the recent season debuts of many popular US shows. The strength of the response to the series apparently even caught its producers off guard."

The Thursday-night repeat of the first episode, which ran only on CBC-owned stations and not affiliates, got 461,000 viewers, which raised the total viewing of the first episode to 2.9 million people. Those are Stanley Cup playoff numbers, not numbers for documentaries and certainly not numbers for Canadian history. In my wildest dreams and hopes I never imagined that that many people would watch. Up against the World Series, against *Who Wants to Be a Millionaire?*, the most popular show on television, against the season premiere of *The X-Files* and *The Simpsons*, Canadian history should have been roadkill, according to all television and marketing rules. "Anyone predicting this a year ago would have been suspected of having an alcohol problem," Laine Drewery mused.

On the Monday and Tuesday following the broadcast, the CBC was swamped with hundreds of phone calls and e-mails that poured in from across Canada and all the American border states – so many that the CBC had to put on an extra shift to handle them. We had struck a deep chord. The response, in fact, was so overwhelming that some columnists predicted it was a result of heavy promotion and early curiosity that would not be sustained. Even historians like Michael Bliss and Jack Granatstein, who had been arguing Canadians were interested in their history, found it too good to be true. We had passed our first hurdle, an episode set in a past so distant that it had less immediate relevance to Canadians' daily lives. Would English Canada now watch three entire episodes about New France? I feared a "Why are we watching all this endless French stuff" reaction. I confessed my fears to Bob Culbert, who had called to congratulate us. "Mark, don't worry," he said. "You've already won the battle."

The following Monday, we went through the same aching wait for the four o'clock ratings. This time the *Globe* horoscope gave me no clues, except to observe that my romantic life was blooming, which dispatched my short-lived faith in astrology. Then came the second miracle. The ratings were sustained. Two million, two hundred thousand people watched the Sunday-night broadcast, and there was still the Thursday repeat to come. The series was shaping into a habit for a huge number of Canadians. Neither the *Globe* nor the *National Post* reported the ratings victories for a long time, even though I pointed out to their editors that, after months of speculating whether anyone would watch, they were not reporting the answer to their own questions. Good news travels slowly.

The CBC research department was in a state of high excitement all this time, behaving like astronomers who have discovered a new planet. All the ratings conventions were being shattered, along with half the truisms of the thousand-channel universe. "They haven't seen family viewing patterns like this," Slawko reported, "since *The Ed Sullivan Show* and *Walt Disney Presents*." A large proportion of the audience was watching television the way nobody is supposed to any more: in family groups of all ages, including children as young as seven. Anecdotally we kept hearing from friends and family that kids were staying up to watch with their parents, and the early figures were bearing this out.

We had aimed the series at age twelve and up, but that was more for future school use. Even I was surprised that we seemed to have seized the imagination of younger Canadians. I wrote in my notes, "They're still two-hour documentaries and you practically have to take the phone off the hook, sit in a straight-backed chair, and pay close attention or you'll lose your place. Something big is happening out there."

One thing I did know for sure now, and I said it in every newspaper and radio interview: "The myth that Canadians are not interested in their history is dead. If it was ever true, which I doubt, it is now statistically, demonstrably, and irrevocably dead." The first two episodes were now the most viewed documentaries in Canadian television history – that means that even with two hundred channels in Canada, this series was getting higher ratings than when there were only four or five channels.

"We're very good television producers," I said, "but we're not *that* good. It's like we've been drilling for gas and struck some giant, pent-up pressure dome that blew us away." I became more fascinated with the scale of the reaction as each episode held onto the audience. There was something in the national mind that had been undetected by the polls, was untracked by the political parties, crossed all political and regional divides, all age and occupational lines, and was *very* big. It would take me weeks to figure out what it was.

In the meantime, I wanted to capitalize on this tidal wave of goodwill for the CBC. The corporation had spent the summer debating whether to shut down its regional stations and was bitterly divided within. In editorials, in letters to the editor, and in Parliament, "This is exactly what the CBC is supposed to be doing" was repeated daily. But the point had to be broadened, because public broadcasting was still fighting for its life.

I had other objectives too. Within a few weeks, most of the first wave of researchers and directors would be leaving the project, which

I thought was a tragedy. I thought it was wrong to let all this accumu-
lated talent and experience seep out of the CBC and Radio-Canada.
These were people who had sacrificed so much for the CBC in the past
three years. But the series had a one-time budget, and as episodes
were completed and contracts ran out, it was our job to shut down.
Gene Allen had applied for a teaching post at Ryerson University in
Toronto. Laine Drewery and Andy Gregg were moving on to projects
outside the CBC. Once again, we were letting the best creators of
content leave. It was corporate madness, I argued.

I was already being asked in interviews, "What's the next big
project?" And I had to answer that there was none so far. People
thought I was being coy, unable to imagine that the CBC wasn't using
this team for an even greater challenge. The moment to announce a
permanent documentary production unit was now.

An ideal opportunity to speak publicly on behalf of documentary production came when I was invited to give the Harold Innis
Lecture at the University of Toronto. It is a high-profile series,
broadcast by the CBC Radio program *Ideas*. I wanted to make the
point that public broadcasting was on its last legs in Canada, and
that market-driven broadcasting policies were strangling Canadian
stories. If we couldn't finance something as fundamental as a history
of our own country in the private marketplace, I argued, what hope
is there for financing anything other than a golf tournament? "It
underscores the cold reality of the market: nothing will be financed
unless it can be demonstrated to sell pop or soap. It just won't happen.
The marketplace will not, operating by its own laws, produce what
is necessary and good for our children and our society. That's not
how it works.

"Public broadcasting is not supposed to be a marginal player for
the elite. It is supposed to be the risk-taker. No other network, no
specialty channel, no institution would have ever embarked on a
project like this. The risk was incalculable. Let's restore the bolder
view of public television. That there shall be, on the airwaves, one
honest player who will act as a counterbalance, who will work not for
the market but the people. And that player shall produce vigorously

in all the constituencies of human discourse and entertainment a news department that is free of special interest, a regional service that is free of local interests, a children's department, a drama department that tells our stories whether or not they sell abroad, because they are important to us, and a music and variety department that nurtures the songs of our sons and daughters.... It is time to bring those studios alive again, bring back the talent we have lost, and open the doors for the next generation. We can restore documentary. We can also restore Canadian drama."

In fact, I did have another project in mind, one that would rally the best talent in the country and cement CBC's position as the principal cultural producer in the country. I had been thinking about it for years. It would be the other core legacy project of Canadian television. I wanted to put the idea on the public agenda at the Innis lecture.

"A modest proposal: I always told people the idea of doing a history of Canada was not original to me. I heard it years ago from my boss, the vice-president of English Television, Peter Herrndorf, who was musing out loud one day. 'There are two great tasks this network must achieve someday,' he said. 'To produce a television history of Canada. And the second great task is – to produce the twenty great classics of Canadian literature.' Sounds like a project to me....

"The lesson of the Canadian History Project is: Canadians want their stories, their music, their history. We just have to have the will to do it. The will that was summoned in 1932 [the creation of public broadcasting]. In the middle of a depression, in the face of a daunting technology, we did not succumb to technological despair and fatalism. We did it then. To borrow a phrase: 'If you build it, they will come.'"

A country has a history and a literature. If we could undertake a ten-year project to produce the great works of English and French literature in Canada, it would have a powerful effect in disseminating our cultural heritage, sharing that heritage across French-English lines, and enriching our schools and libraries. The British had created magnificent productions of Austen, Dickens, and Waugh, translating their literary heritage to the cinematic age. I believed that if Canada did too, it would not only enrich us but project Canadian literature even farther into the world market, where it had already developed a considerable following. The best directors would produce the films, the documentary unit would produce an accompanying literary history of Canada. A year later, the international success of the film *Atanarjuat: The Fast Runner* convinced me that we must do this.

On the eve of Episode 4, "Battle for a Continent," we gathered again, all except Gail Boyd, who was recovering from heavy chemotherapy for her leukemia. I called Gail's home and left a message that we were all thinking of her. I also called Serge, who had gathered a small group of friends at his home, thanked him for putting up with all of us but me in particular, and told him his images would shape a generation's view of that turbulent era. He thanked me for the chance to make this film, and once again we agreed we'd be together on the Îles de la Madeleine.

I knew we were on safe ground in the series now. The rest of the episodes were full of dramatic action, first with the Seven Years War, then the American Revolution and the War of 1812, the epic of the great explorers, and the 1837 Rebellions. The companion book by McClelland & Stewart had shot up to number one on the non-fiction best-seller list as soon as it was released. The video sets sold out in the first week and had to go back to press, then sold out again. Canadian history was the best-selling video for Christmas sales, and we were starting to get complaints daily that people couldn't find it in stores. Caitlin and Madeleine and I went from bookstore to bookstore just gazing at the displays and sending book browsers telepathic messages to buy it.

My picture had appeared in the papers enough that I was being recognized by people. At a parking ticket vending machine, a man waiting behind me startled me by saying, "Are you the guy who's doing that history of Canada? Bloody good on you, we're all proud of you." In a checkout line at Dominion, a young couple with children did the same, and everyone else in the line started shaking hands with me. On two rush-hour subway trips, perfect strangers on the subway called out "Good work" and "Thank you" as I got off at my stop. Before a flight to Winnipeg, the woman at the Air Canada counter recognized my name and upgraded me to business class. At a convention of Ontario high school teachers, five hundred people shot to their feet and gave CBC's Karen Bower and me a standing ovation. *Maclean's* called to inform me I had been voted to its Roll of Honour, the ten Canadians who most made a difference in the year 2000, and the *Toronto Star* picked me for a similar honour. At Pinto's Market near my farm in Cavan, where I appear many weekends looking like an escaped convict, it appeared everyone in the store had seen it and was delighted. Joe Pinto gave me a free movie rental.

The first writer to observe that a significant national phenomenon seemed to be under way was the historian Irving Abella, who wrote a lengthy piece in the *Globe* on November 15 entitled: "The Greatest Show Unearthed – Costly, Controversial, the Canadian History Project Is Accomplishing the Unthinkable." He wrote, "What's going on? A year ago prominent historians and others were lamenting that Canadian history was dead. . . . But suddenly, over the past month or so, millions of Canadians have been glued to their television sets every Sunday night watching, and apparently savouring – guess what – a documentary series on Canadian history." He observed that the series had struck a national chord: "Threatened by internal disunity, racial strife, regional breakdown and menacing globalization, Canadians are desperate for answers and explanations. . . . *A People's History* has . . . restored our history to us with all its vibrancy, surprises and humanity."

Meanwhile the press reviews kept pouring in, almost all of them favourable, many of them commending the CBC, and a few castigating corporate Canada for not backing the project. At the end of December, the *Globe and Mail* columnist John Gray wrote, "For anyone struggling to keep our spirits up here in the silent dark of the Great White North, the most soul-satisfying cultural event this year was the success of *Canada: A People's History*. . . . It was supposed to be a disaster. . . . After press screenings, no surprise, TV pundits proclaimed themselves correct: The series was a well-meaning history lesson, short on entertainment value, certain to fail. Meanwhile, academic pundits – amputated at the armpits, the better to fit the small screen – sniffed that the series wasn't *deep* enough.... Then the first episode aired, and if you heard a great whirring afterwards, it was the sound of opinion vendors, back-pedaling their way to safety.... Who wants to watch that? About 2½ million actually."

There are three striking things for me, as I review the hundreds of clippings. First is an almost universal approval for recognizing the pre-contact history of Canada and treating the aboriginal populations as nations, not tribes. Second, there was scarcely a whiff of the backlash I feared about too much French history or sympathy for the Canadien side in the British invasion. Third, and most striking of all, it's fascinating how the news of the series shifted. The story became not the content of the series but the fact that Canadians *watched* it. In other words, the real story became not the performance on the stage but the audience.

Initially, our contact with the viewers was by mail or by individual encounter. We wanted to avoid an "official launch" in Ottawa at all costs, despite the fact that Head Office wanted a gala on Parliament Hill. We were told that the Prime Minister's Office was very interested in having Jean Chrétien speak at such a launch. To the irritation of CBC's parliamentary liaison people, we refused. It wasn't out of disrespect, we simply wanted to have as little to do with politicians as possible, to avoid any hint of the series being perceived as propaganda for national unity. Instead, we finally settled on a number of regional launches, to emphasize that this history came from everywhere.

The most memorable launch for me was in Winnipeg on November 29, our first large-scale encounter with viewers since the series started. Four hundred guests came to a reception and screening in the grand ballroom at the historic Fort Garry Hotel. There were representatives there from the St. Boniface French community and from the Assembly of First Nations, there were Métis leaders and re-enactors who had helped stage the Battle of Batoche. There were Ukrainians and Mennonites, civic leaders, historians, and people from the Hudson's Bay Company and Manitoba archives, from labour groups, church groups, and immigrant associations, many in traditional dress. The walls were decorated with the earliest photographs of Manitoba's history, and musicians played historic instruments. It was an unexpected and genuine celebration of everyone's harsh pioneer roots. The huge screen played images from the episodes that would air after Christmas – images of the Selkirk settlers landing, the Indians saving them from starvation, the Métis buffalo hunt, the raising of the flag of Riel's provisional government in Manitoba, the diaries of fur traders who married native women, and the remarkable journeys of the voyageurs. The pride in that ballroom was so palpable, the room itself seemed to swell. The applause was like thunder at the end of the screening, and for the rest of the evening dozens and dozens of people came up to us, from former premier Duff Roblin to the Métis leader Steve Racine, who took off the *ceinture fléchée* he had worn for twenty years and put it around my waist.

I wasn't the only one to be struck by the evening – everyone in the group said they'd felt something special was happening. I wondered about it on the flight back. After all, we hadn't shown the various people and groups there anything about their past they didn't already know. And we certainly hadn't dressed it up to conceal the story of privation and territorial struggle that it was. No, by piecing together remarks people had made, I realized that what was moving them was that, finally, their experience and provenance were being valued, given their place. The series was weaving their stories into the national tapestry; the coureur de bois, the Mennonite, the Jewish garment worker were in the same tapestry as Champlain, Donnacona, Papineau, and Mackenzie.

The series went on hiatus for most of December, to make room for Christmas specials. It would return January 7, with the adventures of the great explorers and the opening of the west. But Christmas was pretty grim.

The news we dreaded had come. One month after his episode aired, and two days before Christmas, Serge Turbide died at home with his wife, Jacqueline, and his children at his side. He was forty-five.

No one in Montreal or Toronto got any work done that day, they were too sick at heart. The gentlest man among us, who had given his all, had been struck down just after his greatest accomplishment, just days before Christmas.

In our house it was the last one we spent as a united family. In the home of Gail Boyd and her husband Achille Michaud, Christmas was their best ever. Gail was feeling better. But just weeks later her blood cell count turned bad again, and it looked like only a bone marrow transplant could save her. In Toronto and Montreal, history staffers were volunteering to have bone marrow tests. But the best match was likely to be Gail's sister, who lived in Algeria. We passed the hat in both Toronto and Montreal, and we raised $16,000 to fly her over to be tested. Mecky Furlani, in the meantime, was growing weaker, and her morale sank with the news of Gail's losing battle.

The Montreal team had many pressures on it. Ever since the first episode aired, they had been enduring the hostility of the media and sometimes of their colleagues. My initial suspicions that we were being shut out in the Montreal press sadly proved right. After a small flurry of attention, some of it grudgingly friendly, most television columnists ignored the series, or mocked it.

Le Devoir's television columnist, Vincent Desautels, pronounced the series federalist propaganda: "It's Sheila Copps who should be happy. Happy? The word is weak. The heritage minister should be delirious. Flap-flap-flap, the seal flaps her flippers, shakes her ass, does two or three spins, and jumps back on the floe. It takes more than just a ball on its nose for the little beast to get excited. Flap-flap-flap. Oh, isn't she cute, she's flapping her flippers. Finally someone has understood what the expression 'Canadian content' meant. And Sheila Copps can triumph over all the wicked tongues that mocked her unifoliates. Even better, it's Radio-Canada that is giving her so much joy."

Three weeks later, a commentary by the political scientist Christian Dufour appeared in *Le Devoir*. He savagely attacked the series for "intellectual fraud," saying that the Royal Proclamation of 1763 was the instrument that banned Canadian Catholics from holding office and sitting on juries or sitting in a legislative assembly, and Episode 4, "Battle for a Continent," ignored this.

A week later, our senior historical adviser, Jean-Claude Robert, responded in *Le Devoir*. Dufour was dead wrong: "It's absolutely false to pretend the proclamation forbade the free exercise of the Catholic religion." He also pointed out that the episode detailed the laws against Catholics holding office in considerable detail. Dufour not only had confused himself about the proclamation but had got most of his facts wrong. Mario Cardinal wrote a marvellous article too, defending the unit's integrity.

Dufour's denunciation was all the columnists needed, even if they had never heard of the proclamation. Dufour was raised from the status of pundit to historical oracle and went on a campaign that crossed into slander against the authors of the series. He announced that he would not watch any more, which didn't stop him from criticizing it further, to any audience he could find. Later, he boasted about this publicly: "Every time that I had an occasion since the autumn of 2000, I accused *Le Canada, une histoire populaire* of disinformation and distortion of history."

When the Peter Ingles episode about the 1837 Rebellions aired, I thought there might be a tempering of the hostility. The episode is very vivid about the brutality of the British repression and is second only to "Battle for a Continent" in its dramatic reconstruction and scale. Above all, it deals with the icons of Quebec nationalism: Papineau and the Patriotes. Usually the Saturday papers run advance features and reviews before a big Sunday broadcast like this. Several English papers in Canada did. *Le Devoir* at least acknowledged the episode, but *La Presse* not only almost completely ignored it but ran a full-page feature instead on Ken Burns's new series *Jazz* – a series that, however meritorious, wasn't being broadcast on Canadian television, or even in French.

A new film by the fiercely nationalist Quebec filmmaker Pierre Falardeau, *15 Février 1839*, about the Patriotes, was opening in theatres soon. He was interviewed on the Radio-Canada morning radio show and dismissed our episode as trash and propaganda. Asked about our historian Jean-Claude Robert, Falardeau denounced him: "C'est un *ré-vi-sion-niste.*"

"What does that mean?" Hubert fumed. "No one asked. Shades of Senator Joe McCarthy." For him, this was an example of what he hated most. "The intellectual climate created by Quebec nationalists (by all ideologues everywhere) is suffocating. Nothing new can grow in that soil. The Quebec ideologues feed off ancient grievances. They have mined the past to create a myth that now has the force of dogma. Woe to anyone who dares challenge it. The orthodoxy must be preserved, even if to do so they wilfully have to encourage people to remain ignorant."

Hubert is convinced that the series was a worry for hard-core nationalists. "Our series," he says, "without the on-air participation of those historians who serve as the true guardians of the faith, was dangerous. There was all that raw testimony and no one to tell the viewers what to think about it."

I was disappointed most of all by an article by Lysiane Gagnon in the *Globe and Mail*, from whom I expected a higher calibre. She declared that she hadn't been able to bring herself to watch it, then delivered this kicker: "The production of the series, on the French side of the CBC at least, was deemed a nightmare by many of the people who worked on it. Several historians still have bitter memories of their participation in the project. At almost every step, there were clashes of visions and tense negotiations between Montrealers and Torontonians. There were cries of disbelief when the francophone team saw that the first draft of the scenario, drawn by Toronto historians, didn't even mention Jacques Cartier's explorations." Where she got that idea, we'll never know. The statements are made with no evidence and no attribution. The "clashes of visions" and "tense negotiations" and "nightmares" are at complete variance with all reality, and the idea that we forgot Jacques Cartier is simply absurd.

Given the tepid publicity on Radio-Canada and the eventual newspaper shutout of the series, it was a surprise to find out how many people – 364,000 on average – watched in Quebec. Although there was no "buzz," as there was in English Canada, where the press was now actively urging Canadians to watch, about the same proportion of the French population watched the series as the English. Considering that it was broadcast inconsistently on the Radio-Canada schedule and very poorly promoted, and that some pundits were suggesting it be boycotted, the size of the Quebec audience is almost more impressive than the English.

All winter there were stirrings on the Ottawa front. During the Christmas–New Year hiatus, MPs returned to their ridings, and it appears that many got an earful about the series from constituents. We heard in January that the reaction to the series was discussed at length by cabinet. Sheila Copps was quoted in the press as saying that perhaps there were lessons to be drawn from the private sector's refusal to sponsor the series. Rumours began to circulate that the CBC might get some supplementary funding to ease its crippling budget problems.

I was a speaker at a national conference in Ottawa in early February and ran into Hugh Winsor, the *Globe and Mail* columnist. "Well," he said, "you should feel pretty proud of yourself." I thought he meant about the series. "I hope you get a percentage." I looked perplexed, and he said, "You mean you didn't read my column this morning?" I said I had been in Montreal and had missed it. "You got the CBC millions of dollars," he said.

The Throne Speech earlier that week contained a promise to increase funding for the CBC, and Winsor's sources attributed this to the history series. I said I was very skeptical that the series was solely responsible, as there had been a lot of pressure on the government to help the CBC. "They're just afraid we'll shut down some stations in their ridings, and it will backlash on them at the polls," I suggested. Furthermore, Rabinovitch had brought in many major reforms since he took office. But Winsor insisted his sources were unequivocal: the history series had been an epiphany for the cabinet about how the public supported the CBC when it did what they thought it should be doing. Whether Winsor was right or wrong, it was lovely to hear the compliment.

Around this time, I heard from the University of King's College in Halifax, the oldest university in Canada, that it wanted to award me an honorary degree. I was flabbergasted and genuinely thrilled. Not long afterwards, Bernard Shapiro, the principal of McGill University, called me. "I settled my student loan twenty years ago," I said immediately, but he assured me it wasn't that. McGill also wanted to award me an honorary degree. An honorary degree from your alma mater is a life highlight; one from the alma mater you organized demonstrations against in 1969 for being indifferent to the French in Quebec was an act of tremendous generosity.

The ratings, the public reaction, and the personal awards were gratifying, but we had a mammoth task ahead of us still. The entire second wave of eight episodes was now being put together, and the cycle of rough cuts and fine cuts, rewrites and headlines and promos was happening all over again at the same intensity, but this time with exhausted editors and post-production staff. Gene Allen was suffering from a ruptured disc in his back and was in so much pain that Wilma bought him a special seat that looked like a unicycle; and when that didn't work, he stood most of the day at a lectern, typing on a laptop. Eventually he had surgery and spent two weeks convalescing in his sparse apartment opposite the Don Jail, all the while working on his laptop, e-mailing everyone, and participating in script conferences by phone.

Between meetings and trips to Montreal, I tried to find a place to live. We had agreed, finally, that Anne would get the house, I would get the farm, and I'd find myself an apartment. Circling ads in the paper and driving from one depressing place to another with my daughters was demoralizing, but finally we found one we all liked. There was no time to sort anything before packing because of the series pressures; I just swept everything into boxes. I booked movers for March 3 and then discovered to my horror that Rabinovitch had scheduled a presentation about the history project to the monthly gathering of deputy ministers and heads of agencies for the same day – in Ottawa. I was the speaker, and the event was crucial to the CBC. My friend George Flak, my daughters, and I spent the whole night packing until the taxi came to take me to the airport in the morning. George would handle the moving van for me while I was away.

I arrived in Ottawa barely on time and launched into the presentation. It seemed to go well, and it was clear all the deputy ministers had also experienced the "something is happening out there" phenomenon and were eager to interpret the national reaction. I returned to Toronto in the early evening, to the strange sensation of giving the cab driver a different address for my home than I had when I'd left that morning. The new apartment looked like a trailer park after a tornado, and for weeks we walked through narrow canyons of boxes piled ceiling-high, looking for spatulas, towels, and history scripts. There was no time to unpack as the series was in the midst of another maelstrom of picture-locks. I got the kids' rooms set up, but it was easier for me to buy new shirts and underwear at lunchtime than to search for them at home, and I was grateful for the nights I spent in Montreal, because there I had a hotel room and sheets. When I wasn't at the office, my daughters and I were at Ikea. If Kelly Crichton hadn't taken the helm for me at this point – not to mention all the senior people in Toronto and Montreal who covered for me – I doubt the second wave would have made it to air on time.

In Montreal, Gail Boyd was in hospital, growing weaker while she waited for a suitable donor for a bone marrow transplant. Her sister had arrived from Algeria, but after tests were done, our hopes crashed. She was not a close enough match. Gail's husband, Achille Michaud, was consumed with grief. Hubert was with Gail almost every day or with Achille, helping him cope with keeping his family going. He became like a father to her, and he'd call me several times a week to talk about how she was and what she was saying. "I went over yesterday around dusk," he said, "and she was staring out the window at a glowing sunset, and said, 'Look what beautiful sunsets we have here.'" Somehow, Hubert still managed to write the history of Quebec, including the constitutional storms, from the 1960s to the end of the series. He wrote more original script than anyone else in the series: six hours – and in both languages.

On Good Friday, Gail Boyd died. It was almost too much to bear. I was numb. Death seemed to be picking the nicest and gentlest people in our project, and I had already had more loss in the past five years than I could endure.

On May 2, Prime Minister Jean Chrétien used the Broadcast Centre in Toronto as a venue to announce an injection of $568 million into the arts over the next three years. Sixty million would go to the CBC immediately. Then he made a point of citing the phenomenon of *Canada: A People's History*, congratulating us and quoting this passage from an essay I'd written earlier for *Time Canada*: "While drilling in the fields of national memory and identity, the producers struck a vast pressure dome which erupted with such volcanic intensity of yearning, determination and pride that it left them dazed. . . . Something very big is happening out there." Chrétien looked up from the quote and said, "Well, I completely agree." It was completely unexpected, and gratifying.

In Halifax, a month later, Sally Reardon was trying to make me look presentable, this time as I was being fitted for a red and white doctoral gown for the King's College convocation. As I walked in procession, an elderly man softly called, "Mark." It was Walter Ausserleitner, my first history teacher from high school, with his wife, Martha. I first studied history and became a journalist because of his influence. After the convocation, I recognized another face: Joe Martin, the tireless force behind Canada's National History Society and *The Beaver*. He had flown in from Toronto just to surprise me.

A month later, I met Sally again, this time at the airport in Moncton. Gail Boyd would be interred in the graveyard of her family church in Barachois. Hubert had arrived before us and was staying with Achille and the children at the seaside cabin where Gail and her family spent their summers. That night Achille, the children and their friends, and Hubert, Sally, and I gathered driftwood from the tidal flats and burned a large bonfire late into the night, talking about

Gail, Acadia, and all the centuries of history that flowed on the waters before us.

We buried Gail in the morning. At the reception afterwards, I realized that I now knew Acadian history, but I had no sense of the Acadian present. Here were journalists, painters, professors, playwrights, actors, bankers, and railway employees, all speaking with the same lilt Gail had spoken with, all recalling an aspect of their life with her, leaving me envious of their sense of community.

The next day Sally, Hubert, and I drove across the Confederation Bridge to Prince Edward Island, to the Charlottetown airport. There we boarded a flight that lasted a scant twenty-two minutes before it reached the Îles de la Madeleine, the isolated islands in the middle of the Gulf of St. Lawrence. I had been told to expect a couple of sandbars and a village or two, but what stretched below us were huge arcs of land, fringed with sand beaches and vibrant red cliffs. The islands are an archipelago, linked by sixteen-kilometre sandbars, with large lakes and lagoons, as big as half the countries in the West Indies. This was Serge's home, the islands he left for the first time when he was seventeen. Hubert had promised us a surprise when we met Serge's many brothers and sisters at the memorial service. He was right. Everyone was the spitting image of Serge. There were older Serges, younger Serges, balding Serges, grey-haired Serges, and even female Serges.

At the reception there were fifty guests, half of them children who bounced about like Mexican jumping beans. The men boiled a hundred fresh lobsters and the women laid out a feast of side dishes; then the violins and songbooks came out and everybody sang for almost two hours. I tried to imagine, envious again, what it would be like to have such an extended family. Serge's father recounted for me the days of organizing a fishing co-operative in the 1930s, then going to Halifax by himself, not speaking a word of English, to buy a ship that could carry the islands' catch to market. Sally, Hubert, and I had to leave first, because we had to return our rental car. We shook hands with everyone and as we slowly made our way to the door, it sounded as if everyone was now singing "Auld Lang Syne." For a few moments we didn't get it, then I asked Serge's father, "What's that music?"

"They're singing for the three of you," he said. "The song thanks you for coming and hopes you return soon." We walked down the road to our car in complete silence. Nothing like it had ever happened to us before.

17

The Second Wave

At 4:30 one morning, Bill Cobban, who had worked on *Dawn of the Eye* and had won an Emmy for a documentary on the sale of children in India, was standing in Poundmaker Reserve in Saskatchewan. He was wrestling with a rare problem. The meteor was too small.

Bill was producing the first episode of the second wave of the series – the episodes that aired the following year. It tells the story of Louis Riel and the Northwest Rebellion. Bill had read about a sacred stone, a meteor embedded on the prairie, which held mystical significance for both the Cree and the Blackfoot peoples. If the stone were ever removed, their legends held, their people would face ruin and pestilence. Methodist missionaries considered the rock an object of heathen worship. So they dug it up and shipped it to a Methodist college in Cobourg, Ontario, which sent it to the Royal Ontario Museum decades later.

"I wanted to open the episode with the removal of the sacred medicine stone," Bill says, "because all the predictions associated with it in folklore had actually come true. The Indian peoples were devastated by the railway, by disease, and by war after the rock was taken. When we approached them, the museum made a fibreglass reproduction of the meteor (which is still in its vaults) and this was carefully shipped to us. Then, on the morning of the shoot, when I've got only a couple of minutes of perfect sunrise, we unpacked it and – well, even the camera was bigger than the sacred stone."

With urgent repositioning of the camera to super-low angle and much tweaking of settings, the image of the stone acquired some stature. The crew captured the shot, Bill says, "just seconds before the first shaft of sunrise streaked across the prairie horizon."

Bill would soon have more dramatic challenges than this, during the re-enactments of the return of Louis Riel, the Northwest Rebellion, and the Battle of Batoche. He had become fascinated by the Métis rebellion and taken by the justice of their cause. "Riel didn't come back to start a rebellion," he says. "He came to resolve some outstanding property issues, including over some land he was entitled to personally. We had been told in our history books he was some sort of megalomaniac. I had certainly never learned that he tried to rally the white settlers in Prince Albert to the cause, telling them that they should join the Métis in a petition to negotiate, not to rebel. But the eastern papers were frothing at the mouth and building him up as a monster."

Louis Riel stands on the great fault line of Canadian history for another reason. Saskatchewan and Manitoba would likely be majority-French provinces today if Quebec had listened to pleas from the French communities in the west to send settlers. But at the time, Quebec was losing hundreds of thousands of its people to the new factories of New England and had no interest in losing more to some remote prairie. Ontario also considered the west its backyard. Several Quebec historians have observed that this would be a far different country if a part of the ancestral French root of Canada had been planted more firmly in the west and allowed to flourish.

"Riel was not seen as a great hero in Quebec at the time," Bill says, "more as a bush cousin. And no one listened to his pleas to come out and claim a place in the west. He was told to go and recruit among the émigrés in New England instead. He tried that too, but largely failed. Riel had a great vision of the whole country, a very tolerant one, and I never really understood that before. He only became a *cause célèbre* in Quebec when he was arrested and tried, but his vision had never been embraced." Later on, as the shooting of the second wave progressed, Bill and his team would find out that the ghosts of the rebellion, and its legacy, were very much alive.

Every episode after Bill's was directed by a woman. Nobody planned it this way, but all seven remaining episodes were produced by an extraordinary generation of female documentary directors who had cut their teeth on stories of history in the making – the fall of Communism, the slaughter in Rwanda, the Gulf War, and the Canadian political crisis of the 1980s and 1990s.

Jill Offman was eight months pregnant in 1999 when she decided she wanted to join the history project as a director of a second wave episode. She remembers Anne Emin cautioning her about the magnitude of the decision she was about to make. "If you want to work on the series," Anne warned, "you'll have to come three months after you have your baby, because everyone else is starting before you."

Jill had covered Northern Ireland, Russia, China, Africa, and Bosnia and had been everywhere in Canada for *The Journal* and *The National Magazine*. Now she was determined to be one of the makers of the first television history of Canada. "And I did it," she says. "The baby was my first, and I remember being in a complete state of almost delirium coming into the history project. There were all these little history beavers running around me. Everyone had started before me and knew what they were talking about – it was like a cult.

"I was still tired and sleep-deprived – I had a baby who screamed for the entire first year of her life – and I was kind of shell-shocked. I'd come to work and everyone was speaking in French and English about the Riel Rebellions, staging wars and battles. I was absolutely terrified."

Working alongside Jill Offman was the producer Marcy Cuttler. Marcy had worked on *Midday* for ten years and she quickly became indispensable to the history project. She spent her time and a great deal of care unearthing the essence of the Depression story, and I knew that with Marcy on the case, we would stay true to it. She was thrilled whenever she found a good nugget of information, and from then on, if anyone in the office heard a whoop of delight, it was likely to have come from Marcy.

Jackie Corkery in Montreal was from a Saskatchewan French family that fiercely preserved their mother tongue at home. An ancestor of Jackie's, Abraham Martin, had actually owned the Plains of Abraham (he presciently sold the land a few years before the battle). Jackie had worked at Radio-Canada in Regina and Montreal for eighteen years as a documentary producer before Hubert and I hired her for the history project. She was fluently bilingual but had never worked with English Television.

Her first meeting in Toronto was intense. "I was entering the hallowed halls of English Television in a professional capacity," she says. "I felt nervous, intimidated, and elated. It was the first time I had seen the video. The lights were dimmed to total blackness, and I was overwhelmed with emotion. I sobbed through the whole presentation, hoping no one would turn on the lights. I kept thinking, This is my story, the story of my family, my ancestors, the first French-Canadian settlers, my grandparents. It's the story of the women, the two solitudes with which I live every day."

For Halya Kuchmij, who was documenting the massive wave of immigrants who transformed this country in the years before the First World War, it was a personal mission. Halya was soft-spoken and had a poetic and visual approach to documentaries. She was part of my generation and had lived a parallel experience in Canada. Her parents, Stefan Kuchmij and Marta Wintoniw, were displaced from the Ukraine by the Second World War, and Halya was born in England. The family moved to Toronto in 1952, and she says, "I was brought up in the Toronto Ukrainian ghetto: Ukrainian schools, churches, girl scouts, dancing, and string orchestra. My first language was Ukrainian. As an immigrant and the child of immigrants, I have always felt proud to be a Ukrainian Canadian. Canada was a country that gave me that opportunity to look in both directions at once. One of the largest groups who came over in the era of my episode was the Ukrainians. They played such a huge role in the opening of the west. I felt a personal responsibility that their story be told."

Halya, the cameraman Maurice Chabot, and the producer Andrew Burnstein travelled through the prairies filming the story of Petro Svarich, Maria Adamovska, and other early immigrants to towns like Edna-Star, Two Hills, Mundare, Andrew, and Myrnam. The landscape, the old churches, the community halls, the old cemeteries drew Halya in. "I started to feel an indefinable connection to those first settlers. Those voices from the past wanted to be heard. It was like a chord of music that I had once known and was now remembering."

Marquise Lepage in Montreal, an award-winning filmmaker with the National Film Board, had joined us to do "Years of Hope and Anger," the turbulent history of the 1960s and 1970s. For Hubert and me, her episode was about our era as young journalists; for Marquise, who is a good twenty years younger, this was as much history as the First World War. It was good to have this period seen through the eyes of the next generation, because she could bring the necessary historical distance. If any episode was going to blow up in our face, I feared, it would be this one, because it had to show the clash of Trudeau's and Lévesque's visions of the future. But Marquise's earlier films had shown a deep sympathy for the human story, and we thought she could bring out the sweep and passion of the era. "My tendencies were somewhat sovereignist," she says, "but I was interested in the idea of telling the story of the country fairly, and I wanted to be sure this was an honest journalistic project. I felt comfortable right away. There was integrity and intellectual rigour everywhere."

Each of the directors had a formidable task, because the photo research unit was still swamped by the first wave's picture-locks, and the editors were verging on exhaustion just as the new team of directors walked in with hundreds of hours of fresh raw material for them. But at least these directors had been given enough time to research their era. Two more directors, Susan Teskey and Susan

Dando, were recruited very late and had less than half the time to complete their episodes. They accepted what many considered to be documentary suicide missions.

We were having major problems with the Second World War and Cold War episode. Even after four drafts, the script felt flat and conventional, and production was running late. But to replace directors a year before broadcast was reckless; it was almost physically impossible for anyone to handle. To make it more unrealistic, the task was to produce not only two hours on the war years but a third hour that took us into the 1950s – in other words, half of the next episode as well.

Kelly Crichton raised Susan Teskey's name as a possibility.

"What's she like?" I asked. I had never worked with her, but I knew her reputation as the senior producer of *the fifth estate.* Tough, trenchant, and driven, she was one of the best investigative documentary producers in the country, with a superhuman capacity for work.

"She'll be independent and strong-willed," Kelly replied. "You'll get the episode at the very last minute, and if you're lucky, a few days before air time. But she will do a brilliant job, and if you get her, you won't have to spend another sleepless night about that episode."

Susan and I met on a sunny summer day on the terrace of the downstairs restaurant at the CBC. It was a noisy place, as it is a favourite spot for daredevil skateboarders doing bone-crushing acrobatics on the granite borders of Simcoe Park. There, enveloped in a cloud of my cigarette smoke, Susan heard me out. Lacking the prudence to excuse herself right away, she became more intrigued as I honestly painted the impossible odds she'd face, and I realized Susan Teskey was inexplicably attracted to hopeless but potentially heroic missions. We got along instantly, continuing on to a raucous supper with Kelly Crichton and her husband, Mel Watkins, after which Susan and I ended up in several pubs on Queen Street, pouring out the history of our lives and righting all the wrongs of Canadian history and public broadcasting until the waiters were looking at their watches. The next day, we vaguely recalled that we had struck a deal but couldn't quite pinpoint the exact terms. But the passion she had for the story and the narrative eye and skill that she'd shown in the stories she told me had relaxed every tense muscle in my chest about this episode. Kelly had been right. I never worried another day or night about the episode. And we got the final print thirty-six hours before broadcast.

We had one more nightmare, however. Episode 17 was the last episode, the culmination of the entire series, and its director had to bow out because her partner was having a baby in a few weeks. The episode needed a strong leader who could pull it into shape. The closer we came to living memory, the harder the series became, and this last chapter held every hoary problem from the 1980 referendum to Meech Lake and NAFTA. Done badly, it would look like a warmed-over year-end news special, and we knew that Canadians would rather chew ground glass than watch anything more about the Constitution. I knew exactly where the solution was, but she was inaccessible – in fact, she was on vacation in Australia.

Sue Dando was the senior producer of the biography series *Life & Times* under difficult circumstances. *Life & Times* had been created in the middle of the cuts several years before, and it took Sue forever to get the green light from the network to launch the series. She finally got her budget just three months before she had to be on the air. With one researcher, no cameras, and the reluctance of funding agencies the series would depend on, she had pulled it off. Gordon Henderson agreed that she was who we needed for the episode. "But she'd be crazy to do it," he said. "She has her own series, and this will destroy her summer and the whole ensuing year. She doesn't need us." I knew Sue had wanted to join the history project a year earlier but couldn't because of *Life & Times*. Would she still want to join it now, in the home stretch, with only seven months to complete the final episode? As soon as her plane landed, I set up a lunch and prepared to make the outrageous proposition to her.

At lunch, I knew we were off to a good start when she didn't spill her soup in my lap at the sheer cheek of my proposition. "You want me to take over a two-hour episode?" she asked. "The last episode of the whole series, in both French and English? When did you say it was on the air?"

"November." I tried to sound casual.

"That's seven months," she said.

"Well, it's *late* November," I said.

She said she'd read the outline and decide.

I sensed that something more than my eloquence was exercising a gravitational pull on her. "I thought everything about the '80s would be familiar because I had covered it," she says. "But when I read the material, it seemed different. I was seeing it as history for the first time; patterns, shifts, and influences emerged, and I could see how events fit together in a way I had never thought about before. It seemed more momentous. I usually read an outline and get a sense right away – I either get a shiver of excitement or just a dial tone. I was getting really excited. I told my husband, and he said, 'I guess I won't see much of you this summer.'"

The second wave begins with the story of the Northwest Rebellion of 1885 and the suppression of the western Indian nations and ends in 1990. We picked 1990 – very approximately – because it was an international marker, the real end of the twentieth century, according to many. It was the era of protests in Tienanmen Square, the tearing down of the Berlin Wall, the collapse of the Soviet empire, and the dawn of the Internet.

Some historians thought we should end earlier because 1990 was too recent for us to have meaningful historical distance and perspective; many viewers, however, were surprised we weren't going right up till today. But we thought it important to reach the era that teenagers could remember. I didn't want younger viewers to think of history as something "out there," disconnected from their time; they should see themselves in the flowing current of history. We also didn't want to anoint any single Canadian event, like the free trade agreement or Meech Lake or Oka, with the stature of the culmination of our series. It seemed prudent to pick global turning points in international history and technology and science – the decade when the whole world was transformed.

Many people in the CBC assumed the second wave would be easier than the first because it would be based on still photography, film, and recorded sound. But in many ways it was harder. The directors in the first wave had a blank canvas and could stage critical events; the second wave directors were limited by what images were available, and there were huge gaps in the photographic record. How could they represent the Depression-era dust storms of the prairies, when there was no film of them? How could they tell the story of the Battle of Vimy Ridge with no film? How could we show the massive Quebec City conscription demonstration, where four were killed, without footage? It was vital that we stick to the "history from the ground up" approach. This was still a people's history, but the film and photo record was largely ceremonial and official and favoured the governing classes. The diaries and letters kept by ordinary people had never been published or preserved in archives and had to be found in family attics. Researching the second wave episodes was a detective job, requiring all the skills of investigative journalism.

Using on-camera actors in the first wave had been the only way to reach the past before the invention of photography. But now that justification was no longer valid. After Episode 10, "Taking the West," we decided that we would use no more on-camera actors. We also debated whether to interview the living on camera. Should we interview war veterans? Should we interview Brian Mulroney, Peter Lougheed, Margaret Atwood? After much discussion, we decided we would interview them to get their personal recollections of the time, and have their words spoken by actors in voice-overs, but we would not interview them on camera. An eighty-year-old man on camera, recalling the time he was nineteen in Normandy, would break the sense of being in the period, and it would also bias the content to the memories of the living. We never regretted the decision, once made, and it sat well with the viewers.

Even as the second wave teams kept the edit suites and studios humming all day and night in Toronto and Montreal, the end of the series was coming into focus. By now, we had formed friendships and alliances that made us almost a hybrid third entity within the

CBC and Radio-Canada – an improbable and noisy collection of federalists and sovereignists, Canadians of Ukrainian, Mohawk, and Chinese origins, descendants of Patriotes and Orangemen and DPS who couldn't agree on the time of day but shared an abiding respect for one another. The real capital in a creative organization is any collection of people who have learned to finish each other's sentences and are loyal to an objective. That's how you get anything done, whether it's getting a studio opened at three in the morning or a cameraman to go up in a helicopter in a crushing wind or an artist to spend days constructing one animation. People who feel they are a valued part of a great enterprise will achieve the impossible every time.

Now it seemed that everyone would soon be dispersed to the winds. Gene was leaving to teach at Ryerson University. Gord had already gone back to run his company. Kelly would leave the CBC in the fall and planned to go to Africa. Anne Emin was talking retirement. Maurice Chabot was back at *The National*, Peter Ingles was back at *Enjeu*, and Mario Cardinal, like Cincinnatus, was returning to his fields. "We can't let all this dribble away," Hubert said on the boat back from the Îles de la Madeleine. "It's like breaking up a great collection and auctioning off its pieces."

He had become increasingly anxious as the months went by, because he sensed indifference toward the project at the CBC. The entire Montreal unit felt despondent at the thought of being disbanded and sent back to their old jobs or let go entirely at the end of their contracts. They couldn't believe that some form of history unit would not survive to make more documentaries. "I can't believe we're all talking about cross-cultural production in our public pronouncements," Hubert said, getting angrier, "and we're going to flush this all down the toilet."

Over four years of research, we had assembled thousands of pages of diaries and letters and eyewitness accounts dating back to the first European encounters in Canada. "We've got enough research to produce terrific stories for years," he fumed, "and the collective memory of our units, and the skills acquired, should be preserved and nurtured, not dissipated – this is a crime."

Hubert wanted to draw up a battle plan for preserving a history unit within the CBC and Radio-Canada, and do it right away, because the window of opportunity was closing fast. By Christmas 2001, 80 per cent of the staff would be gone. By March 2002, both units would be disbanded. I had argued for a permanent history unit at both networks in the introduction to the second companion book and in every conversation I had with senior managers and board members at the CBC. At the board level, there seemed to be overwhelming support for preserving the asset. Whenever I met them on public occasions, board members told me that it was "inconceivable to lose all this." Robert Rabinovitch had been emphatic in making cross-cultural programming a priority of his administration, and he asked for a plan that would keep the resources and key people from being dispersed at the end of the second wave.

An extra episode had been added, at our request, because we realized we had miscalculated how much time we needed to do the Second World War and the Quiet Revolution. The closer we got to the end of the twentieth century, we realized, the more detail each chapter required. Rabinovitch and the board authorized funding for that extension, which brought the total length of our series to thirty-two hours. They also authorized a package of special cross-cultural historical programs, including some for the fiftieth anniversary of the CBC in 2002. That injection of extra "work orders" and budget amounted to six hours of additional programming, which allowed us to hang on to the cameras and some of the special edit suites and to keep some key production personnel. It bought us a few extra months, but we needed a long-term commitment to historical programming to maintain modest units beyond 2002. And that is where the dilemma lay.

I had been lobbying for two years for a series to be called *The Canadian Experience*, modelled on the much-admired PBS series *The American Experience*. The series would need a wide brief and could do any story that had shaped the national consciousness. It would be like the Canadian history series, but not tied to one style and not tied to chronological history; instead it would delve for a full hour into a single story.

At the English network, I had support from the beginning. Harold Redekopp had always admired that form of documentary, and Slawko understood the power of narrative history. I wanted thirteen episodes a year but succeeded in getting only six out of the English network. At least I had a solid commitment, air time, and a willingness to discuss budget levels. The initial idea was that *The Canadian Experience* would be a series that ran on both networks – at least part of the time – thereby enabling the retention of the Canadian history units. Claude Saint-Laurent fought for a historical series with his managers at Radio-Canada and reported sadly, "There isn't a scintilla of interest."

So the dilemma was this: the English network had created a modest history unit in the wake of *Canada: A People's History*, and although six hours was a lot less than I was fighting for, it was a beginning and a real commitment. I had assumed Radio-Canada would feel the need to do the same, however grudgingly. After creating an effective two-language unit, one that had had such a profound national impact, how could we dismantle half of it? All winter I had told Hubert that it couldn't happen, it was inconceivable, it went against the will of the board and against all logic. But now it looked like I was dead wrong. I had miscalculated badly.

The French network still had a much greater share of the French market than the CBC had of the fragmenting English market. To distinguish itself, CBC English Television was defining itself more as a focused "public broadcasting" network and as the Canadian alternative. Radio-Canada, on the other hand, saw itself as a general-service network. SRC argued that conditions were different in each market, and the programming strategies should be allowed to be different. History, it appeared, did not fit its broad populist mandate. Ironically, though, as Hubert and I were discussing all this aboard the ferry, the first wave of the series was running again on Radio-Canada, right after the national news, replacing *Le Point* for much of the summer. It had been split into one-hour episodes, and it was getting higher ratings than any program in that time slot in the summer had got before.

All we could do, we agreed, was to work with our respective media lines. I couldn't call the president or board members – one mission to Caraquet is enough for one career – and I didn't need to. I'd put the case to Harold Redekopp, who believed in the dual idea, and he'd press the case in Ottawa for us. Hubert and Mario Cardinal would rally all the support they could in Radio-Canada, and Hubert would put together proposals for programs that could keep his unit going, as well a roster of arguments that would arm Claude Saint-Laurent for one last Hail Mary pass at the French network.

"Maybe I sold you a bag of hammers when I persuaded you to join three years ago," I said to Hubert.

"No. They were the most difficult years of my life," he smiled. "But I'd do it again. We made a difference."

In the meantime, the people we were trying to keep in the CBC were in a frenzy of production. Jill Offman was reconstructing the sandstorms of the dust bowl and the privations of the unemployment camps. Outside Montreal, Jackie Corkery was directing a team with a Model T, reconstructing the posses of federal agents that scoured the backwoods of Quebec searching for French Canadians who did not register for the draft in the First World War. In one Toronto studio, Susan Teskey was recreating a storm in the Atlantic Ocean. To illustrate one sailor's account of how violently the Canadian navy's corvettes pitched and rocked in the Atlantic crossing, set designers had reconstructed the interior of a ship's galley at full scale. In the darkened studio, a structure as big as a cabin was being rocked by groaning stagehands while pipes drenched the interior with water and frying pans and plates of food spilled into the bilge. It conveyed the misery of naval life very effectively.

What I was seeing in her edit suites was also impressive – the Second World War was emerging from the point of view of the lower decks, the trenches, and the factory floor. "God is often in the details," Susan said, and sometimes it needed just one photograph. "Ortona will always be known as the Christmas battle, and the Christmas story is always told through the same little bit of film and the same photograph, a wide shot of men eating at a large square of tables in a ruined church. But I never found that material had much emotional weight. Instead, we used another photograph. A small group of men at a table, looking into the camera, the kind of snap taken by all of us at every Christmas party. Some are young, but not all, some are handsome, others goofy, some are grinning, others seem wistful. It is so beautiful and so poignant, I found it almost unbearable to contemplate their deaths."

Teskey's portrait of Canada at war is like a pointillist painting, made up of a thousand little dots that make a powerful canvas when you stand back. She and her researchers would go to great lengths to get just one of those dots. "One of the most affecting stories was that of the Sidney family in Carcross, Yukon. Angela Sidney, a Tlingit, watches a young daughter die of disease and her son Peter go off to war. After it is over, she welcomes him back with the utterly unique gift of a now almost extinct song called 'Kaax'achgook.' She 'gives' it to him because like the character Kaax'achgook, he drifted away in the ocean but finally comes back. To me it epitomized the difference between our 'people's history' and all the others with scenes of tickertape and dancing in the streets.

"The problem was, Who still knew the song, and could sing it for us? Angela was dead. The author of the book on her told us that the last person in the Yukon who might remember it was Peter, but he too was dead. She suggested there were people in Sitka, Alaska, who knew it, but that might be getting into dangerous territory because there were still clan members who claimed ownership of the song as part of the settlement of a dispute. In the end, Peter's younger sister, Ida, remembered the song. We recorded her in a radio studio in Whitehorse."

Susan's task was to do a history of Canada during the war, and that meant dividing the time between the battlefront and the home front. One of the more memorable scenes taking shape in the edit suite was the "Land of Hope and Glory" sequence, set on the huge factory floor of a munitions plant in Ajax, Ontario. Edna Jaques had told the story of working on the night shift when a young man on the assembly line started singing "Land of Hope and Glory," and one by one, workers added their voices until the factory sounded like a cathedral. When Teskey read Jaques's account, she knew it had to be in the documentary, but there was no footage to support the scene.

The largest munitions factory in the British empire, producing 40 million shells and employing nine thousand people, had been in Ajax. But the town's archives were stored in unheated rooms, uncatalogued in boxes and cabinets. Susan's researchers began what appeared to be a hopeless search. In one box, Roma Andrusiak found two unmarked cans of film, which had been donated to the town in the 1960s by the Wrigley's Chewing Gum Company. It had never been processed. Roma found out that Wrigley's had come out to film the munitions workers as part of a wartime commercial for chewing gum. The CBC processed the film. "We found colour footage of women working in the factory – the glorious footage that forms the 'Land of Hope and Glory' scene," Susan said. "And if you look very closely, you will see that all of them are chewing gum."

In Montreal, Hubert was writing virtually the whole post-war history of French-English relations across several episodes and trying to breathe humanity into the constitutional crises. Mario was buried under the second volume of the companion book, as was Gene in Toronto. Denis Boucher was coping with the torrent of picture-locks from Toronto that had to have French actors inserted and had to go through post-production in Montreal. If any one of those four people got so much as a bad cold, the series would have missed its deadlines; that's how thin on the ground we were. With the departure of the first wave producers, both units were now half their original size, but the workload seemed to have trebled. When we had been producing the first wave, we weren't on the air. But now we had to cope with the same production load, plus all the realities of being an on-air series – which meant hundreds of letters to answer, the Web sites to maintain, curriculum guides to vet, and interviews to do.

Marquise Lepage, like Susan Teskey, had the added load of three hours to edit, instead of the regular two. She had to deal with the suspicion of those in Montreal who believed the series was a federalist propaganda job, but she had also run into something else, something I had noticed too before the first wave went on the air, which was that the federalists in Ottawa were just as suspicious. That diminished after the first wave ran, but a lot of people on Parliament Hill remained nervous about how we would play the rise of the separatist movement.

Other producers were facing different challenges. Sue Dando, director of the final episode with only seven months to complete it, says, "By the time this episode got to audio post, there were 'five dollars and five minutes' available to complete the work." But Ron Searles was not going to let her down in sound effects. For a dramatic shot of an oil well gushing, she asked him for shouts in the background to convey the workers' excitement. Later she learned that Ron had locked himself in the studio at one in the morning, "whooping, yelling, and hollering like a madman," then laying the recording over and over until he sounded like a crowd.

Another producer, Cristina Campbell, should get some kind of award for lowering costs. Sue Dando wanted to shoot a herd of horses in front of an oil rig in Alberta, but "the horse wrangler was used to big, expensive rock videos and commercials and was financially out of our league," Dando says. "When he asked Cristina how many trucks we'd be bringing and if we'd be using a crane for the high shot, she explained it would be a cameraman and a director in a rental van, and they would stand on the roof of the van if they wanted a high shot. She kept deducting horses in order to get the price down, so the herd became a handful. She said the horses didn't even have to move, so did he have any really old or sick horses we could get cheap?"

Tight budgets inspired the assistant director Ian Campbell's ingenuity and Scottish parsimony. To get shots of a float plane taking off and landing, they used Cristina's family cottage. Ian went up in the hired plane and got instructions for when to land by cellphone, while Mike Sweeney stood waist-deep in water, filming. But the pilot said he could do only two takeoffs and didn't want to take the time to bring the plane all the way back to the dock to return Ian. "After shooting two takeoffs and landings, Ian was dropped off in the middle of the lake," Dando says. "All we could see from shore was a bobbing head and an arm outstretched to keep the cellphone out of the water."

Marquise Lepage, in the meantime, was discovering a more complex Canada than she had known. "You think that because you've worked in Montreal, Toronto, and Vancouver," she said, "you know the country." Her episode, like Teskey's and Dando's, was taking the less travelled path. Hers was a story of social and political awakening. It had to touch all the bases, from politics, labour, and women to First Nations and racial minorities. Marquise found jewels like the story of the Catholic school in Ottawa that expelled eight girls for attending an Elvis Presley concert, to illustrate the clash of generations, and she made the destruction of Africville, the black ghetto of Halifax, a metaphor for the hubris of the engineering age. Her most moving experience, however, came when she was shooting the story of the Blue Quills School, near the Saddle Lake Reserve in Alberta. In 1971 native parents occupied a local school and demanded the right to teach their children their own heritage and in their aboriginal language.

The school had arranged for Marquise to meet the elders who had organized the takeover and who could recount the occupation for us. Alice Makokis had been one of the original leaders and one of the first members of the board of directors of this school, the first in Canada to be run by natives. Alice Makokis was dead now, but her daughter Leona stood and spontaneously addressed the elders. She said that since her mother had been dead for some time, she had never had the chance to thank her and to thank all the elders who fought to defend the right of aboriginal people to a good education, and an education conducted by their people. She added, "I am now, thanks to you, a university graduate and I work in this school. Every day I think of you with gratitude." Marquise said, "Her words touched the elders deeply; you could see it in their faces. It also left a profound impression on our little group of whites. I had tears in my eyes, and I suddenly understood, deep inside, the importance of this battle."

The strand of aboriginal history threads through almost all the episodes of the series. So does the strand of immigration, with the ever-changing and broadening definition of the Canadian collectivity. In the last episode of the series, this strand is in the story of Baltej Singh Dhillon, the first Mountie to wear a turban. His battle to hang on to his cultural identity had made front-page headlines for weeks and stirred strong feelings in Canada. Some reactions had a racist undertone, but most of the debate went legitimately to the heart of the importance of Canadian symbols and the nature of assimilation into the country. Initially the chapter told two stories, one of a man who went against tradition and cut his long hair, and the other of Dhillon, who fought to retain his heritage. Loretta Hicks, a Kentucky-raised American who married a Canadian, was the editor on the last episode, and she was very taken by this story, which would never have happened in the United States. "There was a valid argument that the Mountie hat was part of our culture, and if Dhillon truly wanted to become a Mountie, he should adapt to our culture. Although our final structure couldn't use it, I always liked the scene at the barbershop where the Indian man had his hair cut for the first time in order to feel that he fit in. As painful as it was for him, he was treated with respect at the shop. It's the opposite example to Dhillon, but the choice was no less valid."

There is a footnote to that chapter that didn't make the final cut either and showed Dhillon's great sense of humour. When asked what it was that finally made him feel accepted as a police officer, he spoke about being posted to Quesnel, British Columbia, where "one day they called me pig. You know, that was a great day, because now they weren't calling me a Hindu or a Paki, they were just calling me a pig. And to me that was a good day. I was being accepted like everyone else."

The second wave was scheduled to start airing on September 30 on the English network, a month earlier than in the previous year. That didn't worry us, but what did was that the start time was changed from 8:00 P.M. to 7:00 P.M. We felt that was simply too early: people haven't settled down for the evening yet or are having supper, and there is still lingering daylight at that time of year. But the network had been impressed by reports of families viewing the first wave and thought this might be more convenient for them. Also, Slawko wanted to build a Sunday-night viewing habit, and scheduling us at 7:00 P.M. would make room for *Da Vinci's Inquest*. Regardless of what time we aired, we knew we'd have lower ratings. Radio-Canada was not running the series until January 2002, and on CBC there was no Thursday repeat this time, because a new arts series was being launched on Thursday nights. That meant an automatic loss of at least 400,000 viewers on the English network. Furthermore, the late-night Sunday repeat, which was at 11:00 P.M. for the first wave, got us between 150,000 and 200,000 viewers, but this year the repeat was scheduled for midnight. We were worried about the combination of a pre-season launch, no real repeat pattern, and an early-evening start. All those things hurt our viewing levels, but not as much as the catastrophic impact of another historical event.

On September 11, at 9:20 A.M., I was woken by a call from a friend in the States saying, "Tune in to CNN, fast!" I sat in my bathrobe in front of the TV, transfixed, for the next twelve hours. In the office, all production came to a halt. Who could edit or mix or write anything? Office buildings in Toronto were being evacuated. Hour after hour, day after day, it seemed like another calamity might happen. We got back to work on the series, but with one eye on the Newsworld monitor.

By September 30, our launch date, just two and a half weeks later, the North American television universe had been completely rewritten. The audience for CBC regular programming – all network regular programming – had plummeted; everyone was glued to the news channels. Ten days before, President Bush had addressed Congress and laid down his ultimatum to the Taliban to surrender Osama bin Laden, and as we went on air, reserves were being mobilized across the United States.

I organized a launch party at my apartment, and about fifty of us gathered on Sunday. The talk as we waited for Bill Cobban's episode to begin was an unreal mixture of Riel and Afghanistan. Halya's episode, which portrayed the paranoia about foreigners at the turn of the century, then Jill Offman's about the ideological polarization of the world, and Sue Teskey's portrait of the displacement of Japanese Canadians – all suddenly took on a different dimension as reports surfaced of attacks on Muslim and Hindu establishments in the United States.

The advance reviews of the second wave were excellent. The historian Michael Bliss pronounced judgment in a major piece in *Time Canada*: "The second series is as good as the first – even better." Even the issue of sponsorship had been resolved. Rabinovitch had told BCE's executive vice-president, Michael Sabia, that he should not miss a historic opportunity a second time. Two weeks later, BCE committed itself to full sponsorship of the series, a decision I respected because it took some guts to admit it had been wrong the first time around.

But the television universe that fall was radically different. People wanted news about the war in Afghanistan, and then, two weeks after we launched, the U.S. Senate found letters laced with anthrax, and a full panic took over the newscasts. "We're going to get creamed," Anne Emin said, and I feared she was right. The first numbers were respectable for a single broadcast on the English network only, but not uplifting. Comparing the English network's first broadcast with that of the year before, without repeats and the French, we were getting 40 to 50 per cent of the first year's audience. Slawko even considered whether we should delay the series, already in progress, and restart it in January when the Afghanistan frenzy died down. But the ratings began climbing again as the global dust settled.

On October 20, just before Jill Offman's episode on the Depression era, Harold Redekopp, Gene, and I flew to Winnipeg for an awards dinner held by the National History Society. The CBC was being given the Pierre Berton Award for *Canada: A People's History*. The standing ovation from a room full of historians, teachers, and authors was perhaps the most gratifying moment of all. They had laboured all their lives in Canadian history with little national attention and might have been our severest critics, but instead that night felt like a vindication for them. The society's president, Joe Martin, had opened hundreds of doors for us and urged everyone to trust us over the past four years. That night, he was beaming with the pride of a man who had known all his life that Canadian history would be popular someday.

Back in Toronto a few days later, Hubert, Gordon, and I went to the Gemini Awards, where we won, among others, the award for best documentary series. It was a sad night for me. I had signed the pile of nomination papers months before and hadn't noticed that a crucial name was missing. Some weeks later, Anne Emin walked into my office and pointed out the blunder. "Gene Allen has been left off the list for best series," she said. I felt sick. We tried for days to rectify the mistake, but the organizers said it was too late. So when Hubert, Gordon, and I got up to accept the award from Lloyd Robertson, I made Gene the centre of my remarks. It was too little and too late. Gene Allen wasn't in the audience. I had deeply wounded the man who had been my partner when there were only two of us at the very beginning, and who had been the architect and conscience of the whole project. Instead of feeling triumphant that night, I felt as though I had become one of the CBC ciphers I had spent four years criticizing.

"Can I have the statue to take to Montreal?" Hubert asked backstage at the Toronto event. "I'd like to parade it along the corridor to show the bastards who mocked our people that if they're not appreciated in Montreal, they're appreciated in Canada." The Montreal unit had been completely shut out of the earlier French awards, the Gémeaux. All the series got was a well-deserved award for best opening animation for Alain Provost. Nothing for direction, cinematography, writing, music, or sound. The host of the Montreal awards, in his opening monologue, suggested that the best way to fix the financial crisis at Radio-Canada was to lay off the entire Canadian history team in Montreal.

On the English network *Canada: A People's History* ended on Sunday, November 18, 2001. Sue Dando had pulled off the impossible, as I knew she would. The closing party was at her place, and she barely had time to buy snacks for her guests because she was still putting the finishing touches to her final episode the night before. "It was," she admitted, "a close-run thing. But nothing an old *Journal* producer wasn't used to."

The e-mails that poured in Monday morning were read, one by one, by the small unit remaining in Toronto, which was already looking at the experience in the rear-view mirror – exhausted, dazed, and a little sad that it was all over.

Robert Scobel wrote from Calgary, "I'm moved to write to you to congratulate the entire production team, French and English. . . . As a 42-year-old father of two boys, may I say how educational and moving I found the 17-part series. My oldest son of eight watched many of the Sunday night shows alongside of me, a memory I will always hold dear."

Carol Baker from Airdrie, Alberta, reported that throughout the series she had conference calls at each break with her friends, and "at the end of it all, it took about ten minutes for the phone to ring, because we were all having an emotional moment, after hearing your wonderful narrator say 'You are part of an unfolding epic.' We are proud of you for helping Canadians, such as myself and my friends, become proud of who we are and where we came from."

For the past few weeks the Toronto unit had turned its hands to producing a series of goodbye parties, as people's contracts expired one by one. By December, we were down to a core of eighteen, who would turn their attention to *The Canadian Experience* and the new documentary production unit I dreamed of. The Montreal unit, on the other hand, was all at battle stations as it readied to launch the second wave in January, with a daunting load of writing, perform-ance, and scoring to do after the end of the English broadcasts. Nobody got much rest that Christmas.

The accomplishments were already huge: Mario had nursed the second French book to publication in the fall and worked closely with Hubert on finishing six hours of scripts in two languages. Richard Fortin had gone from being a researcher to becoming an accomplished television writer himself. The series ran in the winter of 2002 to very respectable ratings.

But there was never any doubt Montreal would pull the French second wave off, however adverse the odds. The real battle was to save the unit, or some fraction of it. For weeks Hubert came up with program proposals, series ideas, ideas for deals with museums and specialty channels, and most of all ideas for co-productions with his colleagues at the embryonic history unit in Toronto. He and I spent many an evening on the phone during the winter of 2002 trying to save the Radio-Canada history unit.

But finally, in April, Hubert reported that the unit had been told to put everything in boxes and vacate its quarters. He was very worried about what would happen to the massive collection of transcripts, films, photos, videos, and journals gathered over four years in Montreal. "This is a gold mine. It's the history of New France and Quebec – we can't just dump it," he said. Copies of the field tapes were made for Radio-Canada's archives, but Hubert sensed no interest in the rest and didn't trust it would be treated with any care.

In the ultimate irony – one which must have hurt them very much – the men and women who had fought so hard for the proper representation of their people's history in the series insisted that all the material they'd gathered on the history of Quebec be shipped to the Canadian History Project in Toronto, where it would be catalogued and preserved.

"When you think about it, we did the impossible," Hubert wrote when the Montreal unit closed. "But sitting here today, surrounded by dirty cardboard boxes and bare walls, it is a downer. Five years have led to a dead end. For the people that worked for you in Montreal, these five years are not career enhancers; instead, they are being treated, by management, like lost years. But that is a reflection of a malaise here at Radio-Canada, not a failure of the project. We have disappeared because Radio-Canada does not feel that the history of this country is something that warrants any of its air time. That attitude, not our project, is what has sealed our fate. History is the long view and history will judge those responsible for that decision.

"But the public, the French-speaking public, drank at our well. They found the water refreshingly clear and they are still thirsty. I have plenty of e-mails that I will happily share with you."

In his next note, he wrote, in the habit we had acquired of addressing each other with Seven Years War titles: "We have taken the hill, *mon général*. We have won the battle, but I am sad to report that I have lost the regiment. – Le Maréchal."

18

Opening Pandora's Box

On Sunday, October 22, 2000, the myth that Canadians are not interested in their history was finally laid to rest, with cold, hard numbers. The massive interest in the series also had an effect on many Canadians themselves. Hundreds of thousands of people were delighted to discover that they were not alone in their thirst for Canadian history. "I was amazed to find out that everyone in our township was also watching," the local veterinarian told me in Cavan. "I thought it was just me who wanted to learn our history. I thought I belonged to a secret society. It turned out everyone I knew belonged to the same society." It was a phenomenon that cheered those of us who had almost given up hope that Canada even cared about itself.

The phenomenon cannot be just a passing phase. It was just too big an explosion of interest not to have something subterranean underlying it. It revealed a deeper current of national pride and a stronger sense of national identity than most of us ever imagined. And despite a cranky press, the viewing levels on Radio-Canada were as significant as on CBC. I think there was a pent-up desire among Canadians to know more about ourselves and that we have arrived at a period of national introspection, prompted by the unease over globalization and the near-rupture of the country during the referendum in 1995. We are embarking on an uncertain voyage in the uncharted waters of a global economy and new political constellations. For a long voyage, you pack the essentials, so the issue of who we are and what we represent becomes pertinent. So if we are connecting with our history, what will we do with it? How will it inform a very fluid present?

I am struck, first of all, by the attitude of viewers toward the pre-contact history of Canada and the aboriginal strand that runs through the entire series. In particular, as I mentioned earlier, that map of "A Continent of Nations" registered deeply in people's minds. The diversity and complexity of that map of a thousand years ago may be resonating with a view of Canada today as a gathering place of diversities.

The broad sympathy for the aboriginal strand in the series also suggests to me a lot more public willingness to rethink the place of aboriginal people in Canada. The idea of "two founding nations" – French and English – is already being replaced in the popular culture and in the schoolyards by the concept of three founding nations.

I learned that there can be no true understanding of Canadian history if it is taken solely as a post-contact history. That just makes it a "settler history," like a chronology of South Africa that begins with the arrival of the Afrikaners and then concerns itself for the rest of the time only with their squabbles with the British. There was not an unpopulated land here when the Europeans arrived but a number of long-established and developed nations. I am not saying this as an expression of sentiment or political correctness. Denying this history until recent years is as absurd as insisting that the history of Mexico started only after the defeat of the Aztec empire. There were civilizations here of extraordinary complexity, and our history begins with them.

Those civilizations exercised a defining force on the shaping of the two hundred years following first contact. The interplay of aboriginal and European peoples developed new forms of warfare indigenous to this place, forms of trade and hunting and agriculture unique to this land, cosmologies and views of our place in the universe that were particular to these societies. That interplay also produced a new race of people, the Métis. French and English traders and settlers intermarried with the First Nations to such a degree, we know now, that there is probably no ancestral Canadian family that does not have native blood, and most aboriginal people, except in remoter areas, have the bloodline of the newcomers in theirs.

The history is as intertwined as the bloodlines. For the first hundred years of the European (largely French) presence in Canada, the Indian nations were in control. The French survived here, after many perilous decades of war, through an intricate system of trading alliances and social accommodation, in which the French and the aboriginals treated each other as different yet equal.

The English penetration of the interior, through the Hudson's Bay Company and the North West Company, took place with the sufferance of the First Nations and continued only because it was mutually beneficial. Every exploration and mapping of the continent was led by native guides. Many cities west of Montreal evolved from trading posts, which survived only because the Indian nations agreed to bring furs to trade, or from military forts built to protect that trade.

The first settlers on the prairies could have been eradicated by the Plains nations. The record shows, instead, that they survived only because of the initial protection and support of those Indians. The first provisional government of Manitoba under Riel was based on respect among the Métis, the Indians, the French, and the Irish-Scottish settlers, who formed councils representative of all their races and nationalities.

To suggest that the only residue of four hundred years of contact, commerce, and intermarriage is a fondness for maple syrup and canoes is patently ridiculous. *Canada: A People's History* was only a step toward discovering the history that takes account of the aboriginal story. There is a buried history of Canada waiting to be brought to life, a way of seeing ourselves that we have completely, and perhaps intentionally, neglected. Some excellent historians have begun to take apart this mental barrier, but the real research into our buried racial heritage, one that recognizes that we are a racially hybrid people, remains to be done.

The series also stirred the silt at the bottom of the French-English pool of suspicion, and I'm glad it roused the passions it did. English viewers clearly knew little of the French history of Canada and, from the hundreds of letters I've read, seemed to have been mightily impressed by the scope and depth of that history. It's clear to me now that there is a vast current of opinion in English Canada that accepts that the French are the founders of post-contact Canada, that recognizes that their language and culture suffered for the better part of two hundred years after the Plains of Abraham, and that has come to understand that many of the steps Quebec has taken in this generation were necessary to protect its language and culture. In other words, just as there is a growing recognition that the First Nations played a vital role in the founding of modern Canada, there is an acceptance of Quebec's "distinct society," which English Canada rejected in the Meech Lake and Charlottetown accords.

Quebec is building a multinational society, enriched by Haitian and Vietnamese immigration and now by new waves of migrants. The nationalism in Quebec is one of language and culture, not race. But at the core of that nationalism is Quebec's history. The Québécois are the product of a very particular and unique New World experience.

Mario Cardinal helped me understand how almost all Québécois, Acadians, and French Canadians carry the past with them as a fundamental part of their identity. Most of us in the Toronto unit of the history project couldn't trace our families back more than two or three generations. In the Montreal unit, most could. Mario's family history is not untypical.

We left on September 7, 1659, from La Rochelle aboard the *Saint André* with Jeanne Mance. My European roots are in Marans, near La Rochelle. It's a tiny strategically placed village built around a fortified castle on the Sèvre Niortaise, a small river which was used as an invasion route, usually by the English, to penetrate French territory. La Rochelle was a bastion of Protestantism at the time of the Reformation, and Marans was its granary. It was captured and recaptured time and again by the Catholics and by the Protestants, so that the tiny village produced some of the most celebrated military leaders of the time, the most notable being Henry of Navarre, the future King Henry IV of France.

Tired of these wars, three sisters named Michelle, Louise and Marie-Marguerite, and their husbands, became interested when Jeanne Mance arrived in October of 1658 to recruit priests, nuns and settlers. On July 2 of 1659 three families – Charbonneau, Goyer and Cardineau – left for the New World on a death trap of an old transport ship, where a tenth of the 107 passengers died of the plague. On arriving in Quebec in September, the three families borrowed 225 pounds from Jeanne Mance to pay for their passage – a debt it took them a decade to repay. In the next generation the name Cardineau changed slightly to Cardinal, and two brothers, Pierre and Jacques, became farmers and fur traders on the island of Montreal, trading as far as Detroit.

From this lineage came Joseph-Narcisse Cardinal, a notary at Laprairie, a *patriote* in the 1838 rebellion wave. He was betrayed by the Amerindians of Kahnawake, turned over to Colborne's troops, condemned by a court martial, and hanged at Pied du Courant on December 21, 1838. He wasn't my direct ancestor but I am very proud of him, just as I was proud, at the beginning of my career, to work for ten years at the paper founded by the grandson of Louis-Joseph Papineau.

In my attaching myself to *Canada: A People's History*, I was assuring that this history would be the story of what had been my country, New France, but also the story of Lower Canada, with its Rebellion, and the United Canadas, before becoming the vastness which followed from the conquest of the West.

This rootedness is not exclusive to the French; Maritimers and Newfoundlanders are equally anchored to their provenance, and any Macdonald can be triangulated by three or four questions along the lines of "Are you from the Canso Macdonalds or the Sydney Macdonalds?" But the sheer length of the French experience in Canada exercises a defining effect. History is so central in Quebec that the very idea of making this series was a major controversy there. In Montreal, I must have been asked a hundred times whose history we were telling. "Can you teach the same history in Toronto as in Montreal?" one *La Presse* columnist asked as soon as the project was announced. I soon realized that many Quebec intellectuals thought that a history of Canada would inevitably drown the particularity of the French-Canadian story.

Some sovereignists argued that we could not tell the history of an entity that doesn't really exist. That objection wasn't too hard to deal with. Whether they wanted it to continue existing or not, Canada has existed in various forms for centuries, and it was obviously possible to write a history of it. Others, like the Quebec historian Jacques Lacoursière, argued that the only real way to do a history of Canada would be to do three histories – written in three parallel columns on the page – one of the aboriginal experience, one of the French, another of the English. I argued that that was not unlike what we were doing, only we were weaving the strands throughout the narrative, and adding a fourth perspective, the immigrant experience, as well as highlighting women's and labour history. Professor Lacoursière's argument is not a negative one but rather a view that respects three distinct views. But others were positively enraged at the idea of doing a history of Canada.

What we were doing was a "bastardization," they argued. It would be impossible to reconcile the radically different interpretations of events held by the diverse groups in Canada. I could never fathom this argument. By that logic, no one should attempt a history of Europe. Can no one do a history of the Second World War because there are at least three – if not thirty – radically different perspectives on it? "This must be the only place left on earth," I argued at one conference, "where serious intellectuals argue that it is wrong to write a history because there are contending versions of it. This is juvenile. This denies the works of some of the greatest historians who wrote about wars and empires, from Herodotus to Shelby Foote. This stance leads to nowhere but total paralysis." One can disagree with the overall view taken, but let's not pretend it cannot be done.

We took pains to explain that journalists cover the Middle East on the news each night without taking one side, that we covered every constitutional crisis fairly; why then was it forbidden to cover the conscription crisis of the First World War? We could honestly describe the arguments of both sides and give voice to the leaders of both sides, without acting as a Supreme Court that imposes its own judgment. "It's what we do for a living every day," I said. "Why are you trying to ban us from the past?" But it remained, from start to finish, the most constant objection in the Quebec press.

Nowhere in this country is the subject of history more volatile than in Quebec. But as the hostility in Radio-Canada and in the press mounted, the more amazed I became at the defensiveness. Whatever flaws I have as a journalist, I have never been suspected of being a lapdog for any government or political party. Everyone in the industry knew the reputation for integrity of Louis Martin, Mario Cardinal, and Hubert Gendron, Gene Allen, Gordon Henderson, and Kelly Crichton, or could establish the fierce independence of their credentials with one phone call. But apparently reputations didn't matter. The very act of doing a history of Canada meant that we were twisting it to suit some federalist fiction. We were agents of the federal Liberals.

After it was all over, I asked Mario Cardinal to explain to me the journalistic hostility to the series. His reply is worth quoting at length.

For many Québécois, the word "Canada" is a synonym for frustration, deception, combat and humiliation. For the *indépendantistes* (that is to say, almost half the population and the majority of intellectuals, including journalists) the word "Canada" is taboo. I have lost friends who no longer speak to me simply because I agreed to work on this series.

The series was announced not long after the 1995 Referendum. The Quebec population knew that the English Canadians had had the fright of their lives and were determined that it wouldn't happen again. In other words, the Québécois expected that the ROC – Rest of Canada – would take all the measures necessary to prevent "the next time." In Canada, everybody quickly forgot the Meech Lake accord. Not in Quebec: here one remembers that English Canadians refused, even at the lowest minimum that Quebec requested, to recognize Quebec as a distinct society. When the series was launched, in the autumn of 2000, Meech was only ten years old. When you've been wounded, ten years is a pretty short time to expect people to forget.

Yes, I knew the media wouldn't be burning any incense in our honour. I know the Quebec journalists pretty well. I also know Radio-Canada and the programmers. I knew we shouldn't expect to get any favours from anyone. But what I didn't antici-pate was the silence of the historians. One political analyst told me, "But what did you expect? The academics are not interested in public debates. What they want is to publish in specialized reviews. It's good for their careers and gets them known abroad. They're certainly not going to go against the current of ultra-nationalist Quebec thought."

At the base of the sovereignist argument is history itself and the conviction that, without the events of 1759, New France would have become an independent nation sometime in the nineteenth century. Since this history was deflected by an external event – the British conquest – it is possible to restore the normal evolution of the French people in North America by removing the lingering verdict of that distant event. The French in North America are still concen-trated in a coherent geographic unit, Quebec, and are a distinct culture and people. The only instrument this people lacks to protect its identity, the argument goes, is the powers of an independent state, powers that every other former European colony in the Americas has, from Brazil to Chile to Costa Rica.

This "normal trajectory of history" argument is debatable, of course. The first country the American Revolution invaded was Canada, which was then entirely French with a weak British army garrison. George Washington published a dire warning that the Canadiens had better support the Revolutionaries, since the Canadiens were a small people at the mercy of their neighbours. I'm not convinced the eighty thousand Canadiens of that era would have survived in a hostile, anti-Catholic, and unilingual republic of over a million American colonists. I suspect they would have become the Louisiana of the north. But who knows in these might-have-been games?

Sovereignists make another point that is less debatable: Quebec is the homeland – in fact the *only* bastion – of the French language in the western hemisphere. Montreal is the second-largest French city in the world. *La Presse* is the second-largest French-language newspaper on the planet. This, for sovereignists, puts a special responsibility on Quebec to ensure that it has all the instruments of national self-preservation. Even if one is not sovereignist, this responsibility to preserve the French language and culture and identity in the New World is an article of faith.

"You have to understand one central difference about the French in British North America," Hubert once explained to me. "As a culture and as a people, we were completely cut off from the metropolitan mother culture. There were no replenishing waves of new immigrants from France, bringing new ideas, as there were for the English, the Scots, the Irish, the Germans, the Ukrainians, and all the other immigrant peoples who established themselves here. The French in Canada are alone in a way that almost no other ethnicity in North America is."

English-speaking Canadians who think there is an emotional link between Quebec and France today couldn't be farther from the mark. First, the continental French have a linguistic arrogance that looks down on the Quebec and Acadian accents and vocabulary, and they exhibit a near-total ignorance of their history. Periodically, a Quebec singer like Robert Charlebois or Céline Dion will become hot in Paris, but it tends to be transitory. The Québécois do not suffer from the syndrome of respecting their artists only after they've become accepted in France, as sometimes happens to other Canadian artists who become hot after they've scored in the United States. It's striking how *little* emotional, social, or political attachment the Québécois, Acadians, or other French communities in Canada have to France.

Many Québécois – perhaps even most – consider themselves an indigenous people of North America. "The view is that there are perhaps two tiers of indigenous people here," Hubert said. "On the very first tier are the aboriginal nations, and then the French on a second tier – but certainly not on the same tier with the English and the nineteenth- and twentieth-century immigrations." I know that my francophone friends and colleagues are also more inclined to see themselves as an American people – in the broadest sense – than my anglophone colleagues and friends.

Even the word "Canadian" is contentious. It was a revelation to most of our Montreal colleagues that William Lyon Mackenzie, in rallying the citizens of Upper Canada to rebellion, said, "Canadians! Will we allow ourselves to be no better than slaves?" and urged them to support their insurgent Canadian brothers in Lower Canada. As Jean-Claude Robert observes, "In my grandfather's day, a Canadien meant a French Canadian." The anglophones were "les anglais," and most of them defined themselves as Britons. One phenomenon of the last fifty years is the wholesale abandonment of the word "Canadien" by millions in Quebec, where the vast majority now call themselves Québécois. I can't think of a similar occurrence anywhere else in the world, where a community abandons its name because others have adopted it.

The popularity of the series on CBC was seen by some in Quebec as evidence that English Canada is in full nation-building mode. There is some truth to that, in the sense that Canadians are trying to define who they are and what they stand for. But it is more: the experience of the past five years makes me think that two parallel journeys of self-definition are underway. Both have a considerable nobility to them. In Quebec, the journey is toward being understood to be an indigenous American people who survived against all odds and have a mission to protect the French language and culture in the New World. In English Canada, the journey is toward a pluralistic vision of equality, of ourselves as a people who have come from all parts of the planet to create a place of tolerance and civility. The contradiction comes because the Québécois understandably do not see themselves as just one of the patches in the multicoloured quilt of a new Canada – this reduces them to one ethnicity among dozens, and their land, in the current constitutional arrangement, to one province among ten.

The history I have just finished living with suggests that once we truly understand the others' positions, mutual accommodation will be within the grasp of the Canadian genius. It has been before, and it will be again. I doubt that accommodation, when it comes, will be a "one-size-fits-all" arrangement.

It is possible to accept the whole package, with all its contradictions, and feel quite at peace. As an immigrant of Polish descent, I feel no need to choose between one heritage and another. Louis-Joseph Papineau, Louis Riel, John A. Macdonald, and Thomas D'Arcy McGee belong to me, as do Emily Carr, David Thompson, Tecumseh, Donnacona, and Champlain. The Great Peace of Montreal in 1701 is a bigger event in my heritage than the Poles defeating the Germans at Grünwald in 1410. I identify more with Papineau than with Pilsudski. Canada, with all its interplay of forces and histories, shaped me and shapes my daughters. I get goose bumps when I read about the Assembly of the Six Counties and when I read the diaries of Loyalist refugees. It's immaterial to me whether those Patriotes and those Loyalists would have gotten along. My daughters and I are the product of their existence and their struggles, even if there is not a drop of their blood in our veins. We are from here.

Similarly, we are so defined by the immigrations of the past century that the histories of those who settled here have become a part of the collective memory. The Holocaust, the Ukrainian and Irish famines, the wars in Vietnam, the Horn of Africa, and the Balkans are all part of our history too.

Is there a theme running through Canadian history? I think so. You can find the shadowy outline of a pattern. A river does run through it. So many of us here are descendants of a great migration of the unwanted and the disenfranchised, the landless and the persecuted, that it has shaped the collective identity. Yes, there were gold-seekers and carpetbaggers, there were those who travelled here in business class, but they mostly came and went. We are the children of those who stayed, the desperate, the adventurous, and those who sought nothing more than a better life for their children. All of them came with little more than hope. This is not true of most countries on earth. It is true of the United States, of Australia and New Zealand, and perhaps of parts of South America. But it is most clearly true in Canada.

America was wealth and opportunity. Australia was exile. Canada was hope.

The river that runs through Canadian history is a current of refuge and hope. It is starkly clear to anyone who bothers to look at the waves of newcomers. New France was founded on the migrations of the poor, the *filles du roi*, and the adventurous. The English migrations that followed the Conquest were the Loyalist refugees from the American Revolution, the Scots fleeing the devastation of the Highland clearances and the slums of the Industrial Revolution; they were followed by the waves of those dispossessed by the Irish famines, by the economic desperation in China, then the great migrations of the landless from eastern Europe and Scandinavia. The twentieth century is a constant tide of refugees coming to Canadian shores, from Stalin's forced famines in the Ukraine, the Holocaust, and the Second World War, extending through those who fled the Hungarian uprising, the Vietnam War, right till today, as every day a jetliner lands with refugees from the Balkans or Africa.

There are three parts to almost every Canadian family biography I have encountered, at least in non-aboriginal families. First, there is the "adversity," the reason for the migration. This is always a story of religious war or intolerance, invasion, famine, or landlessness, of political ideology being imposed in the form of draft, duress, or economic ruin. In the description of the adversity there is the "pioneer" – the person, most often a woman, who determined on the great trek. I have a close friend whose middle name is Hector. Every man in his line of descendants has the middle name Hector. It is the name of the ship that brought the first migrant, the progenitor.

The second part is the "passage." It is usually a turbulent story of a difficult journey and dismay at the harshness of the winter climate and the two, five, or twenty years of hardship in the new land, clearing land, working as a janitor.

The third part is inevitably the "redemption." The first successful crop. The first child to complete school. The first story of acceptance.

The adversity, followed by the passage, followed by the redemption, with particular honour paid by every descendant to the pioneer.

There was one funeral I omitted in my story. It was that of Peter Allnut, the *McGill Daily* editor before me. We shared the 1960s together, lived on each other's living room floors, and started a radical magazine together. Then he got crippling multiple sclerosis and spent twenty-five years in an institution. Hubert Gendron and I went to his funeral in the Eastern Townships. They buried him in an old Loyalist cemetery, and as his coffin was lowered into the fresh-dug earth, his brothers stood by, solemnly holding a large gilt-framed portrait of a woman. Afterwards, I asked them who she was. She was Anne Truax, the Loyalist who brought her refugee family from Vermont through the swamps into Canada, and to this place. "Over there, near the garage at the bottom of the hill," Peter's brother said as he pointed, as if it had happened yesterday. I had never thought of Peter as being of Loyalist descent, though I now understood why his will stipulated he be buried in Quebec soil. It doesn't matter who Anne Truax's parents were. She was the progenitor. History begins here, and it remains intensely alive.

This heritage of refuge – or migration of hope – has shaped our national character. We are disdainful of class, and the biggest social gaffe one can make is to try to pull rank or assert privilege. We are inclined to boast about the hardship of our ancestors, and to be proud if our fathers were bricklayers; having a privileged background scores no particular admiration. It is unacceptable to be rude to a waiter or a waitress, because our son or daughter is probably going to be one at some point.

We are very jealous of our rights, and vigilant lest any other person or group have more than us, leading to an almost litigious streak in the national character. This is why we are acutely sensitive to queue-jumping or petty fraud in any arena of civil life, from immigration to social services. We are innately suspicious of government and ideology, because so many of us are refugees from political regimes and ideology. Far from being docile and deferential to authority, as some writers have suggested we are, Canadians harbour deep mistrust of and disdain for politicians.

Some find my view of the theme of refuge that runs through our history rather bleak; one critic characterized it as a vision of "a nation of losers." I'm perplexed by this. Americans don't find the words at the base of the Statue of Liberty bleak: "Give me your tired, your poor, your huddled masses yearning to breathe free, the wretched refuse of your teeming shore. Send these, the homeless, tempest-tossed to me. I lift my lamp beside the golden door." I always thought these words, however romantic and overwrought, more aptly describe the Canadian national ethic. That's who we really are. And it's worth celebrating. We are both the unwanted and the adventurous, who formed and continue to form a unique New World society.

William Thorsell, the former editor of the *Globe and Mail*, told me a story which speaks to that point and gave me my ending. He went on to become the director of the Royal Ontario Museum, and in that capacity found himself in Ottawa at a dinner for the retiring secretary general of the United Nations, Javier Pérez de Cuéllar. A secretary general receives a lot of precious artifacts and gifts from heads of state during his tenure. Pérez de Cuéllar was donating all of his to Canada, hence the dinner of appreciation. Thorsell was at his table.

"Why are you giving all your gifts to Canada?" he asked. "Why not to Peru? After all, you are a Peruvian."

"Because," Pérez de Cuéllar replied, "of all the countries I came to know in my tenure, Canada most approximated the world as I thought it had to become. All races, all nationalities, in a peaceful coexistence."

There are three major histories, aboriginal, French, and English. There are histories of women, labour, gays, among many others. It is within the wit of man to construct the systems and constitutions that respect the particularities of them all.

The mystery of Canadian history is that we have every single ingredient for every Old World conflict, yet we are peaceful. Every toxin is here: two languages, two religions, different races, contested land, a devastated indigenous people. How we *haven't* become Kosovo, Northern Ireland, or the Middle East is a far more intriguing story, and more pertinent to the modern world. Canada is in a constant, cranky, and litigious negotiation of its constituent parts, which has created a grumpy civility that may not always be pretty but has attracted the envy of those in more wounded parts of the world. The point of studying Canadian history is to examine when that civility and accommodation broke down and when it worked, the better to assure that the eternal equilibrium is maintained and the constant negotiation goes forward. It is the struggle no one can afford to win.

Gene Allen told me on the first day of the project: You always encounter, in the constant negotiations of Canadian history, the eternal frustrated question, When are we finally going to settle this?

The answer, of course, is never.

That's not the problem. That's the point.

Postscript: "The Company of Adventurers"

And where is everyone now?

Jim Byrd, who took the big risk in announcing the project in 1996, was pushed out of the CBC and now lives in Newfoundland, dividing his time between the Banff Television Festival and nurturing independent projects. Bob Culbert, the executive director of CBC news and current affairs and Newsworld, who incubated *Canada: A People's History* in his department, left the CBC and is now vice-president of documentaries at CTV.

Gene Allen, the brains of the project, had no offer to remain within the CBC when his contract ended and left to become an associate professor of journalism at Ryerson University, a job he loves.

Jill Offman couldn't wait the many months for *The Canadian Experience* to become a reality, and left the CBC to become director of programming at the Discovery channel. Andrew Burnstein left the CBC to become an executive producer at Discovery.

Andy Gregg returned to independent production, where he works frequently for Gordon Henderson's company, 90th Parallel.

Michelle Métivier, who directed Episode 6, "The Pathfinders," left to become an independent producer. Gail Gallant, who worked on the first episode, now works for Alliance Atlantis. Julia Bennett, who worked with me on "Battle for a Continent," now works at the Life Channel. Fiona McHugh, who worked on the Confederation episode, returned to the independent world, and Grazyna Krupa, who worked on the War of 1812, left CBC/Radio-Canada to have her second child and work as an independent producer.

Kelly Crichton, the senior producer who came into the series late and brilliantly led it to completion, left the CBC after decades as a director, after running *the fifth estate* and heading the news department. She went to travel in Africa.

Sally Reardon, the *Journal* veteran and senior producer who was my closest confidante during the series and producer of "Battle for a Continent," is now a senior producer with *The Canadian Experience*, working out of Halifax.

Laine Drewery went back to independent production outside the CBC, as did Bill Cobban and Marquise Lepage. I'm trying to lure them all back.

Of the Montreal unit, those on short-term contracts, like Claude Berrardelli, were left with no choice but to leave Radio-Canada, and those on staff were given other jobs: Richard Fortin is now with Radio-Canada's all-news channel, Peter Ingles and Frédéric Vanasse work in documentaries. The Montreal cameramen, Pierre Mainville and Gaétan Morisset, returned to staff duties, and the editors to new assignments. André Daigneault works with a combined English and Cree unit. Denis Boucher and Pauline Payette went back to independent production.

Mario Cardinal, the Émile Zola of Quebec, who lent his stature and pen to the defence of the series, returned to his farm and a retirement that no one seriously expects to last.

Stephen Phizicky, the CBC *éminence grise* who was Nick Auf der Maur's closest colleague, Maurice Chabot's federalist nemesis, and my secret agent in recruiting Hubert Gendron, left the CBC to become an independent, which nobody thought would ever happen.

Our senior visual researcher, Ron Krant, is, as I write, recovering from heart bypass surgery, and, by the time you read this, will have resumed his research work with *The Canadian Experience*, amid all the files and films and volumes of the adventure we lived through.

Michael Sweeney, the first cameraman on the series, is director of photography for the documentary production unit and *The Canadian Experience*. The cameramen Maurice Chabot, Hans Vanderzande, Pierre Mainville, Gaétan Morisset, and Derek Kennedy are just waiting for the call. Ian Campbell, who almost drowned to save his cellphone, is still in charge of impossible assignments, and Pat Goodland, our post-production supervisor, is ready to process the first six hours of *The Canadian Experience*, along with the composers, mixers, and the eccentric foley studio.

Rachel Brown Rollerbladed her way out of the CBC and is now a big shot at the Canadian Cancer Society, which is fitting, given whom she worked for. I, however, gave up smoking a year ago, possibly my greatest achievement. Rachel was replaced by Nathalie Bibeau, whose instructions from Anne Emin, like Rachel's, were "Make sure you fly anything Mark does past me first" and "Watch out for Gendron and the French." She was assured, "They're both nice people, but neither one can be trusted alone, or, much worse, together." She has been of enormous help to me in writing this book.

Jim Williamson, the suavely diplomatic director of the Confederation episode, became the senior producer of *the fifth estate* but "wouldn't mind another kick at the history cat."

Susan Teskey, a sucker for overwhelming jobs, who saved the Second World War episode, became the senior executive producer of CBC Television's *Disclosure*, the big-budget weekly documentary series that needed a lot of refitting after its first season. She says she plans to moderate her work habits. No one believes her.

Susan Dando, the founder of *Life & Times*, who had seven months to rescue the entire last episode, and with it the summation of the history of Canada, learned nothing from the experience and agreed to become the senior producer of *The Canadian Experience* and our new in-house documentary production unit, CineNorth, while also producing a mammoth documentary about Susanna Moodie and Catharine Parr Traill at the same time.

Murray Green is the senior editor of *The Canadian Experience* and CineNorth, although he probably hasn't left his dark time-compression chamber long enough to notice. He is editing a documentary on the origins of public broadcasting in Canada. That documentary, entitled *Dominion of the Air*, was the centrepiece of the CBC's fiftieth-anniversary television celebrations for the fall of 2002. It's directed by Jackie Corkery, the Fransaskois girl who produced the First World War episode. She had to move from Radio-Canada to CBC Toronto to find a job after it was all over. The documentary is in both languages and ran on both networks; Marcy Cuttler is the producer. Casey Kollontay is the new production manager of *The Canadian Experience*, and our business manager, Wilma Alexander, grudgingly agreed to buy new bookshelves for my office. Anne Emin, the project manager, is still talking about retirement. No one takes her seriously.

Slawko Klymkiw is still the program director, and though I gave up cigarettes, he smuggles a much-appreciated Cuban cigar to me now and then.

Hubert Gendron and his wife went to Venice and Prague for a few weeks after it was all over in Montreal, and he returned determined to try to rebuild the French history unit he and Claude Saint-Laurent believe should exist. A night hasn't passed without Hubert calling me. I shouldn't be surprised if, by the time this book is printed, he has succeeded – if only to give the documentary production unit in Toronto a run for its money.

The CBC that I describe here is recovering from the turbulent years. The devastation caused by the decade of cuts has calmed, and the air of gloom is lifting. It no longer feels like an institution occupied by outside bailiffs. Financially, though, it is still weak, and the government doles out small budget increases only year by year, making it difficult to recoup the production strength it once had. Most of the figures at Head Office have changed and the network's relationship with the production sector is no longer so tense. The experience of the Montreal history unit notwithstanding, there are more CBC/Radio-Canada joint productions all the time, the Trudeau mini-series with Colm Feore being the most visible example so far.

When he became president, Robert Rabinovitch firmly settled the direction of the CBC on the production of Canadian stories and put a priority on joint French-English programming. He did that before *Canada: A People's History* even aired, and the success of the series underscored the wisdom of that direction. The message from viewers that the series was what the CBC is supposed to be all about was received loud and clear by all of us, and gave us the confidence to be the Canadian institution we were meant to be, instead of a copy of a private network.

Guylaine Saucier was very proud of the history project's success and in the remainder of her time in office fought hard to get new funding for the CBC. She left the position of chair to work on reforming the Toronto Stock Exchange and sits on the board of several corporations. Many members of the board of directors, which always supported the series, made a point of going to public events and personally thanking the cameramen, historians, and producers who worked so hard to assure its success. Clarence LeBreton, from our mission to Caraquet, is now the senior member of the board. Perrin Beatty was no longer president when the series he approved aired. He presided over the gloomy years without the reward of being there for the success of the series. But it must afford him satisfaction. He wanted the project to signal that there was a future for the CBC, despite all the bloodletting, and it did just that. He is now president and CEO of Canadian Manufacturers and Exporters.

Too many good people have left the CBC, and you've met some of them in these pages. But just as many new and young talented people are coming in every day, some of them into CineNorth, and into the Canadian History Project, which still exists and which is now developing *The Canadian Experience*.

Only the CBC, even battered and internally divided as it was, would have undertaken this project. No other television network in the country would have risked what the CBC risked. And certainly no institution would have gambled so boldly in its darkest financial hours. But by betting on the good sense of the Canadian people, it not only succeeded but redeemed itself and found its clear direction. Graham Spry, the founding father of the CBC, said over fifty years ago that every generation would have to refight the battle for public broadcasting. In the end, I think that's what the Canadian History Project was all about, and all of us mentioned here were privileged to have been part of that struggle.

As for me, the experience of those years transformed me. Sometimes it was a nightmare, sometimes a ball, but I had to write about it. Serge Turbide, Gail Boyd, Bill Fortais had died. Mecky Furlani died today, as I was writing this conclusion.

For months after the series aired, people asked me what my next project was. This book, my inadequate tribute to my extraordinary colleagues, and to the people throughout the corporation – from the boardroom in Ottawa to the remotest Arctic field unit – who fought to retain the integrity of the CBC, was my next project.

Index